KARAMANLIS
The Restorer of Greek Democracy

KARAMANLIS

The Restorer of Greek Democracy

C. M. WOODHOUSE

CLARENDON PRESS · OXFORD

Oxford University Press, Walton Street, Oxford OX2 6DP

London Glasgow New York Toronto
Delhi Bombay Calcutta Madras Karachi
Kuala Lumpur Singapore Hong Kong Tokyo
Nairobi Dar es Salaam Cape Town
Melbourne Auckland
and associated companies in
Beirut Berlin Ibadan Mexico City Nicosia

Oxford is a trade mark of Oxford University Press

Published in the United States
by Oxford University Press, New York

British Library Cataloguing in Publication Data
Woodhouse, C. M.
Karamanlis: the restorer of Greek democracy.
1. Karamanlis, Konstantinos
I. Title
949.5'074'0924   DF836.K37
ISBN 0-19-822584-9
            822794-9 (pbk.)

Library of Congress Cataloging in Publication Data
Woodhouse, C. M. (Christopher Montague), 1917-
Karamanlis, the restorer of Greek democracy.
Includes index.
1. Karamanlis, Constantinos, 1907-
2. Statesmen—Greece—Biography. 3. Greece—
Presidents—Biography. 4. Greece—History—
1950-1967. 5. Greece—History—1974—
I. Title
DF836.K37W66   949.5'07'0924[B]   83-15137
ISBN 0-19-822584-9   AACR2
            822794-9 (pbk.)

First published 1982
Reprinted (New as Paperback) 1983

Typeset by Graphic Services, Oxford
Printed in Great Britain
at the University Press, Oxford

Preface

'INSTABILITY' is the word most frequently applied to Greek politics. Foreign observers repeat it compulsively; Karamanlis has often used it himself. It is therefore worth recording that Karamanlis held office as Prime Minister for a total of fourteen years—longer than any British Prime Minister since Gladstone, and perhaps longer than any Prime Minister of a democracy in the twentieth century. He won twelve personal elections, held five different ministries, and formed seven governments, each of them based on a single party. He dominated the political scene in Greece to a degree rivalled only by Elevtherios Venizelos, who was indeed his favourite model, but whose mistakes he succeeded in avoiding.

His career as a politician lasted forty-five years (1935–80), though it was twice interrupted: once by the pre-war dictatorship of Metaxas and the Second World War, and again by his self-imposed exile in Paris and another military dictatorship. It ended with a political transition of exemplary smoothness, when the Presidency of the Republic, the leadership of his party, and the premiership changed hands within a few days in May 1980. It is at that point that this essentially political biography also ends.

I undertook the work with the approval of the President, who gave me access to a great quantity of his personal archives, for which I am much indebted to him. In using this material I have been greatly helped by Mr Panayotis Lambrias, Mr Ioannis Poulos, and Mr Constantine Svolopoulos, who each organized certain sections of the archives in chronological order for me, and supported them in many cases with valuable commentaries. I have identified the documents quoted only by date, since the President's archives are not yet catalogued.

In addition I have had the benefit of many conversations both with the President himself and with members of his family, personal friends, public servants, and fellow politicians.

I am especially grateful to the following, whose names I give in Greek alphabetical order: Evangelos Averoff, George Athanasiadis, George Avtzis, Angelos Vlakhos, Helen Vlakhos, Lambros Evtaxias, Theodore Theodoridis, Panayotis Kanellopoulos, Aleko Karamanlis, Akhilleas Karamanlis, Nikolaos Linadartos, Amalia Megapanou, Constantine Mitsotakis, George Oikonomopoulos, Andreas Papandreou, Dr Iordanis Propatoridis, George Rallis, Costa Triantaphyllidis, Professor Costa Tsatsos. I have also benefited from the friendly help of many members of the Greek Embassy in London, and from the advice of the editorial staff of the Oxford University Press.

C. M. Woodhouse

Contents

List of Plates
between pages 120 and 121

PART I

Apprenticeship
1907–1955

Chapter 1
A Man of Macedonia

EVERY Greek is born into a part of his country's history. For Constantine, the eldest son of George and Photeini Karamanlis, it was Mount Pangaion in eastern Macedonia, where he was born on 8 March 1907. The mines of Pangaion were the source of the gold and silver which laid the economic foundations of the Macedonian empire in the fourth century BC, under Philip and his son Alexander the Great. Ten miles to the south-west of his native village lay Amphipolis, over which Athens and Sparta fought in the Peloponnesian War. About the same distance to the east lay Philippi, where Mark Antony and the future Emperor Augustus defeated Brutus and Cassius, the assassins of Julius Caesar, in 42 BC. There too St. Paul preached the Gospel for the first time in Europe a century later. Thirty miles to the north-west is the county town of Serres, where the Ottoman Sultan Bajezid once held court and summoned the Christian rulers of the Balkans as his vassals in 1394.

Karamanlis' village was called Küpköy, the 'village of jars', which were a famous local product. The area was liberated from the Turks in the Balkan Wars of 1912–13, which Karamanlis could just remember. The name was then changed to Proti ('the first'), after a Byzantine princess who was said to have spent her summers there. So history still lay over Karamanlis' birthplace, but it was Turkish and Bulgarian history as much as Greek and Roman. Like other great men in Greece's history, including his predecessor Elevtherios Venizelos, he was born an Ottoman subject. Not until he was six years old did he become a free citizen of the Kingdom of Greece, when the Treaty of Bucharest brought the Balkan Wars to an end in August 1913. Even then his family was not secure, for the Bulgarians, who had been allies of the Greeks in the first Balkan War and their enemies in the second, were still hoping to annex eastern Macedonia. They made two more attempts to do so during the two world wars which followed.

Despite its Turkish name, Küpköy was a Greek village. A handful of Turkish families lived there in great poverty, working as labourers or domestics. Turkish officials, police or soldiers from Serres, were rarely seen. If they came to seize Greek nationalists like George Karamanlis, the village was a labyrinth of alleys between the houses through which wanted men could escape. But the Bulgarian nationalists were a more serious danger. Their irregular *komitadjis* ('men of the Committee') provoked a nationalist reaction among the Greeks, of which George Karamanlis became the local leader.

He had also been born at Küpköy, and had started life as a schoolmaster at Kerdyllia, twenty miles away to the south, in 1903. In the same year he was enrolled by the Greek nationalist organization as an 'agent, first class'. His activities became known to the Turks, who dismissed him from his teaching post in 1904. Returning to Küpköy, he never taught again, though he was called 'the schoolmaster' as a title of honour. He took up tobacco-growing, which was the basis of Macedonia's economy, and he prospered. In 1905 he wanted to marry Photeini Dogloglou, also from Küpköy. Her parents objected, so the couple eloped: 'a kidnap', their son proudly called it.

A year later, in 1906, George Karamanlis started to build himself a new house on ground adjoining the humbler cottage where he had been born. The cottage remained standing for some years as a storehouse and cow-shed, but eventually it was demolished as the new house grew. Only the eldest son remembered it at all. All the eight children of George and Photeini Karamanlis were born in the same room of the new house: Costa in 1907; Athina in 1909 (who died in 1914); Olga in 1911; Aleko in 1914; a second Athina in 1917; Antigoni in 1921; Grammenos in 1925; Akhilleas in 1929. As they grew bigger, one bedroom housed the girls and another the boys. Only Costa had the privilege of the eldest: a room of his own, with a table for his books.

George Karamanlis continued his nationalist activities, and his son's earliest memories were linked to the troubled life of Macedonia. Under the cow-shed was a cellar, where his father stored arms for the Greek irregulars. The little boy would pretend to go and look at the cow, in order to visit the secret armoury and examine the weapons. He recalled the sight of men carrying arms up from the cellar, the slaughter of the Turks in 1913, 'the flame of savagery burning in the eyes of our village neighbours', the forcible baptism of Turkish women. 'Even now when I think of it, my heart contracts,' he told his French biographer.[1] Fighting and violence were a way of life for the peoples of Macedonia, each of them believing that only so could their own nation survive.

It was the same for the village boys. They fought miniature battles with stones against the boys of neighbouring villages, Greeks like themselves—for of course they could never play with Bulgarian or Turkish boys. The schoolmaster's son showed an early talent for leadership in these 'stone-battles'. He also learned that guerrilla war was not just a children's game. His father had been appointed in 1908 by the Bishop of Drama to the leadership of the committee of liberation for the area of Pangaion. One day the chief organizer of the movement in eastern Macedonia, known as Capetan Tsaras, came to Küpköy to see his father. The little boy met the great man and told him that when he grew up he too was going to be a guerrilla captain (*kapetanios*). Later, when the guerrillas became regular soldiers after the Balkan Wars, there were no more *kapetanioi*, so his ambition changed: 'I am going to be a leader!'

It was a risky ambition, for he had seen his father pay the penalty of leadership. George Karamanlis was arrested, imprisoned, and maltreated more than once: by the Turks in 1908 and by the Bulgarians in 1917. His first conflict with the Bulgarians was caused by his refusal to issue orders to the village in Bulgarian when they occupied Küpköy. On that occasion the little boy clung to his father's legs, and his tears and screams induced the Bulgarian officer to let him go. When the First World War spread to Macedonia, George Karamanlis was less lucky. He was arrested and carried off to Bulgaria for eighteen months in 1917–18. Photeini refused all financial help, knowing that her husband would hold out. His reward came only after his death, when the medal commemorating the liberation of Macedonia was posthumously conferred on George Karamanlis in 1936.

There were also happier memories of childhood, especially

[1] Maurice Genevoix, *The Greece of Caramanlis* (translated from the French, London, 1973), p. 45.

after peace came and his father returned and Küpköy became Proti. But it was never an easy life for a child, even in the better times. As a ten-year-old, while his father was a prisoner, he would climb Pangaion, not to enjoy the view but to collect firewood and the herb which makes mountain-tea; and as he grew older, to shoot hares and quails for the pot. He learned to ride bareback, and to swim on occasional trips to the sea. Like all his brothers and sisters, he had to work in the tobacco fields. Planting tobacco needed three workers on each furrow, one behind another: one to make a hole, one to place the seedling, one to cover and water it. Today the whole process is carried out by a single machine, but in those days it was a back-breaking toil.

George Karamanlis' business flourished again. His holding grew to ten acres, and he bought a lorry to carry his crop to the nearest railway station. He lent money freely to his friends, to invest in their enterprises. He was the great man of the village, owning one of the largest houses. As a former school-master he naturally wanted to give his sons the best education possible. (Daughters did not qualify for much education, by the provincial conventions of the day.) At Proti there was only a small primary school. So in 1919 he sent his eldest son, at the age of twelve, to board with friends at Nea Zikhni, fifteen miles away, where there was a secondary school of two classes, for boys up to thirteen.

The boy was miserable at first, and twice tried to run away home. In the end, locked in the house of his family friends, he accepted his fate. After a year at Nea Zikhni, he moved on to the larger secondary school at Serres for three years. Education became more congenial. But George Karamanlis doubted whether local education would ensure him a place at the University, so he decided that his secondary education must be completed in Athens. It was 1923, and Costa Karamanlis was sixteen years old.

He was accompanied on the journey to the capital by his father and his younger brother Aleko. As the family had no close relatives in Athens, the boys were placed in a private boarding school known from the headmaster's name as the Megareos Lyceum. A year later, in September 1924, the elder boy moved on to the Eighth Gymnasion (secondary school) in the district of Kypseli, where Aleko later followed him, but both boys continued to board at the Megareos Lyceum. The headmaster's daughter remembered the elder brother as a paragon, as headmasters' daughters are apt to do with boys older than themselves. But others too recalled him as a model pupil, impeccably dressed, handsome, and strong-willed.

He enjoyed life in Athens and made lasting friendships at school. Even as Prime Minister, he would attend reunion dinners of his class. Two schoolfriends in particular remained close to him for over a half a century. They both came, like Karamanlis' own family, from distant outposts of Hellenism where Greeks had to fight for their nationhood. Iordanis Propatoridis had escaped from Izmir (Smyrna) when the Turks occupied the city in 1922. Two years later Theodore Theodoridis was deported from Rhodes by the Italians for the crime of hoisting the Greek flag. Karamanlis was touched by the experiences of these two 'old refugees', as he called them.

Propatoridis became an eminent surgeon. Theodoridis opened a pharmacy in central Athens, where even as a Minister Karamanlis would stroll in to hand over his prescriptions in person, and sometimes argue politics with other customers. A fourth member of the youthful group, Nikos Yannopoulos, who also became a surgeon, met a tragic end. A woman patient on whom he had operated failed to recover. Her husband, out of his mind with grief, shot and killed Yannopoulos in the street. He had been, according to mutual friends, the closest of all to Karamanlis in their youth.

'Youth pleases youth', as the Greek proverb puts it; and it is often translated: 'Birds of a feather . . .'. But those who flock together are not always birds of a feather. Unlike his friends, Karamanlis was hot-tempered and quarrelsome: 'I was the terror of the neighbourhood,' he admitted; 'everyone I met, I fought.' Nor was he quite the model student his headmaster's daughter imagined. He attended classes so irregularly that his friends could not understand how he passed all his examinations near the top. The secret was that he went home in the vacations and 'read till my eyes fell out'; sometimes retreating to the congenial isolation of a monastery on Mount Pangaion where 'I read in four months what I had failed to read in four years.'

With his three friends, he entered the University of Athens in November 1925. While Theodoridis took a four-year course in pharmacology and the other two a five-year course in medicine, Karamanlis took the four-year course in law. They remained inseparable, though their interests diverged. Karamanlis, who was already set on politics, often attended debates in Parliament, where he was befriended by Athanasios Argyros, an influential Populist Deputy from Serres. There was a natural affinity between them, since George Karamanlis, conservative and royalist in outlook, also supported the Popular Party. But refugees from outside the frontiers of Greece, like Propatoridis and Theodoridis, were more inclined to support Venizelos and the Liberals.

The issues between the parties over the constitution were still alive and bitter. In the year Karamanlis came to the capital as a schoolboy, King George II was exiled and the monarchy was overthrown. The republic which took its place was often shaken by military coups. There were troubles also with Greece's neighbours: a terrible war with Turkey in 1921-2; the Italian seizure of Corfu in 1923; and an ill-judged attack by the Greeks on Bulgaria in 1925. The quarrel between royalists and republicans lasted from 1915, when Karamanlis was eight years old, until 1935; and even after the restoration of the monarchy, it was to break out again and again. All these events helped to shape Karamanlis' pessimistic philosophy of politics. But according to his friend Propatoridis, he was already looked upon by fellow students as a man destined to govern Greece; and he did not deny it.

Reflecting on the misfortunes of the times, he concluded that the essential bases of the state which he was to govern one day were stability and continuity, tolerance and reason. Revolution and change for change's sake were the perennial enemies of constitutional government. The Greece which he wanted to build was precisely what the Greece he saw as a student was not. That was why, while he would tease his friends the 'refugees' for supporting Venizelos, he would never quarrel with anyone for being a Venizelist. He never found it hard to make friends with political opponents. Yet this demanded more of a young man who took his politics seriously than it did of his Venizelist friend Propatoridis, who took them lightly.

They had other differences too. Propatoridis considered Karamanlis' tastes philistine. He liked the opera, while Karamanlis preferred detective films and night-clubs. 'How can one sing and kill somebody at the same time?', asked Karamanlis. Propatoridis persuaded him to come to a performance of *Tosca*. He watched his friend anxiously during the first act, expecting him to walk out. But as the curtain fell, Karamanlis admitted grudgingly that it was 'not so bad'. He sat through to the end, but enough was enough. The cinema remained his chief entertainment; and his favourite reaction to a film was to subject it to political analysis.

Despite his close friendships, he had also the reputation of a 'lone wolf'—what the Greeks call an *agrimi*. He would not conform to a conventional pattern, even in friendship. To say 'thank you' in a commonplace way, he once admitted, was a formality he found difficult; so he resolved to be indebted to no one. Later, from 1935, he developed a physical defect which further isolated him: he suffered from otosclerosis, which caused deafness and was then thought to be incurable. There were also more immediate problems in his university years, for his father's business was in trouble.

The tobacco industry in Macedonia collapsed in 1925, largely because of the competition of American tobacco in European markets. George Karamanlis had been over-ambitious in the prosperous years. He expanded his holding from ten acres to forty, borrowing at high rates of interest. There were enemies who were jealous of his plans to give his sons a private education. Moreover, he had brought them up to be open-handed. 'If anyone stands you a cup of coffee,' he told his eldest son, 'stand him two in return.' There was also the problem of dowries for his daughters. By 1927 the finances of the family were in a state of crisis.

In the ordinary course of events, the young Karamanlis would have been due to report for military service in 1927, but he was granted a postponement to finish his university course. Before taking his degree, he found employment as agent of an Italian insurance company, for which he worked throughout 1928-9. (Fifty years later he could not remember the name of the company, but his brother Aleko supplied it: the Anatoli.) It was a valuable experience, not only financially.

For two years he travelled indefatigably up and down, across and across his own province, earning enough to pay off his father's debts as well as meeting the family's expenses. He also acquired contacts and a knowledge of the world which were to be helpful in his political career. At the same time he was preparing to qualify as a practising lawyer. All this equipped him with more than a student's experience when he took his degree on 13 December 1929. Three months later, on 8 March 1930, he reported for duty at the headquarters of the Nineteenth Infantry Regiment in Serres.

Because of his family responsibilities, his period of service was reduced. Instead of serving eighteen months, he was released after four, having been promoted corporal, with a record-sheet which concluded: 'conduct excellent'. He had continued his studies while in the Army, and was now ready to begin his legal career. With the help of a loan from a family friend, he opened an office in Serres and awaited his first client.

It turned out to be a peasant charged with murder. In later years Karamanlis would say that he could not remember anything about the case, but under pressure he would admit that it never came to trial. Some said the man escaped, but Karamanlis thought he was released for want of evidence. Such an anticlimax befalls every young lawyer at the outset. But soon his practice flourished, making him financially independent within three years. He moved to a larger office and built up a handsome library of law books and Greek classics.

Olga, his eldest sister, came to Serres to keep house for him. It was not a demanding task, for his diet was very simple. Frugal meals left more time for thinking and talking about politics. All that Olga had to do was to keep her brother supplied with plenty of his favourite dish of spinach pie (*spanakopitta*), made strictly according to their mother's formula.

The career of a provincial lawyer, however successful, could never satisfy his aspirations. He knew that his vocation was politics. In 1932, having reached the statutory minimum age of twenty-five, he agreed to stand as a candidate for the Popular Party in his native county. But his father strongly opposed the idea, going so far as to say: 'I would not vote for you myself!'

He pointed to his son's need to earn his living, he warned him of the pitfalls of politics. Either he would be untrue to himself for the sake of success, or he would remain an honest man and fail; and in either case he would suffer torments.

In a Macedonian village it was a bold man who contradicted his father, but Karamanlis was convinced of his vocation. Long afterwards he recalled the substance of his reply:

If what you have in mind is my settling down, living an orderly family life, you must realise that I will never be reasonable in that way. If I am ambitious, it is because I am concerned with other things, much more important than myself. Is that naïvety? Perhaps I am naïve. But I still don't believe that one's existence on earth is justified by cultivating a bit of personal happiness. Everyone is a man in relation to other men—you know that very well, you have given proof of it. But everyone gives himself in his own way, according to time and circumstance. Today, for me, politics offer this opportunity. It is to my people that I want to devote myself, for them and through them I would justify my passage through the world.[2]

Nothing would shake his father's opposition. 'It is a long way from words to deeds,' said the old man, as if that would change his son's mind. His last uncompromising words were bitter: 'I do not want this disease to infect my house'. Aleko, the only brother old enough to understand what was going on, recalled it fifty years later as a terrible scene.

Part of George Karamanlis' disillusionment with politics was due to the events of the 1920s. As a royalist, he could see no merit in the unstable republic. Its only period of effective government had been under Venizelos from 1928 to 1932. It was in the latter year that the fateful conversation between father and son took place. What the father could not see was that it was precisely because of the instability and irresponsibility of contemporary politics that his son was set on becoming a politician. But the quarrel made it difficult for Karamanlis to take the decisive step immediately. He withdrew his candidature from the general election of September 1932 and returned to his work in Serres.

He did not see his father again until two months later, when he revisited Proti. It was their last meeting, for a few weeks later, on 21 November, George Karamanlis died. 'I have the feeling', said his son, 'that my father died with bitterness in

[2] Genevoix, pp. 68–9.

his heart. He thought that one day or another, beyond doubt, I should end by ignoring the advice he had given me.' And so he did. But in 1974 a group of his admirers, without his knowledge, added an inscription to his father's gravestone assuring the dead schoolmaster that his son had done right to take up a political career.

At least the day did not come in his father's lifetime. There was another general election in March 1933, but naturally Karamanlis did not take part, four months after his father's death. A heavy burden now fell on him as head of the family, with three young sisters to be married and three young brothers to be educated. But two years later, thanks to his success as a lawyer, his circumstances were secure enough.

A candidate of the Popular Party could hardly fail in the election of 9 June 1935. Three months earlier a military revolution had been attempted by a group of Venizelist officers who feared that the republic was about to be overthrown. They were briefly successful in the north-east. Karamanlis was among the known royalists who were seized and held by the rebels in Serres, where Aleko brought bedding and food to him in prison. But the coup was soon crushed by the government, and Karamanlis was freed after a fortnight. When the general election followed, its outcome was a foregone conclusion. The Venizelists and other republicans did not even put up candidates.

Although there had been friction among the Populists in Serres, and even talk of rival candidates within the party, the attempted coup removed any risk of a split. The party easily won all eight seats in the county, with Athanasios Argyros at the top of the poll. Over the whole country, the Populists and their allies won 287 seats out of 300. The rest went to two small parties of the extreme right, one of which was the Union of Royalists led by General Ioannis Metaxas, a former Chief of the General Staff, of whom much more was to be heard.

There was little satisfaction for Karamanlis in such a walkover. His apprenticeship to national politics had barely begun, and had not begun as he would have wished. But when he returned to Athens for the first time since his student days, he found new circles open to him as a Deputy. At first Argyros was his political mentor, but he soon formed a group with two or three other Deputies of his own generation. Among them was Lambros Evtaxias, a wealthy bachelor who owned one of the few surviving mansions of the last century, in Klavthmonos Square. Immediately opposite stood the Hotel Athinon, where Karamanlis rented a room in much more modest circumstances. It was to be the scene of many future triumphs, for up to 1963 Karamanlis always delivered his final speech as party leader in general elections from a balcony overlooking the square.

Other politicians soon noticed him, including the Prime Minister, Panagis Tsaldaris. A young lawyer, George Oikonomopoulos, who was later a close friend, first met him in Tsaldaris' private office, and heard the Prime Minister describe him as a man with a future. Although he might still have seemed a self-conscious provincial, his natural dignity and forthright speech attracted notice. An *arkhontas*, he was later called by one of his ministers, George Rallis—himself an *arkhontas*: a patrician, a natural aristocrat. But he never forgot his origins in a Macedonian village nor lost his Macedonian accent.

His early progress, however, was soon interrupted. The main task of the 1935 Parliament was to vote in October for the restoration of the monarchy. It was to be confirmed by a plebiscite, but before that could be held Tsaldaris' government was overthrown by militant royalists. The plebiscite on 3 November, which was known to be fraudulent, restored King George II by an overwhelming majority. But the King, who had spent most of his exile in London, returned with British ideas of parliamentary democracy. He dismissed the government which had restored him, appointed a non-partisan Prime Minister, and dissolved Parliament to hold new elections in January 1936. Even Venizelos declared himself reconciled to the monarchy shortly before he died on 18 March 1936.

The Liberals and republicans contested the new elections, but they were unsatisfactory in a different way from the previous occasion. Although Karamanlis had a personal success, the Popular Party fared badly. It won only two seats out of eight in the county of Serres. Argyros lost his seat; four Liberals and one Communist were elected; but Karamanlis was top of the poll. Over the country as a whole the major parties were so evenly represented that the Communist Party (KKE) held the balance with fifteen Deputies. The difficulty of forming a government was aggravated by the death in rapid succession of several of the country's established leaders. As a result General Metaxas, who had become Vice-Premier at the head of a minuscule party, succeeded as Prime Minister almost by default.

Once again Karamanlis' personal success was short-lived. The government of Metaxas, who had no respect for democracy, soon turned into a dictatorship. On the pretext of danger from the Communists, Metaxas persuaded the King on 4 August 1936 to dissolve Parliament, to suspend parts of the constitution, and to grant him emergency powers. His dictatorship, known as the 'Fourth of August', lasted until his death in January 1941, by which date Greece was at war with Italy and about to be invaded by the Germans. No Parliament met again for ten years. Karamanlis had not yet even had the opportunity to make a speech in Parliament.

The experience of the Fourth of August was traumatic for him. He had witnessed earlier coups, but only as a child or from a distance. This was the first time he found himself in the front line, and it was not the last. Naturally his reactions to the threat of military intervention thirty years later were conditioned by the experience of 1936. But it was harder to react against the Fourth of August because the dictatorship came about in an essentially constitutional fashion. The dictator was already the legitimate Prime Minister, and his powers were granted by a constitutional monarch. To have resisted the dictatorship would have been to support revolution. This would not in itself have been abhorrent to Karamanlis, who once described himself as having a 'revolutionary character'. But the purpose would have to be a serious one. Who can say that his caution was not a source of strength in a country which had so often embarked on reckless adventures?

His real strength could be described in another way. It lay in his capacity for patience and silence, for biding his time and keeping his own counsel. He showed it during ten years of political inactivity from 1936 to 1946, and again during eleven years of self-imposed exile, from 1963 to 1974. It is a striking fact that in a political career spanning forty-five years, twenty-one of them were spent out of action. But although the world saw his aloofness and reserve in those years, beneath the surface the political fervour was unquenched.

The first decade of inactivity was perhaps worse than the second, for the second was a matter of deliberate choice. In 1936, like most provincial Deputies, Karamanlis simply went home two or three weeks after Metaxas' seizure of power. Some, who had wider experience, like Panayotis Kanellopoulos on the right and George Papandreou on the left, as well as the Communists, openly opposed the dictatorship. Karamanlis did not, though he was under surveillance. He rejected any proposals of co-operation with the dictatorship, and resumed his law practice in Serres. There he stayed, apart from two or three visits a year to Athens, until war broke out with Italy in October 1940.

One of the few contacts he retained in the political world of Athens was with Evtaxias, who also visited him in Macedonia. Once when they were together in Kavalla, Karamanlis momentarily showed the depth of his resentment against the dictatorship. Seeing the crowded streets and squares of the city, which had once so nearly become part of Bulgaria, he remarked to Evtaxias: 'How I would love to be free to make speeches to these people!' But no such freedom existed. Merely to have tried would have invited arrest.

He was leading a solitary life at this time. The deafness was becoming acutely painful: sometimes he thought that he would never have a political career again. A visit to Austria and Germany—his first journey abroad—in quest of a cure was fruitless. He was working long hours to pay for the education of his younger brothers and his sisters' dowries. The family was still living at Proti, except for Olga who was with him at Serres. Another blow came in the early part of 1940, when his mother died. Only a small group of friends from Athens was present at the funeral.

His loneliness was also a matter of temperament. He did not enjoy social life, he had few amusements, he would not accept favours or obligations. He would be his own man, dependent on no one, watchful for opportunity but never compromising his destiny, however dark it might be. It became darker than ever when the Italians marched into Greece from Albania on 28 October 1940.

Greece then became Britain's only free ally in the world, a year after the outbreak of the Second World War. Karamanlis was thirty-three years of age, still liable for military service. He reported for duty at Sidirokastro, with his brother Aleko, who was twenty-six. Aleko was embodied in a unit bound for the Albanian front, but he himself was categorized as unfit for active service because of his deafness, and placed on the reserve. He returned to Serres with the intention of closing his office and moving the family to Athens. Long afterwards he admitted that he had been ashamed to stay at home as a reservist when his contemporaries were at the front, even though he had not applied for exemption but had it forced upon him.

In March 1941 the Karamanlis family left Macedonia for Athens. They never returned to the house at Proti, though it remained in their possession until it was sold in 1951 (but later repurchased by the younger brothers). In Athens they took a flat in the northern suburb of Kypseli. Karamanlis registered at the Law Society on 23 March in order to open an office in Athens. Aleko was sent back to Athens from Albania about the same time, to enter the officers' school. The three sisters were now grown up: Olga was thirty, Athina twenty-four, Antigoni twenty; but Grammenos and Akhilleas were still schoolboys, fifteen and eleven.

Soon the family was separated again, when the German invasion of Greece began on 6 April. The Greek Army and the small British expeditionary force were no match for the new enemy. Salonika fell to the Germans within ten days, Athens by the end of the month. The British withdrew as best they could, taking with them the King and his new Prime Minister, Emmanuel Tsouderos, a former Governor of the Bank of Greece. Although the Greeks surrendered, many hid their weapons for future use. The Italians followed the Germans into Athens, and the Bulgarians followed them into Macedonia and Thrace.

Some Greeks hoped at first that life under the occupation would not prove intolerable, but Karamanlis had no illusions. Although he remained in Athens to keep open his office, he soon realized that the bare necessities of life would be almost unobtainable. So the family must move back to Macedonia, with the exception of Aleko, who stayed to begin his own career as a lawyer, and Antigoni, who took a job in the Bank of Greece and kept house for her brothers.

The elder sisters were soon to be married, both of them to Macedonians: Olga to a doctor in 1940, Athina to a lawyer in 1941. It was natural for the family to move back to Macedonia, but not to Proti, which lay in the Bulgarian area of occupation. They settled instead at Nigrita, west of the River Strymon, where the German occupation seemed by comparison to be the lesser evil. Thus the family was divided: four of them in Macedonia, three in Athens. From Nigrita food parcels occasionally arrived in Athens, but Karamanlis did not see his family in the north again until the liberation. It came as a surprise to him to learn at the end of the war that his brother Grammenos had joined the Communist-controlled resistance force of ELAS.

The flat in Kypseli was Karamanlis' only home in those years. Like every home until he married, and even afterwards, it was a temporary accommodation which acquired an accidental permanence. Antigoni and Aleko were both at work, but he himself gave up his legal practice after the Germans commandeered the building where he had his office. The years of occupation were far worse in Athens than in the provinces. To make a living was almost impossible, except by collaborating with the enemy. Karamanlis rejected collaboration as uncompromisingly as he rejected armed resistance, which he saw as pursuing unacceptable aims. As he put it later, 'No movement of that period reflected my own political ideas.'

It was not for lack of approaches that he remained detached. The collaborating authorities offered him employment, either as a nomarch (the chief executive of a county authority) or in the Agricultural Bank. He refused all such offers, saying that after the war he intended to return to politics with an uncompromised reputation. But he did not remain entirely idle, for idleness was always intolerable. His main activity was to help in the administration of relief to the Macedonian colony in Athens. It entailed a walk of several miles every day from Kypseli to the centre of Athens and back, but at least it also ensured a meal of sorts.

While in the centre, he occasionally visited old friends, such as Lambros Evtaxias. Otherwise his life was a melancholy routine: reading at home, studying English, gossiping with his sister, occasionally visiting the Café Gambetta, where the Macedonians forgathered. But there was little joy there, for he had no money to buy a cup of coffee, nor was there anything worth calling coffee to be had. After once being told by a truculent waiter to remove himself if he had nothing to order, Karamanlis went there no more. He sat at home and brooded on his obscure destiny.

A faint inkling of what that destiny might be emerged during 1942. There was a group of Athenian intellectuals on the fringe of politics who had been meeting from time to time since before the war to discuss their nation's future. During the occupation they widened their scope by recruiting a few politicians, though they were determined not to become involved in the political squabbles of the wartime years. Many of them later played leading roles: Professor Costa Tsatsos as President of the Republic; Professor Xenophon Zolotas as Governor of the Bank of Greece; George Mavros as Foreign Minister and leader of the revived Liberals; Petros Garouphalias as Minister of Defence; Professor Angelos Angelopoulos as Governor of the National Bank, despite a brief flirtation with the extreme left.

The points of view within the group ranged from liberalism leftwards. Its members felt the need of a contributor from the conservative side. One of the group, the lawyer George Oikonomopoulos, suggested his friend Karamanlis. None of the others knew him personally, but they welcomed him to the group. His forthright views impressed them. He in turn enjoyed the intellectual company, though he found many of the discussions theoretical and trivial.

In the spring of 1944 the group broke up, for a variety of reasons. Angelopoulos broke ranks by going to the mountains, where the left-wing resistance, controlled by EAM (the National Liberation Front), had set up a committee known as PEEA (Political Committee of National Liberation). This was virtually an alternative government, challenging the authority of the King's government in exile. Its establishment was followed by the murder of a respected leader of the non-Communist resistance, Colonel Psaros, and a mutiny in the armed forces in Egypt.

Karamanlis shared in the general horror at these events. He

saw that the time for action had come, and that the centre of action must lie outside Greece, in the Middle East. A conference of leading politicians met during May 1944 in the Lebanon, to form a government of national unity under George Papandreou, who had recently escaped from Greece. Karamanlis did not have a high opinion of Papandreou, to whom he sent a critical letter while still in Athens. But he resolved at last to make his own escape from the occupation, and to make contact with the new government and the world outside.

It was well known that caiques slipped across the Aegean from time to time, and that places on them could be bought at a price. But being well known, it was also known to the Germans, who took what steps they could to block the hazardous traffic before the refugees reached safety in Turkey. Karamanlis was under surveillance. He no longer slept regularly in his flat, but moved from house to house. When he decided to leave, at first he told only his old friend the pharmacist Theodoridis. But later he needed Aleko's help, and let him into the secret.

The first chance came while the Lebanon conference was assembling. He was to be one of the 'second mission to the Lebanon', as he put it, with a group of politicians which included Constantine Tsaldaris, the nephew of the late Prime Minister and his successor as leader of the Popular Party. The plan was to sail from Porto Raphti on the east coast of Attica. It was abortive because it became known to the Germans, but fortunately the Greeks learned in time that they knew.

Some days later Tsaldaris told Karamanlis of another opportunity, but the price was thirty gold sovereigns. He replied that he had not even thirty lice on him. ('Pounds' and 'lice'— *lires* and *pseires*—rhyme in Greek.) But a better chance came in July, through a British officer of the clandestine services. This time Aleko was to drive him to the rendezvous, which was at Anavyssos, a small harbour near the southern tip of Attica.

The group which assembled there had to wait for two days, hiding in a ravine. It was not a bad time of year for sleeping rough, but Karamanlis never slept at all, and the days were intolerably hot. On the second night a caique from Peiraeus put in and embarked the waiting party. They sailed without lights through the islands, making for the gap between Tinos and Andros. There they met heavy seas, which forced them to anchor in a bay on the north coast of Tinos.

They were found, no doubt not accidentally, by men belonging to ELAS. Since ELAS depended on EAM and the KKE (Communist Party of Greece), they were unlikely to be sympathetic to Karamanlis. When he admitted who he was, they took him to the small port of Panormos and locked him in the Customs shed. The rest of the group were released. No Germans were to be seen; but for Karamanlis the Communists rather than the Germans were now the prime enemy.

He was held there for many days: he lost count of the time. At last he persuaded an officer of ELAS to let him out on parole, to have his shoes repaired. At the cobbler's shop he again identified himself, with better success. The cobbler put him in touch with a sailor, who told him of a caique, anchored at an uninhabited islet nearby, which was due to sail with a party for Turkey that night. A rendezvous was fixed, and Karamanlis returned to the Customs shed as he had promised. But soon after midnight he broke a window, jumped out, and found his way to the rendezvous. A small boat took him to the place where the caique was anchored.

It was the night of 14 August. The story is taken up by an Army officer, Captain Andreas Papalionardou, whose diary records that Karamanlis joined his party that night. Papalionardou's group had set out from Attica on 10 August, but had also been held up by bad weather between Tinos and Andros. With its crew, the caique had some fifty persons on board, including two Generals and a well-known violinist. The diary covers the next seven weeks, during which Papalionardou was seldom out of the company of Karamanlis.

On the day after they set out, bad weather again drove them back. They anchored at Gioura (Gyaros), an island later famous as a place of exile for dissidents. Three other caiques were also held up there, with passengers for the same destination. They were delayed for several days by the harsh, dry wind known as the *meltemmi*. After the wind dropped, they set out again, but this time they were held up by engine trouble. Ten days passed in this succession of frustrations. It was not until 25 August that they passed through the gap between Tinos and

Andros. After that, sailing was easier. They passed between Ikaria and Samos on the twenty-sixth, to arrive on the Turkish coast that evening.

Three Turkish soldiers saw them land at an otherwise uninhabited spot. They were not unfriendly, and asked them only the puzzling question, whether there were any Jews in the party. Other Turkish officials later wanted to know if any of them were Anatolian Greeks. But there was no attempt to delay them, for the Turkish authorities had a well-established arrangement with the British to receive Greek refugees as well as escaping British and American servicemen.

On the twenty-seventh they were taken on foot to a neighbouring village, and from there to Cheshmé, where Greek consular officials met them. Later that day they were driven by car to Izmir (Smyrna), where Karamanlis was installed in the Ankara Hotel. He and his new friend, Captain Papalionardou, who was at a neighbouring hotel, were allowed to move freely about the town—a town full of emotional memories for any Greek—during the next four days. Papalionardou had carefully concealed from the Turks that he was an officer, for fear of internment. It was better to be a civilian in the hands of the Turks, but the other way round, as Karamanlis was to discover, once they passed into the hands of the British.

They were put on a train for Syria on 1 September, and arrived at Aleppo two days later. There the British took charge of them. Many days passed in frustrating inactivity at a military camp. Papalionardou remembered only receiving injections and preparing lists of officers; Karamanlis remembered a concert in which the Greek violinist played with an orchestra of the RAF. The rest of his memories were hazy: 'I managed somehow—how, I don't know—to get to Egypt.'

It was a frustrating process. The first officers left the camp on 13 September; Papalionardou said goodbye to Karamanlis on the twenty-ninth; but still the civilians remained behind. Finally Karamanlis was allowed to leave for Cairo in the first week of October, after some five weeks in British hands. He was already too late to play any part in the political developments which had been launched by the Lebanon conference, for on 7 September Papandreou's government had left Egypt for Italy on the penultimate stage of its return to Greece.

Karamanlis arrived in Cairo almost destitute, hungry, shabby, and penniless. At the Greek Club he was refused admission because he was not wearing a tie. He was recognized, with difficulty and incredulity, by a fellow Deputy, the retired General Binopoulos, who lent him money and helped him find a hotel. He enquired after an old friend, John Livanos ('not the big shipowner, a poor Livanos'), and learned that he was at Alexandria.

He left Cairo for Alexandria, where he was warmly welcomed. The next morning he awoke to find Greek flags flying all over the city. Their meaning was plain: Athens was free. He stood on his hotel balcony with tears in his eyes. It was time to return home, after four months' vain travelling.

His friends urged him to stay in Alexandria for a time to recuperate, but he was in a hurry to be off. He returned to Cairo, where he obtained a flight to Athens on 26 October, in a British aircraft carrying other politicians, among them Tsaldaris. He summed up his adventures with blunt realism: 'I left without a tie, I came back without a tie.'

Athens was already in a state of tension between the Greek and British authorities on the one side and the left-wing resistance on the other. Although there were Communists in Papandreou's government, they refused to accept his plans for disarming ELAS unless the Greek regular forces were also demobilized. At last the tension burst into open violence on 3 December, which lasted until the British forces drove ELAS out of Athens in January 1945. A truce was eventually signed at Varkiza, a coastal resort near Athens, on 12 February.

Karamanlis played no part in these turbulent and bloody events. He was again living at the Hotel Athinon, short of food and occasionally under fire. A revolution was no place for him, just as he had no place in a dictatorship, occupation, or the resistance. His place was only in a responsible, constitutional system, and he would not compromise himself. For the same reasons he took no part in the extra-parliamentary manœuvres which led to the appointment and replacement of successive governments by the British authorities during 1945.

During that summer he made his first post-war journey abroad, travelling to England, where he stayed for two months with a friend, Stavros Papastavrou, who taught at Cambridge. His main object was to improve his English, but he made few acquaintances and saw little of the country, apart from visits to Oxford and London. While at Cambridge he tried to set down his political philosophy in writing for the first time. He formulated it in a letter to an old family friend, George Avtzis, a lawyer from Rodoleivos, near Proti, a few years older than himself. Avtzis published the letter (though not in its entirety) in the newspaper *Vradyni* on 2 November 1974.

'You want to have my thoughts on our political affairs,' Karamanlis began, going with characteristic bluntness straight to the point: 'I find them heart-breaking.' He found the country suffering from 'incurable political incompetence'. The problems were essentially simple, but they were complicated by stupidity and bad faith. The political leadership of the country was completely discredited. He went on:

I am sure that neither the right nor the left—what misunderstandings, to be sure, those terms cause in our country!—would choose to be where it is if it could clarify its position logically. But where can you find logic in this blessed country? Or even if you could once find it, you will find it lacking in that generous spirit which alone makes it creative. And yet, as I have said to you before, without a spirit of generosity nothing significant can be done in life, above all in political life, which is the fullest expression of life. So for the salvation of this country there has to be a profound change in its political life. But when?

He rejected the popular view that crushing the Communist rising in December 1944 and winning the forthcoming plebiscite on the monarchy would prove a sufficient renovation of political life. 'Once the impression left by the crime of December has faded and our national effort is finished, what will be left to unite us with the soul of the people?' Nothing, he implied, unless the coming election were used as the basis of an evolution in political life towards 'the creation of such conditions as to liberate people from the need to follow parties which fail to inspire it, and to establish the prerogative of innovation somewhere other than at the street corner'. The purpose of politics must become not simply to win elections but to use power responsibly. 'People cannot safely be left to carry on politics in future as if they were simply taking a pill.'

How was this to be achieved? 'By learning to practise politics,' he answered. The highest form of politics he defined as consisting in 'the will and the ability of even the most insignificant of men to sacrifice himself for his country'. But this will was almost entirely lacking in public life. It was no use talking about the lack of personalities: although true, this was not the explanation of 'our political disaster'. The fault lay in the Greeks' incapacity for political consistency: 'It is an incapacity which runs through the whole of our age-long history. Hellenism, you see, has always lived in a state of improvisation and extremism. It can perform momentary miracles, but it cannot make a continuous effort. And politics is above all a continuous effort.'

The Greek people, he continued, 'is intelligent and therefore capable of identifying what is right, but is incapable of carrying it to a conclusion because of psychological defects.' No Greek, for example, could forgive himself if he helped to bring about the promotion of somebody else. The traditional poverty of the Greeks merely led them into political opportunism. So where was a new breed of politicians to be found? His answer was pessimistic: 'Politics is not like poetry, which you can create far from the world. The politician needs the strength which he draws from the confidence of the world. But we have no confidence in anything or anybody.'

He ended with a striking reference to Elevtherios Venizelos, the only Greek politician before his own time who might have been regarded as an exception: 'Venizelos, my friend, had already made his name before he came here. He came as a figure from outside Greece. If he had made his début in free Greece, I fear that he would have been sunk from the first. For me that is the secret of his immediate domination.'

Such was the melancholy conclusion of Karamanlis' first statement of his political theory. It seemed to preclude from the outset any prospect of success for himself on his own austere terms. The rest of his career was devoted to proving himself mistaken. Like Venizelos, after all, he came from 'outside Greece'—that is to say, from a province which had not yet become Greek when he was born there. And when he returned from exile in 1974, he too 'had already made his name before he came'.

Chapter 2
The Path to the Top

It was not until the last day of March 1946 that the first general election for a decade could be held. Even then conditions were unsatisfactory and growing worse. The disorders which had reached their first climax in December 1944 were breaking out again. In some areas, particularly Macedonia, the government was hardly in control. Many politicians, including the Prime Minister, Themistocles Sophoulis, wanted the elections postponed until security was assured; but no one could say when that would be. There had been several postponements already, and the British authorities, who held the reins of power in Athens, would not tolerate another. The extreme left refused to take part in the elections, and was perhaps already planning an armed rebellion again. On the night before polling day a guerrilla raid on Litokhoro, a small town at the foot of Mount Olympus, caused the poll there to be postponed for a week. It was later hailed as the first blow in a new civil war.

The election was nevertheless recognized as reasonably free and fair by an international team of observers from Britain, France, and the USA. The Soviet government refused to send observers. It had already referred the Greek situation to the United Nations, which gave its complaints no support. Naturally the Soviet government gave moral support to the Greek Communists, who claimed that all those who failed to vote would have voted Communist. In the conditions of 1946 a victory of the right was certain in any case. Constantine Tsaldaris, the leader of the Popular Party, formed a government based on a large majority. At Serres Karamanlis was top of the poll, as he was to be at every subsequent election until he retired as Prime Minister in 1980.

He had no expectation of being included in the government at once, but he soon attracted notice. He was appointed to two important parliamentary committees, covering foreign and economic affairs. Not only his own party but also leading figures of the Opposition regarded him favourably, among them Sophoulis, the Liberal leader, and Sophocles Venizelos, the son of the great Prime Minister. Still, Karamanlis was doubtful even if he would be able to continue his political career. He had first to find a cure for his deafness, which was becoming intensely painful.

His hopes were revived by his friend Xenophon Zolotas, who wrote to him from the USA about a newly developed operation to remedy otosclerosis, known as 'fenestration'. He set out for New York, where the operation was successfully carried out in the summer of 1946. With this assurance of the renewed possibility of a political career, there also came the news, while he was in New York, of his appointment to an economic mission, which had been sent to Washington in July under Sophocles Venizelos. Karamanlis went straight from New York to Washington to join it.

The mission had many topics to discuss, arising from the devastation of Greece in the war and the increasing inability of the British government to supply sufficient aid. One of the topics was the export of Greek tobacco, in which Karamanlis had both a special interest and personal experience as a Macedonian, but there were other far graver issues to be discussed. President Truman himself received the mission, and detailed talks went on with Dean Acheson, the Assistant Secretary of State and future architect of the Truman Doctrine, together with other officials.

Karamanlis found the Americans well-meaning but dangerously naïve about the Soviet threat. 'You are a great country', he told the President, 'but we are nearer to them.' The Venizelos mission bluntly warned the Americans that Greece was in danger of total collapse, but they obtained little relief. The US government allotted them a hundred Liberty ships, which became the basis of the Greek merchant marine, but also pressed on them the advice that their government must be broadened if more aid was to be forthcoming. On their way home, they stopped in Paris, where Tsaldaris was attending the Peace Conference, and they conveyed to him the unwelcome message from Washington.

Tsaldaris twice tried to form a wider coalition, but each time his discussions with the Opposition broke down. So on

4 November he formed a new Council of Ministers drawn exclusively from the Popular Party, and three weeks later he invited Karamanlis to join it as Minister of Labour. For the first time, on 24 November 1946, Karamanlis entered ministerial office, at the age of thirty-nine. By the standards of Greek political life, he was still a very young man.

The problems facing the successive governments of Tsaldaris were formidable, and labour relations were not the least among them. Greece was still living with the legacy of the German occupation, the consequences of which were to last for many years. Everything depended on British support, but Britain's capacity to meet her overseas obligations was visibly failing. The only problem which Tsaldaris could claim to have settled so far was the persistent question of the monarchy. King George II had been restored to his throne by a plebiscite in September; but the result was to increase the antagonism of Greece's Communist neighbours in the north and of the KKE at home. The growth of violence was met, with little effect, by a new Security Law. Soon the very existence of the state was threatened.

The Ministry of Labour was at the centre of the conflict. Industrial law had been left in a state of chaos by the occupation, and it was aggravated by the appointment of a Communist as Minister of Labour in Papandreou's government of national unity. He had immediately installed a Communist-controlled executive of the General Confederation of Greek Workers (GSEE). After the uprising of December 1944 was crushed, many Communist trade-unionists were held in prison. Nevertheless the first elections to the new executive of the GSEE in March 1946 were won by the Communists. Four months later the courts invalidated the elections on the ground that the organizing committee was not properly constituted. With the help of an adviser sent by the British TUC, a compromise was devised in November, by which the previous executive of the GSEE was restored to office with the addition of five representatives of the 'reformist' wing of the trade unions. It was further agreed that the imprisoned trade-unionists should be released, apart from those charged with murder.

Karamanlis took office at this difficult point. He had also

to grapple with the complex problems, inherited from the war, of wages, pensions, health and accident insurance, unemployment benefits, and even Christmas bonuses. There had been no recovery yet from the ravages of war and occupation; the economic situation was worse even than in 1944; and the urban Communists in the trade unions were acting in concert with their colleagues in the mountains, in trying to destroy the state. Nevertheless Karamanlis carried out the agreement to release the imprisoned trade-unionists: 121 out of 162 were set free, the remainder all being held on charges of murder.

Beyond that, the problems which Karamanlis inherited were insoluble during his short term of office. Despite interminable discussions in the Ministry, obstruction by the left-wing union organizations made progress impossible. Perhaps the most significant and characteristic step Karamanlis took was to spend almost three weeks in northern Greece, visiting Salonika, Serres, and Kavalla to study the deteriorating situation at first hand. That tour occupied almost a quarter of the duration of his first ministerial appointment. But he had little opportunity to apply the lessons he learned, for in January 1947 Tsaldaris' government was forced to resign, and gave way to a wider coalition under Dimitrios Maximos.

When Maximos took office on 24 January, at first he re-appointed Karamanlis along with other less senior ministers. But on 17 February he reconstructed his government, and Karamanlis was dropped. It was his first personal set-back, made the more disappointing for him by the fact that his post was not simply taken over by a new member of the coalition but amalgamated with the Ministry of Agriculture. In reporting the reconstruction, the Press barely mentioned his name, and gave no reason for his exclusion from office. Nor did he ever receive any explanation.

He remained out of office for the next fifteen months. It was a frustrating period, in which Greece was almost destroyed beyond recovery by the Communist rebellion, aided by the Communist powers to the north. Macedonia in particular was in mortal peril. But there was little that an ordinary Deputy could do. Karamanlis' parliamentary commitments were limited to membership of the committees on reconstruction, foreign affairs, and the Press. Few opportunities for initiative were open to him. One of the few was a proposal, which he initiated in February 1948, to provide compensation for drivers attacked and lorries destroyed by the rebel forces. These were risks to which his own constitituents were particularly exposed.

Before Karamanlis came back into office in May 1948, history had taken a new course. In March 1947 the American President launched what became known as the Truman Doctrine, with the primary object of protecting Greece and Turkey from Soviet aggression. A few weeks later King George died, to be succeeded by his younger brother Paul. In July Greece joined other European countries in a conference to discuss the Marshall Plan, the United States' second great initiative of the year. On 24 August the Maximos government was replaced by another coalition under Sophoulis, but there was not yet a place in it for Karamanlis. In October the United Nations passed a resolution setting up a Special Commission on the Balkans, to investigate the Greek charges against Albania, Yugoslavia, and Bulgaria, and also the countercharges of the latter.

One of the few cheering events of the years 1947–8 was the cession of the Dodecanese by Italy to Greece under the peace treaty. Not surprisingly, this event was accompanied by a campaign for the cession of Cyprus by Britain. In March 1947 the Greek Parliament unanimously passed a resolution expressing its hope for *enosis* (the union of Cyprus with Greece). But the only response from Britain was a proposal for a new constitution, published on 7 May 1948. Its terms held out no hope for *enosis*.

On the same day, as it happened, Karamanlis returned to office. Sophoulis re-formed his government, after the assassination of one of his ministers in the streets of Athens by a Communist six days earlier. In the reconstructed government Karamanlis was appointed Minister of Transport. It was a less politically contentious office than his previous one, but it was entangled in administrative problems. The country's communication system had been wrecked by the occupation, and its restoration was now held up by the civil war. Equipment, fuel, and money were all in short supply. Karamanlis was responsible not only for roads and public vehicles, shipping, railways, and civil aviation, but also for electricity and all liquid fuels. Strikes were frequent; so were complaints about inadequate services. Karamanlis also found himself involved for the first time in serious disputes with British and American representatives.

It was his policy always to bring his problems out into the open. Within a month of taking office, he found himself criticized in the liberal newspaper *Vima* for the shortcomings of the public-transport system. He replied in a short, vigorous letter on 5 June; and *Vima* at once apologized to him, explaining that the criticisms had been directed at his predecessor. Complaints continued in Parliament, but each of his critics was now careful to say that Karamanlis was not personally to blame.

Blame for the inadequacies of the electricity supply naturally fell on the British-owned Power and Traction Company, with whose resident Director Karamanlis found himself more than once in conflict. Upon his insistence that the Company had an obligation to install new equipment to meet increased demand, the Director flew to London for consultation, and returned with the reply that the Company could not afford it. Karamanlis then proposed that American aid should be used for the purpose, with a revision of the Company's charter in the light of the new situation. The Company refused, and asked the British government to intervene.

Ernest Bevin, the Foreign Secretary, accordingly made representations to Tsaldaris in London. Tsaldaris asked Karamanlis to discuss the problem with the British Ambassador. Relations between the two men became strained, and the discussions broke down. Karamanlis then proposed to the Council of Ministers that the necessary capital should be raised from Greek sources and the Company's charter revised. Although the government agreed, action was not completed until after Karamanlis left the Ministry. In the event, the required capital was found from US funds. But the revision of the charter was not carried out until the end of 1959, when the Company was replaced by the Public Electricity Corporation on 1 January 1960.

Meanwhile Karamanlis had the unenviable task of explaining

the delays to the exasperated people of Athens. On 2 October 1948 *Vima* complained that he was not vigorous enough in dealing with the Power and Traction Company. The same paper complained again on 5 October about the dilapidated buses still in service. Karamanlis replied with a letter giving details of the steps he had taken for their replacement and for relieving the congestion of the central squares of Athens. As a result of these exchanges *Vima* became a discriminating supporter of Karamanlis, at least during the lifetime of its proprietor, Dimitrios Lambrakis.

More important than answering the nagging criticisms was the task of laying the basis of reconstruction. Inevitably it now depended on American support. Thanks to Marshall Aid, the Corinth Canal was reopened in July 1948 and the network of motor-roads was extended into the areas threatened by the rebels. Together with an investment of six million dollars in the electricity supply for Athens, these were essential contributions to Greek recovery; so too was Karamanlis' energy in exploiting them.

As a provincial himself, he recognized the importance of extending all public services into remoter areas. His were the first plans to be carried out for the electrification of the provincial towns and islands. He established a company to run the trams and electricity supply in Salonika, emphasizing the importance of creating industries in the north to avoid congestion round Athens. He introduced legislation to co-ordinate road and rail transport, with a fund to equalize freight rates, and also to improve coastal communications, which were important because most of the major towns of Greece were on the sea.

In Drama, the town neighbouring his own constituency of Serres, he was once greeted by a newspaper article calling for 'the sympathy of our compatriot'. Drama benefited from that sympathy, which gave the town its first electricity supply; but so did dozens of other provincial towns. For Karamanlis was careful to protect himself against charges of favouritism. When the new road programme was eventually completed, the villagers of Proti complained that their area had been left to the last.

Karamanlis took his own decisions in these matters, dependent though he was on the Americans. Sometimes he took their advice—for instance, in declining the offer of a power-station from Bremen as part of war reparations, on grounds of cost and delay. Sometimes he rejected their advice—refusing, for instance, to agree with the recommendation of American experts that the railways of the Peloponnese should be closed. In October 1948 he introduced legislation to reform the basis of concessions to foreign companies, which would affect not only the British Power and Traction Company but American and other foreign interests as well. Their opposition to the proposal led to the transfer of Karamanlis on 18 November from the Ministry of Transport to a new department, the Ministry of Social Welfare. It was part of a general reconstruction of Sophoulis' government, and gave Karamanlis his first great opportunity.

Although he had been at the Ministry of Transport only six months, that was twice as long as his first post at the Ministry of Labour, and long enough for him to have made his mark. His tenure of the Ministry of Social Welfare was twice as long again, from 18 November 1948 to 5 January 1950. It was decisive in establishing his reputation, for as *Vima* wrote two days after his appointment, his was the most difficult task in the government. Apart from the normal problems of a relatively underdeveloped country, there were now nearly 700,000 refugees from the civil war, including some 400,000 in northern Greece. 'On his handling of the refugee problem', said *Vima* on 20 November, 'will be judged not only the person of the Minister but the competence of the whole government.'

He responded with the energy which was his most conspicuous characteristic. The mere catalogue of his movements in the following twelve months illustrates both his determination and his method of work. Within a week of his appointment, he was in Ioannina to organize preparations for the return of refugees. He was in central Macedonia in early December, and in Karditsa in the middle of the month, immediately after the rebels had temporarily occupied the town and been driven out. He was in Ioannina again a week later to make sure that his earlier plans were being executed; in western Macedonia during January 1949, to visit Naoussa, which had also just been attacked; in central Macedonia during March; in Rhodes during

April: back in Salonika in May; in central Greece and Thessaly during July, and then again in central Macedonia; in Larisa, Ioannina, and Salonika during August; in central Greece, Thessaly, and Ioannina during October; in Macedonia and Thrace during November, and in Evvia (Euboea) later in the same month. The refugees everywhere knew who was looking after them.

The tours were not simply intended to enhance Karamanlis' popularity, though they had that incidental result. The Press noted with respect that he was in Karditsa and Naoussa within days of their relief, and that when Karpenisi was besieged in January 1949 he was immediately on the telephone to Lamia to organize relief. No other minister had such a good press, but no other minister did what he did. On two of his visits to the north, in March and August 1949, he was accompanied by leading officials of the US missions to Greece and by other ministers; but there was no doubt who was playing the leading role, and the Americans could not fail to see it. In the intervals between his tours, a spate of legislative and administrative action was launched in Athens.

His first week in office set the pattern. During three days in Ioannina he set up a housing committee for the refugees, ordered clothing and prefabricated huts, increased allowances for food and fuel, commandeered buildings—including cinemas, cafés, schools, and a theological college (which was designated to become a *paidoupolis* or kindergarten)—and held a press conference to tell people exactly what he was doing. 'Within ten days all the refugees will have a roof over them,' he announced; 'and before the end of the month they will all have new clothes.' These were not idle boasts. He called for patriotic efforts and a spirit of sacrifice. Boldly he declared that private rights must take second place to national needs. Returning to Athens, he told the Council of Ministers what he had done, emphasizing that they were dealing with a state of war rather than a problem of social policy. His colleagues agreed, and authorized him to do the same elsewhere. They were thankful to have a colleague who did things.

The Press too recognized that a new star was rising. A leading newspaper in Ioannina, the *National Struggle*, praised Karamanlis for 'cutting the Gordian knot'. Similar praise came from *Makedonia* in Salonika. There was qualified approval from *Vima* on 27 November 1948, and even from the habitually critical *Estia* a week later. When he had laid his detailed plans for co-ordinating relief before the Council of Ministers on 14 December, *Vima* commented two days later: 'We believe this was the first time that the problem was faced as a whole in a systematic way.' But Karamanlis was not in Athens to read his praises: he was in Karditsa, and then on his way to Ioannina again.

It was true that his plans were for the first time comprehensive. There was to be a national census of refugees, which began on 12 December, but there was no need to wait for the figures to see where action was most urgent. Security zones were established in the endangered areas by the selective arming of villagers. 'Children's towns' or kindergartens were set up in half a dozen areas on the same model as at Ioannina. The number of food-distribution centres was doubled. Subsidies were offered to re-establish agriculture. The distribution of clothing and prefabricated housing was accelerated. Relief funds were augmented by taxation and US grants. A scheme of 'Welfare-Work' was set up with the dual object of providing employment for refugees and accelerating reconstruction.

All this activity was to be co-ordinated by two government committees. One was an Advisory Council under the chairmanship of the Minister of Social Welfare, comprising senior representatives of the Ministries of Co-ordination, Reconstruction, Agriculture, Economic Affairs, Health, and Supply. American advisers might also attend this body. The other was a Co-ordinating Committee under the Minister of Co-ordination, comprising the Ministers of Economic Affairs, Social Welfare, Reconstruction, Agriculture, Health, Supply, and the Interior, together with the Chief of the General Staff. The only man who had a seat on both bodies was Karamanlis himself.

His proposals were supported in the Press, which helped to give the public the encouraging feeling that at last something decisive was being done. But some resistance was inevitable. Other ministers resented the apparent subordination of their departments to the Ministry of Social Welfare. The Chiefs of Staff feared the consequences of giving arms to civilians. The funds for 'Welfare-Work' were not easily granted. Sophoulis asked Venizelos and Markezinis to arbitrate between Karamanlis' demands and his colleagues' opposition. Venizelos was nervous about supporting Karamanlis, but Markezinis did so more readily. So Karamanlis finally had his own way, and the repatriation of the refugees was carried out far more rapidly than the American advisers had thought possible.

Karamanlis had become indispensable. A crisis in the conduct of the civil war led to another reorganization of Sophoulis' government in January 1949, and to the appointment of General Papagos as Commander-in-Chief of all the armed forces. The new government was an even broader coalition, but Karamanlis remained Minister of Social Welfare and continued in the same post after Sophoulis died on 24 June. For a short period, from 24 February to 14 April, he combined the Ministry of Health with his principal post. It was a striking reversal of his fate in the reconstruction of February 1947.

On 26 January 1949 he submitted to the Council of Ministers those of his proposals which required legislation. The objections to them had been overborne. His draft bill 'On the co-ordination of measures for the remedy of all categories of needs of the victims of the bandits' became Law No. 894 on 2 March. It was by far the most important legislation passed by the government of the day.

There was no delay in putting it into effect. The Advisory Council met for the first time, with US officials present, on 23 March. By 2 April the census of refugees was completed, showing a total of 706,092. By the middle of June Karamanlis was able to announce that 456 schemes had been approved under his 'Welfare-Work' plans. The budget for the refugees was approved on 6 July. A few days later it was announced that the repatriation programme had been completed in the Peloponnese, the first area to be cleared of rebels.

A meeting of the Co-ordinating Committee on 14 July was attended by General Papagos as well as the ministers concerned. Karamanlis reported that 146,000 refugees had already been repatriated, 227,000 more would be repatriated by the end of September, and 53,000 had been deleted from the lists on revision of the census. He also asked Papagos for more small arms for the security zones. This could now easily be agreed, for the supply of American weapons was ample and the defeat of the rebel forces was only a few weeks away. The autocratic Commander-in-Chief perhaps did not enjoy having to meet the requirements of a rising politician who had never risen in the Army above the rank of acting corporal. But he complied.

Although it was the refugee problem which brought Karamanlis into the public eye, he won the respect of his subordinates also by his attention to less spectacular tasks unrelated to the Communist rebellion: routine matters such as the relief of chronic poverty and the care of the war-wounded; acts of God such as disastrous storms in Crete and an earthquake in Chios; and the elimination of corruption in his department, which resulted in two criminal investigations during his term of office. He also won the respect of the Press by his blunt refusal to raise false hopes. The Macedonian paper *Tharros* reported on 12 July 1949 that 'when faced with unreasonable demands and claims from the mayors, he had the courage to blurt out the painful truth that "All Greeks make demands but none of them wants to pay!"'

But as final victory over the Communist rebellion approached, the pressure to accelerate repatriation grew again, and with it came a renewal of criticisms. Karamanlis frankly admitted delays in his programme for Epirus 'owing to lack of technical preparation'. He was obliged to ask Parliament for wider powers and the Americans for increased funds. The main reason was that his earlier plans, made before the rebellion was finally crushed at the end of August 1949, had assumed a slower rate of repatriation than was now feasible. On 16 October the Communist leaders announced that they were 'discontinuing the armed struggle'. Ten days later Karamanlis made a statement, to forestall false optimism, describing the magnitude of the remaining problems and the stages by which he proposed to tackle them.

It was not long before the relief of victory gave way to grievances. A Deputy complained that the extended powers given to the Minister by new Orders introduced under Law No. 894 would enable him to influence local elections in the provinces. Although *Vima* wrote on 11 August that 'we cherish exceptional regard for Karamanlis', a month later, on 18 September, it was calling for 'a co-ordinating Commander-in-Chief' to conduct 'the battle of repatriation'. The military metaphor suggested that the writer had Papagos in mind. Karamanlis made no reference to the hint when he replied in Parliament that he was himself the co-ordinator appointed under the law. But on 7 November, after an audience with King Paul, he called on the Field Marshal, as Papagos had now become, to request his help in the provision of professionally trained men from the Army for tasks connected with repatriation. Whether Papagos liked it or not, this was a pointed reminder of the proper relationship between the civil and the military power.

Early in December Karamanlis issued a progress report on his work for the refugees. He described the difficulties and the solutions he had adopted, in spite of the inadequate means available. He reported that nearly half a million refugees had been repatriated up to 30 November. He gave statistics of the allowances and the housing provided for them. He estimated that nearly two-thirds of the agricultural land abandoned during the war had been brought back into cultivation. He reported 411 projects completed under the 'Welfare-Work' programme, out of the 456 which he had announced as approved in June. In a frank conclusion he admitted that there had been 'weak points' in the programme, but he emphasized that the government claimed no more than to have made a beginning.

It was a good beginning, but so far as Karamanlis was concerned it was also the end of his responsibility. The coalition which had ended the civil war broke up early in January 1950. As the four-year term of the Parliament elected in 1946 was due to expire shortly in any case, it was immediately dissolved. The general election held on 5 March resulted in deadlock. Although the Popular Party won the largest number of seats, it fell short of an overall majority. The three centre Parties, led by Venizelos, Plastiras, and Papandreou, were able to form a precarious coalition. Although the civil war had ended barely six months earlier, a number of supporters of the extreme left were elected under the banner of the Democratic Front. Some justification for Karamanlis' pessimistic view of Greece's political system could be found in the fact that no less than forty-four parties contested the election.

As usual, Karamanlis headed the poll at Serres. But he was

now in opposition. His interventions in the new Parliament were naturally directed chiefly to the interests of his constituency. During May 1950 he spoke four times on the problems of tobacco and wine production in Macedonia. After a visit to Kerdyllia, where his father had once taught, he also warned Parliament on 15 May that guerrilla activity was again threatening the population. These were his only speeches in Parliament during the first half of the year.

It was also natural that with his wide experience of office he was assigned to an unusually large number of parliamentary committees—on foreign affairs, social welfare, health, housing, and reconstruction. The first of these committees gave him a timely expansion of his political horizon, for two events of great importance to Greece's foreign relations occurred in 1950. In January the Cypriot Ethnarchy, in which one of the most active leaders was Bishop Makarios of Kition, organized a plebiscite on *enosis*. A delegation of Greek Cypriots was charged to carry the results of the plebiscite to the United Nations. They called in Athens on the way, but had a discouragingly cool reception on 20 May from Plastiras, who was then Prime Minister. Soon afterwards, on 25 June, occurred the second major event of the year, the outbreak of war between North and South Korea.

The Greek government supported the UN resolution to intervene on behalf of the South Koreans, and offered six transport aircraft and later an infantry brigade to the UN force. In August Venizelos replaced Plastiras as Prime Minister, and on 13 September he appointed Karamanlis, as a representative of the Popular Party, to be Minister of Defence. The appointment thus came at a challenging time, but it lasted only seven weeks. Such was the instability of the political balance that four different governments (three of them led by Venizelos) succeeded each other between the general election and the end of the year.

Short as Karamanlis' tenure of the Ministry of Defence was, it gave him the opportunity for a characteristic display of energy. While the force for Korea had to be prepared and equipped, there was a renewal of guerrilla activity in northern Greece. Clashes with the Bulgarians also took place on the River Evros, which formed part of the frontier. At the same time the Americans were proposing to cut their military aid, while Papagos was insisting on an expansion of the Army.

An increase in soldiers' pay had to be postponed, but Karamanlis succeeded in extracting additional funds from the Americans to improve some allowances. It was pointed out to the Americans by Venizelos, prompted by Karamanlis and Papagos, that without a substantial increase in American aid, there was a danger that defence commitments would once more, as they had nearly done in 1947, swamp the national economy.

The threat to security at home and abroad at this time made questions of personnel and appointments to the staff and commands more important than ever. A senior General who served under Karamanlis wrote later (in an article in *Vima* on 20 December 1955) with warm admiration of his attention to detail and impartiality in such matters. He insisted on the rule, which had recently been neglected for political reasons, that Generals must retire automatically after eight years in the highest ranks. Unlike his predecessors, he personally attended meetings of the Supreme Military Council to examine the cases of officers who had been subject to criticism. But his strict insistence on the proprieties between senior officers and himself did not always please Papagos.

Karamanlis himself described a serious incident involving the Chief of Personnel, a high-ranking General, in the Ministry:

One day this General came into my office improperly dressed, with his tunic unbuttoned and a cigarette in his hand. I ordered him to leave my office for insubordination. The General complained to Papagos, who was his personal friend, that I had humiliated him in the presence of third parties. Papagos demanded of me, through the Prime Minister, an explanation of the affront. When I refused, he threatened to resign. In the end the episode was put right by the transfer of the General to a post outside Athens.

It was a rare opportunity—the first but far from the last—for Karamanlis to assert the primacy of the civil power over military arrogance. Such episodes apart, most of his work was normal routine. There were many unfulfilled schemes of his predecessors which required legislation to bring them to a conclusion: the reorganization of technical staff and the creation of a supply corps for the Air Force; the formation of a corps of reserve officers under the Ministry of Defence; the establishment of an autonomous housing authority for officers of the three services. The necessary legislation was speeded through Parliament during Karamanlis' brief tenure of office. He knew that they were matters of importance to professional servicemen, even if they did not have the glamour to attract public attention.

Not that public attention was lacking in his few weeks at the Ministry of Defence. His post naturally led him to speak openly for the first time on foreign affairs. He repeatedly emphasized the danger from the north—at two press conferences in October, and at the inauguration of the Staff College and Defence College, which he attended with Papagos in the same month. He identified the danger clearly. It did not come from Yugoslavia, whose growing friendliness with Greece he welcomed. It did not come from Turkey, which was invited simultaneously with Greece, during Karamanlis' period of office, to co-operate with the North Atlantic Treaty Organization. The source of danger was Bulgaria. A dispute over the course of the River Evros, which the Bulgarians had tried to divert, had been referred to the UN Balkans Commission. The Bulgarian government ignored the Commission. Karamanlis pointed to the contrast with Greece's loyal support of the United Nations.

His period of office ended abruptly on 2 November, when the Populists withdrew their support from Venizelos, who formed a new government without them. But Karamanlis continued, out of office, to speak on foreign affairs in Parliament. On 30 November he supported the restoration of full diplomatic relations with Yugoslavia. At the same time, as a patriotic Macedonian, he recommended caution on the issue of allowing the Slavophone refugees of the civil war to return to Greece. There were, he pointed out, 36,000 of them in Yugoslavia, whose return would disturb relations between the two countries. It was a short but pungent speech—twice interrupted by a Deputy who made the strange assertion that there never had been a Slav minority in Macedonia—and it was received at the end with applause.

Karamanlis' main interest was taking a new direction, for the Popular Party was disintegrating. It was not clear what would replace it, but he began to speak publicly of the need for a fundamental reform of political life. The theme was the same as that of his letter to George Avtzis five years earlier, but it now carried the weight of experience in four public offices.

A new party was proposed at this time, to be called the 'Popular Unionist Party', under the leadership of Stephanos Stephanopoulos and Panayotis Kanellopoulos. The latter wished to include Karamanlis in the leadership. But Karamanlis would have been an uneasy ally, for he advocated joining the government now led by Venizelos, to which Stephanopoulos would not agree. The Popular Unionist Party was in any case short-lived. So was another 'New Party' of the right, led by Spyro Markezinis.

It was Papagos who ended the period of uncertainty, by resigning his post as Commander-in-Chief at the end of May 1951 and declaring his intention to enter politics. Venizelos' weak coalition fell in July, and Parliament was dissolved. On 30 July Papagos formed his new party called the 'Greek Rally', clearly modelled on de Gaulle's *Rassemblement Français*. Karamanlis was one of the first to join it, as did Stephanopoulos, Kanellopoulos, and Markezinis.

The general election held on 9 September was fought under a new voting system known as 'reinforced proportional representation', which was expected to ensure a working majority for the winning party. But it failed to do so: the result was another deadlock. The Greek Rally won the most seats, but without an overall majority. Papagos refused to consider a coalition, and forbade his Deputies to offer any advice to the King. Karamanlis nevertheless advised the King to send for Papagos to form a government, and urged Papagos to accept. His reasoning was that this step would repair Papagos' uneasy relations with the Crown, but he also had electoral motives. He was opposed to frequently recurring elections, and he feared that a government under Plastiras or Venizelos would reintroduce simple proportional representation, which would damage the prospects of the Greek Rally. However, as he later wrote, 'Things worked out differently, and justified those who held the opposite opinion to mine.' Papagos rebuked him for his interference.

In principle Karamanlis shared Papagos' dislike of coalitions.

But Plastiras and Venizelos did not, and they duly formed another government together under the former. Venizelos even sent an emissary to Karamanlis offering him the post of Minister of Defence, which Karamanlis declined. The foredoomed Parliament had little interest for him. He served on only two parliamentary committees, for the social services and communications.

The state of Greek politics exasperated not only the leaders of the Greek Rally but also the Americans. They had hoped to see a strong government under Papagos, but it was clear that this could be achieved only under a straightforward majority system of election. They had also noted Karamanlis as a coming man, who shared their views on the need for political reform. In December 1951 he was invited by the State Department to spend three months in the USA. On his return he made one of his only two major speeches in that Parliament, during a censure debate on 20 March 1952.

In this speech he severely criticized the instability of the political system, and attacked the practice of government by coalitions. He called for government by a single, strong, homogeneous party to solve the country's problems. Everyone knew that only the majority system could bring this about. Similar advice was pressed on the government by the US Embassy.

A new electoral law introducing the majority system was accordingly presented to Parliament in September 1952. Karamanlis naturally supported the change in a speech in Parliament on 4 September, on the ground that it would help to eliminate 'the formulation of policy in the wings rather than in the Chamber'. He went on also to support other innovations, such as votes for women and for serving soldiers, who had formerly been disfranchised. 'Why', he asked, 'should sixty per cent of the Greek people be denied their political rights?'

The introduction of votes for women fulfilled a provision of the new constitution, introduced at the end of 1951. In general, though not in this respect, the new constitution met with objections both from the left and from the Greek Rally, partly because it extended the powers of the King to suspend certain constitutional rights in a national crisis. It was a curious extension of the royal prerogative to be introduced under

General Plastiras, who had, as a colonel, deposed the King's father thirty years earlier. It also proved useful to another revolutionary colonel fifteen years later.

Such major political changes sometimes occur, by the chance of history, under undistinguished governments. The new constitution and the new electoral law were not the only historic changes to take place during the short-lived Parliament of 1951–2. In February 1952 Greece and Turkey both became members of the North Atlantic Treaty Organization. Friendly visits were exchanged between the Greek and Turkish Foreign Ministers. In June the Greek King and Queen visited Ankara, in November the Turkish President visited Athens. All was goodwill between the two countries, though it was soon to be compromised by the re-emergence of Cyprus into the news.

Makarios, who had become Archbishop of Cyprus in October 1950, was pressing the Greek government to raise the question of *enosis* at the United Nations. Colonel Grivas was organizing demonstrations in Athens, and making reconnaissances in Cyprus. Plastiras allowed the subject to be mentioned informally by the Greek representative at the UN General Assembly and the NATO Council in November 1951, but otherwise gave Makarios and Grivas no encouragement. The Greek spokesman at NATO was the Under-Secretary for Foreign Affairs, Evangelos Averoff, who was then a Liberal but later a devoted supporter of Karamanlis.

There was also a major event in Karamanlis' private life in this period. On 2 July 1952 he married Amalia Kanellopoulos, the niece of his political colleague, Panayotis Kanellopoulos, with whom his relations were already close and friendly. The one significance of the marriage for his political career, which was already assured, was to add the asset of a charming and talented hostess. But it also opened new horizons for him in other directions.

Amalia's interests were intellectual and artistic rather than political. She spoke excellent French and English; she introduced her husband into new circles of the theatre and the arts: she thus helped him to enjoy, in a new milieu, a year which was in political terms stagnant and unprofitable. She also made it possible for him to establish a real home, instead of living in rooms at the Hotel Athinon, as he had done since 1944.

The period of political stagnation ended with the dissolution of Parliament in September 1952 and the general election on 16 November. Karamanlis accompanied Papagos on his electoral tour of northern Greece. Under the new voting system Papagos' victory was virtually certain. Even Papandreou and Tsouderos had now joined the Greek Rally, which won 239 out of 300 seats. The former Prime Ministers, Plastiras and Tsaldaris, were among those who lost their seats. Karamanlis naturally increased his majority. Although his relations with the Field Marshal were not warm, he immediately returned to office as Minister of Public Works.

It was not thought to be one of the more glamorous posts in the government, and Karamanlis was not among the most senior ministers. Higher policy was in the hands of five men; the Prime Minister, who also held the Ministry of Defence; two Ministers without portfolio, Kanellopoulos and Tsouderos, who were in effect Vice-Premiers; the Foreign Minister, Stephanopoulos; and the Minister of Co-ordination, Spyro Markezinis, who controlled economic policy and was regarded by many as the strongest member of the government. It seemed possible that Karamanlis' operations, which depended heavily on finance, would be hampered by a lack of sympathy with Markezinis. But those who doubted his prospects had misjudged their man. In his three years as Minister of Public Works he consolidated and extended his reputation.

Ambitious programmes had been announced by ministers before, only to be abandoned by their successors or even by themselves. Karamanlis' programmes, in contrast, were addressed to identifiable needs, closely supervised, and carried to completion. Some of the needs were long-term, such as the infrastructure of industry, communications, and tourism. Some were immediate, such as the utilities and public services of Athens, Peiraeus, and Salonika. Some programmes were completed only after Karamanlis' term of office. For example, his struggle with the Power and Traction Company as Minister of Transport ended in success only after he had left the Ministry, when restrictions on electricity were finally lifted in April 1949. His projects were always conceived as part of a strategic plan, and they were always monitored by himself.

Just as he had made the electricity supply his primary target in 1948, he now gave the same priority to Athens' water-supply. He let it be known that he was determined to solve the perennial problem of enlarging the capacity of the Marathon reservoir, which supplied Athens and Peiraeus, and also to change the contractual basis of the Water Company, OULEN. There was a long history of disagreement about the best way to replenish the reservoir from Lake Yliki, north of Thebes. One scheme, favoured by the American experts of OULEN, proposed a thirty-mile aqueduct via Thebes; the other, favoured by Greek consultants, proposed a forty-five-mile aqueduct via Khalkis. The Press, politicians, and experts took sides with intense bitterness, while the capital was starved of water.

Karamanlis described his approach to the dispute with characteristic bluntness:

I put the following question to the responsible officials: 'Here we have two points to connect: Yliki and Athens. One route is via Thebes, the other via Khalkis. Is there any other possible route?' Answer: No. So I told the appropriate department to look into the position on the quiet. A month later they told me there could be an intermediate route which would be shorter and cheaper. I immediately called for a feasibility study, again very quietly so as to avoid untimely opposition. As the problem was urgent, I also invited competitive tenders for the execution of the work, with an order that the feasibility study should be carried out concurrently. Then there was a tremendous fuss, both sides accusing me of making irresponsible decisions. The outcome, anyway, was that I brought the water from Yliki to the Marathon reservoir in three years and two months exactly, before it was entirely exhausted and Athens faced with the dramatic problem of a total drought.

No one had dealt with practical problems in this way before. The Opposition, led by Venizelos, was outraged at the procedure; but Karamanlis carried the necessary legislation through Parliament in April 1953, barely five months after taking office.

He never forgot that Athens was not the only city in Greece, and that others had suffered just as much in the last decade. The most important were Peiraeus and Salonika, Greece's two major ports. In March 1953 Karamanlis introduced legislation to reorganize the administration of the harbour of Peiraeus, and he initiated a programme of building new highways and reconstructing old ones between Athens, Peiraeus, and the coastal suburbs.

Salonika was especially significant to Karamanlis for many reasons. It was the second capital of Greece; it was the centre of his native province; it had been a bone of contention with Greece's northern neighbours; and it was the natural area to which the de-centralization of the industrial congestion of Athens could be directed. Karamanlis' first visit in his new post was therefore to Salonika in January 1953, and he returned three more times during the year. His drive for efficiency and modernization did not please everyone, however. When he planned, for instance, to amalgamate the harbour administration with that of the Free Zone, the incumbent administrators resisted. The arguments were tedious and frustrating. He broke them off with a promise to re-examine his proposal, but in the end he insisted on carrying it through.

There were incidental pleasures accompanying his visit to the north. One was the coincidence of a by-election in the city, in which women had their first opportunity to vote in a parliamentary election. The innovation was particularly welcome to Karamanlis, who had argued vigorously in favour of women's franchise, and later was the first to include a woman minister in his government. Still more personal was the opportunity to pay his first visit as a minister to his native village. His father's house had other occupants for the time being, but there were many old friends present to cheer him. He also revisited Nea Zikhni, where he had once crept like a snail unwillingly to school and tried to run away.

During his tour of Macedonia he avoided giving premature promises, but during a later visit he claimed that in a few years the whole appearance of the city would be completely changed. It was a justified forecast, and one which could be judged by already visible results in Athens. On 26 July the newspaper *Kathimerini* wrote that Athens had changed 'not in a few years but in a few months', and praised Karamanlis for refusing to make idle boasts. Similar judgement was pronounced by *Vima* on 11 December: 'Karamanlis does not speak about his work himself; he lets his work speak for him.' Another aspect of his character was revealed when it was proposed to name after him the new coastal road between Phaliron and

Glyphada: he declined the honour.

Unavoidably there were also disputes and criticisms. Once more he found himself at loggerheads with the Power and Traction Company, this time over the obsolescent trams which obstructed the traffic of Athens. He reached agreement with the company to abolish them in six months. Then, to save time, he began road-works on either side of the tracks. But when the six months expired, the Company tried to make new conditions for withdrawing the trams. Karamanlis' reaction was characteristically robust. One night, when the trams had returned to their sheds at midnight, he went personally to the terminus on Patissia Street to supervise the removal of the rails. 'The next day naturally there was a colossal uproar,' he recorded afterwards: 'the Company threatened to take me to court; the public applauded.' And that was the end of the trams.

Other schemes also ran into opposition. Various interests resisted his plan to build a new highway over the dry bed of the River Ilissos, which is now King Constantine Street. His administrative reorganization of Peiraeus was attacked as imposing political control over the port. Accusations of corruption were published in an Opposition newspaper on 13 September 1953. Two days later Karamanlis published a detailed reply, which was declared conclusive by both *Vima* and *Kathimerini*. Even the unsympathetic centre newspaper *Elevtheria* rebutted criticisms of his plans for Athens with the comment, on 6 October, that 'motorists believe he is the only member of the government who actually works.'

Such praise was dangerous. It had a converse in the criticism by provincial Deputies that Karamanlis was neglecting the provinces. But the criticism was easily answered with statistics of the five-year road programme published early in 1953. There were to be 750 miles of new motor-roads and 950 miles of road improvements; and on 9 February Karamanlis announced in Parliament that 380 bridges damaged in the war were already under repair. He also announced a new system of classifying roads (national, provincial, and local), with corresponding provision for their finance. To promote industrial development in the provinces, hydroelectric power was to be increased by dams on the Rivers Aliakmon and Axios (Vardar) in the north and on the Akheloos in central Greece.

These vigorous replies failed to silence the interested charges that he was favouring the capital at the expense of the provinces. But he was never at a loss for a retort. A letter in *Vima* repeated the complaint; he answered it on 8 August 1953 by drawing attention to an article in *Ta Nea* (*Vima*'s sister evening paper), which had circumstantially refuted the complaint a week earlier. The complaint was nevertheless repeated in Parliament on 28 May 1954. He rebutted it with detailed statistics, concluding that there had been 'a campaign recently to create a false impression of the scale of the work in Athens' with the consequence of causing 'a sense of bitterness and misunderstandings in the provinces'.

A more serious though less open critic was his colleague Markezinis, the Minister of Co-ordination. At times Karamanlis suspected that he was being deliberately starved of funds. On one occasion, unknown to Karamanlis, Markezinis tried to persuade Papagos to dismiss him, but Kanellopoulos intervened with the threat that in that case he would also resign. A popular joke of the time rumoured that Markezinis and Karamanlis were in dispute over the former's wish to extend the underground railway in Athens. 'His underground activities', it was said, 'are intended to neutralize Karamanlis' work above ground.' Nor was Markezinis the only one jealous of Karamanlis' success. When Markezinis quarrelled with Papagos himself, and resigned in April 1954, Stephanopoulos was reported to have opposed the suggestion of Karamanlis' promotion in his place. Papagos did not in fact give him the post, but later in the year he added the Ministry of Communications to Karamanlis' responsibilities, and looked on him thereafter with a more approving eye.

An important occasion for jealousy among his colleagues arose from the tragic earthquakes which struck the Ionian Islands in August 1953, followed by other tremors in the area of Volos and the island of Santorini. At first Markezinis insisted on taking responsibility for reconstruction, but the work was not well planned, and for many months progress was slow. Then on Kanellopoulos' initiative the responsibility was transferred to Karamanlis, who undertook it with his customary energy. The infrastructure of roads, water-supply, drainage, and foundations was laid with the help of the army;

72,000 houses, and all the public buildings—schools, hospitals, churches, town halls—were rebuilt; the work often continued up to midnight under the glare of searchlights. Karamanlis included several visits to the islands in his constant round of provincial tours. When he attended the King and Queen at the inauguration of new buildings on Zakynthos on 6 April 1955, he made a typically terse reply to an admiring journalist: 'I just did my job.'

By 1955 Papagos recognized that Karamanlis was indispensable, but a last attempt to displace him was still to come. Early in July it was reported in the Press that he had submitted his resignation over a disagreement with his colleagues about a contract with a German company to supply telephone and telecommunication equipment. It was in fact true, but the disagreement was in the end overcome. The contract was still being negotiated, and eventually, on Karamanlis' advice, the negotiations were terminated. The Greek agent of the German firm thereupon brought accusations of corruption against Karamanlis' colleague and close friend, Constantine Papakonstantinou, who was Minister of Communications. Papakonstantinou issued a writ for libel, and Karamanlis gave evidence in his support at the trial on 28 September. The agent was convicted and sentenced to eighteen months' imprisonment. It was almost the last event of Karamanlis' tenure of the Ministry of Public Works, and he suspected that it was deliberately contrived to discredit him.

Few ministers ever won so great a public esteem in a comparatively routine department. The Press showed extraordinary unanimity in his praises. Even *Elevtheria* sardonically admitted on 27 June 1953 that it was 'beginning to think that if he would leave the Greek Rally, he could do some service to our country'. Conservative and liberal newspapers were less coy. On 18 August 1954 *Kathimerini* wrote that 'Karamanlis' rare energy sets an example that should be copied'; *Vima* on 2 September called him 'a man of rapid and right decisions'. His praises were not confined to journalists. A Professor of Architecture wrote in October 1954, 'as one who has often in the past criticized the planning anarchy of Athens', that he could not omit to describe 'the truly tremendous work of Karamanlis as unexampled in the history of Greece'. The municipality of

Peiraeus awarded him a gold medal in August 1954, and Athens followed suit six months later.

It was true that Karamanlis' work spoke for itself. He laid the infrastructure of Greece's future development: for industry, with hydroelectric power and modern roads; for the major cities, with modern streets, lighting, and water-supply; for tourism, with new hotels and seaside resorts, and improved access to sites such as the Acropolis; for communications, with the modernization of harbours and aerodromes, and a new railway link in Macedonia. Comparatively few of his initiatives required legislation, but those which did were important: to unify the technical services of different ministries, to reorganize the harbour administrations of Peiraeus and Salonika, to bring all the machinery used in public works under his own control, to bring building regulations up to date, to designate and finance the different classes of roads, including the introduction of tolls on the motorways. He was also the first to think of the desirable innovation of notices in foreign languages on the main routes. No detail was too small for his attention.

His journeying in the years between 1952 and 1955 was indefatigable. A rough tally of his visits shows almost a dozen to Salonika and Macedonia, five each to the Peloponnese and the Ionian Islands, four to Epirus, three each to Thessaly and central Greece, two to Crete, as well as innumerable inspections of local works round Athens, Peiraeus, and the coasts of Attica. Only one of his travels took him abroad, but it was one of the most significant.

In February 1955 he flew to Istanbul to meet the Turkish Minister of Public Works, and to sign an agreement on anti-flooding works to be carried out on the River Evros, where it forms the Greco-Turkish frontier. On 1 June he attended the inauguration of the flood-works with his Turkish colleague, who then visited Athens. This first contact with Greco-Turkish relations came about on the technical level, which was the level on which Karamanlis always preferred to work. But it came also at a politically opportune moment.

Only six months before Karamanlis' visit to Istanbul, the Balkan Pact had been signed between Yugoslavia, Greece, and Turkey. While Karamanlis was entertaining his Turkish visitor in Athens, the British government was planning to invite the Greek and Turkish governments to a conference on Cyprus, which eventually met in London on 29 August. But the conference was doomed to failure, chiefly because of the outbreak of violent anti-Greek riots in Istanbul and Izmir on 5 September. Karamanlis was to inherit the unhappy consequences.

During September some curious speculations appeared in the Press about Karamanlis' own views on the Cyprus problem, followed a few days later by a more remarkable speculation about the possibility of a new government under his premiership, which he promptly denied. There were other signs that the spotlight was turning on Karamanlis. Three times in April and May 1955 he was present beside the King on public occasions—in Zakynthos, at the Peiraeus harbour-works, and at the works on the Acropolis. During the same months it became known that Papagos was seriously ill; and his administration was visibly faltering.

There were two Vice-Premiers at the time, Kanellopoulos and Stephanopoulos, but neither was designated as Papagos' deputy. Either might preside at the Council of Ministers, on no settled principle. Kanellopoulos saw Papagos only once during the summer, and did not know that he was dying. Stephanopoulos was better informed, being a friend of Papagos' doctor. It was believed that Papagos intended Stephanopoulos to succeed him, but there was no evidence in writing.

Those who knew that Papagos was dying began consultations on the succession during the summer. One of them was the American Ambassador, who spoke to a number of leading politicians, among them Costa Tsatsos, the future President of the Republic, who was then in opposition. Tsatsos confidently recommended the name of Karamanlis. Later he learned that others, including Liberals such as George Mavros, had given the same advice. Karamanlis' name therefore had inter-party support; but there was no question of American pressure in the choice.

More important was the attitude of the Palace. Two courtiers were used by the King to take soundings during July and August. On the first occasion Karamanlis was invited, together with Mavros and Panayotis Pipinelis (a retired Ambassador, formerly political adviser to King George II), for a general discussion of the succession to Papagos. On a later occasion Karamanlis alone was approached with the suggestion that the King should request Papagos' resignation and appoint Karamanlis in his place. Karamanlis expressed his gratitude for the King's confidence, but advised against the suggestion, partly because it would be fatal to Papagos and partly because it would be attributed to the unhappy relationship between Papagos and the Court. He confided in Tsatsos that the suggestion had been made, but said he would remain loyal to Papagos so long as he remained alive.

The King was naturally holding private audiences with many ministers at the time, including Kanellopoulos and Stephanopoulos as well as Karamanlis. These were routine occasions, but they led to speculation in the Press. Only occasionally did the King reveal his mind openly. One such occasion was to George Rallis, who accompanied him on a state visit to Belgrade in the second week of September. He asked Rallis, who did not know that Papagos was dying, whom he would recommend for the succession. Rallis named Karamanlis. As the Queen came into the room at that moment, the King remarked to her: 'He too says Karamanlis.' Rallis had no doubt that their choice was the same.

Papagos, however, was extremely reluctant to recognize that he would never return to work. The politicians were becoming impatient with the virtual abeyance of government. Venizelos twice demanded that the King should dissolve Parliament during September, once in writing and once through the King's private secretary. But the King was powerless to act without Papagos' resignation. He wrote to the Field Marshal on 1 October, and again on the third, tactfully hinting that he should resign, but the response was unsatisfactory. Only at the last moment would Papagos even go so far as to sign a letter naming Stephanopoulos as his deputy until he should recover.

Meanwhile a consensus was emerging in favour of Karamanlis. He was not a heavyweight in comparison with older politicians, and at forty-eight he was young by Greek standards. But his record of achievement was impressive. The fact that he was a new face also weighed in his favour, both with the King and with the Americans. So did his handsome appearance, his popularity with junior Deputies, his unpretentious background, and perhaps even his heavy Macedonian accent.

His appointment nevertheless came as a surprise. Papagos died at 11.30 p.m. on 4 October. Although Athens Radio announced the same evening that he had nominated Stephanopoulos to be his deputy, the King received both the Vice-Premiers together the next morning. They submitted the resignation of the government, and the King asked them to arrange for the election of a new leader of the Greek Rally. Stephanopoulos replied that it would be wrong to do so before the funeral, which was to take place on the seventh. The King had not yet committed himself to the choice of a successor, but he was under no constitutional obligation to await the election of a new party leader.

On the two days before the funeral ministers in groups of four were to form a guard of honour round the coffin lying in state, one at each corner, for half an hour at a time. Kanellopoulos and Stephanopoulos were in the first group; Karamanlis was in the second, which indicated his ministerial rank. As soon as he came away from his vigil, at 8.30 p.m. on 5 October, he was summoned to the Palace and invited to form the new government. Having accepted, he went straight to tell Kanellopoulos and sent an emissary to tell Stephanopoulos. There was an immediate outburst of indignation, in which Stephanopoulos played a leading part but Kanellopoulos maintained an honourable silence.

Karamanlis' personal impression was that the indignation of the politicians was largely artificial. Privately, he believed, they were content with the King's solution, because they assumed, in his own words, that 'my role would be transitional and short-lived'. If so, they made a fatal error of judgement; and certainly their indignation, while it lasted, was noisy.

Venizelos, Papandreou, and Markezinis spoke of 'favouritism' and a 'royal *coup d'état*'. Stephanopoulos collected signatures to a motion of protest within the Rally. A meeting of Deputies of the Rally was convened under the chairmanship of Emmanuel Tsouderos, as the senior ex-Premier, on 6 October. Stephanopoulos spoke first and denounced the King's action as 'unconstitutional'. Kanellopoulos, speaking next, pointed out that it was not in the least unconstitutional, though undeniably surprising. Both were applauded, but no decision was taken.

Karamanlis was not present, being already busy forming his government. Another meeting of the Rally Deputies was held in the afternoon of the seventh, after the funeral, and yet another the same evening. By then feelings were calmer. Some 180 of the 208 Deputies were present at the third meeting, which agreed without dissent to support Karamanlis but to entrust the leadership of the party to a five-man committee consisting of Kanellopoulos, Stephanopoulos, Tsouderos, Rodopoulos (who was President of the Chamber), and Karamanlis himself. For reasons which later became clear, Karamanlis did not want to be elected as sole leader.

Denunciations of 'favouritism' still continued; but what did they mean? Obviously the King chose the man he favoured and favoured the man he chose. But it was impossible to deny Karamanlis' record of achievement. What the accusers meant was that the King's judgement had been influenced by outsiders—probably the Americans or the Queen. But no kind of intrigue involving Karamanlis personally had taken place.

He had warned the King that it was doubtful whether the Rally could agree on a new leader—certainly not on himself. He was doubtful even whether he could win a vote of confidence. On learning this, the King offered him the right of dissolution, but he would not accept it before presenting his government to Parliament. His conduct in accepting office was impeccable. It was also, of course, carefully considered. He had already decided to disencumber himself of the past by dissolving the Greek Rally.

On 10 October, five days after accepting office and three days after Papagos' funeral, he presented his government to Parliament. The interval was unusually short; so was his first speech as Prime Minister, which occupied barely two and a half columns in the Official Report. He began with a fitting eulogy of his predecessor, and then turned at once to his central themes: the economy and foreign policy. He forecast austerity and a balanced budget, but without new taxation. He promised a stable currency and increased investment. His government would not 'remain unmoved by the marked upward trend in the level of prices'. Such sentiments are familiar on the lips of all Prime Ministers. But the terse and determined way he expressed them made a good impression, abroad as well as at home.

Under the heading of foreign policy he began by declaring that history and geography had placed Greece naturally at the side of the Western democracies. But he deplored their failure to understand the 'just demands' of the Cypriots. He denounced the hostile conduct of, the Turks in Istanbul and Izmir, for which he demanded material and moral amends. In contrast, he spoke warmly of Yugoslavia. He promised to consult the party leaders on foreign policy, and not to confront them with *faits accomplis*. Again there were no surprises in his speech, but it was skilfully constructed: not a word was wasted.

Finally he announced his intention to ask for a dissolution with a view to elections in the spring. He hoped first to secure agreement on a new electoral law, 'because one of the basic causes of our political troubles is the lack of a firmly based electoral system'. He ended with something more than a conventional appeal to patriotism, discipline, and co-operation, 'for the government knows that the Greek people becomes agitated and rebellious not so much when it is suffering but chiefly when it has the feeling that it is being mocked and cheated by the state and its experts.' Surprised by the brevity of Karamanlis' inaugural speech, the Opposition found little in it to criticize directly. On 12 October he received a vote of confidence by 200 votes to seventy-seven. But the clamour against the 'royal coup' continued outside Parliament.

The speech in effect defined three major aims. The first was to solve the Cyprus problem; the second was to modernize the national economy; the third was to reform public life. All three had the same ulterior purpose: to integrate Greece more closely with Western Europe. This was not necessarily their order of importance—in fact, all three had to be started simultaneously—but it was likely to be the order in which they could best be achieved. The history of Karamanlis' first eight years in office is the history of his efforts to achieve these three great aims.

It was a refreshing innovation that a Prime Minister should

set out with such clear-cut and relevant aims at all. The Liberal newspaper *Vima* foresaw on 13 October an era of 'fewer words, more action, greater determination'. Right-wing governments did not ordinarily appeal to *Vima*; but Karamanlis did not belong in any ordinary sense to the right wing.

It was against the right wing of the Rally that he had first to secure his position before he could tackle the great problems. The right-wing Press, echoed on the left, called him a 'Quisling', as being a nominee of the Americans. To dissociate himself from the extreme right, he announced on 4 January 1956 that he would form a new party, the National Radical Union (ERE), to contest the forthcoming general election. It was a subtle stroke to steal the term 'radical' from the extreme left.

Out of just over two hundred members of the Rally, 170 joined him. Kanellopoulos and Stephanopoulos did not; but important recruits came across from the Opposition, including Tsatsos and Averoff. With George Rallis and Papakonstantinou, who were his staunch followers from the first, this group formed the core of his support. It was a striking fact that a quarter of a century later, at the end of his last administration, all of them were still at his side: Tsatsos as President of the Republic, Papakonstantinou as Deputy Premier, Averoff as Minister of Defence, Rallis as Foreign Minister and his eventual successor.

The conduct of the general election caused no real criticism. Although the Opposition demanded that Karamanlis should resign in favour of a non-political or 'service' government, as was the custom during elections, Karamanlis considered it sufficient to replace the men in the key posts (Defence, Justice, the Interior, and Northern Greece) with neutral Ministers. He also introduced a new electoral law, embodying a compromise between proportional representation and the majority system, which favoured the Opposition. As he once remarked, changes in electoral law were invariably made to please Oppositions.

With an appeal for a campaign that should maintain a high level of debate, he began on 22 January an election tour which set a pattern, occasionally modified, for the future: first Salonika, his own local and the country's northern capital; then Serres, his own constituency; then back to western Macedonia and Epirus; south into Roumeli and north again to Thessaly;

then to the major islands of Crete and Rhodes; northwards to the other islands of the Aegean; thence to western Thrace and eastern Macedonia; finally to Athens to address a huge crowd in Klavthmonos Square. There he spoke for an hour and a half, without notes.

The themes of all his speeches elaborated those of his first speech as Prime Minister in Parliament. But he added a new warning. He was fighting, he said, 'alone against all'. To some extent this was his own choice. The left-wing parties had formed an electoral coalition because the voting system deliberately favoured large parties. Venizelos and Tsaldaris offered to co-operate with Karamanlis, but he declined. They too then joined the opposing coalition, which comprised eight parties ranging from the extreme right to the extreme left. Karamanlis attacked his opponents particularly for collaborating with the Union of the Democratic Left (EDA), which was well known to provide a cover for the outlawed Communists. He called it 'the formation of a new EAM'.

His decision to form a new party, his refusal to consider electoral alliances, and the speed and vigour with which he presented himself to the electorate, were all abundantly justified by the outcome. Although he could not expect to repeat the overwhelming victory of Papagos in 1952, he emerged from the poll on 19 February 1956 with 165 seats out of 300. His share of the popular vote was forty-eight per cent, so the Opposition had a small popular majority; but it was inconceivable that the leaders of its eight parties could have formed a coherent government even if they had had a majority of seats. Karamanlis was therefore able to form a government drawn exclusively from ERE, which was sworn in on 29 February and secured a vote of confidence by 165 votes to 125 on 11 April. A striking innovation was that for the first time the Council of Ministers included a woman. She was Mrs Lina Tsaldari, the widow of Karamanlis' first party leader; and she held what had been one of his own successful posts, the Ministry of Social Welfare.

PART II

The First Term
1955-1963

Chapter 3
Settling Cyprus

KARAMANLIS had been in office four months, and events had
not waited for him to secure his position. In Cyprus particularly they had taken an alarming course. A history of the
Cyprus problem cannot be compressed within the scope of a
biography, and must be sought elsewhere.[1] But as it dominated
the early days of both his periods of office, something must
be said of the difficulties he faced. They may be placed in
order of importance: the incomprehension of successive British
and American governments; the tough and skilful obstinacy
of the Turks; the irresponsibility of the Greek Opposition; and
the narrow egocentricity of Archbishop Makarios and Colonel
Grivas.

The problem had been handled hitherto in a small committee of ministers consisting of Papagos, Kanellopoulos,
Stephanopoulos, Tsouderos, and Markezinis (until his resignation), but not Karamanlis. Most of the committee wanted
to settle the matter bilaterally with the British, but that required a degree of patience unacceptable to public opinion in
Greece and Cyprus. Markezinis had been the first to advocate
an appeal to the United Nations. But such an appeal would
automatically give the Turks a voice in the matter.

Unfortunately it became plain, after a fruitless meeting between Papagos and Eden in Athens in September 1953, that
negotiation with the British was impossible. This difficulty
was reinforced by the fateful use of the word 'never' by the
Minister of State for the Colonies in the House of Commons
on 28 July 1954. By then Papagos had already given way to the
pressures of Makarios, Markezinis, and others. He announced

[1] I have used particularly the following: François Crouzet, *Le Conflit de Chypre
1946-1959* (Bruxelles, 1973); Stephen Xydis, *Cyprus: Conflict and Conciliation
1954-1958* (Columbus, Ohio, 1967); Nancy Crawshaw, *The Cyprus Revolt: An
Account of the Struggle for Union with Greece* (London, 1978); Angelos Vlakhos,
Deka khronia Kypriakou (Athens, 1980); and Stanley Mayes, *Makarios—A Biography* (London, 1981).

on 18 March 1954 that he would appeal to the United Nations unless bilateral talks began within a few weeks. The Turkish government then formally stated its claim to express its views. But the Turks did not withdraw from the negotiation of a tripartite treaty with Greece and Yugoslavia, the Balkan Pact, which was signed on 9 August.

The appeal to the UN went slowly through its accustomed stages, to the great exasperation of Greek opinion. It achieved the limited success of being inscribed on the agenda of the General Assembly, but the substantive debate in December 1954 ended in a decision not to adopt any resolution for the time being. Meanwhile Grivas had arrived in Cyprus to start his campaign. After some hesitation, Makarios authorized the outbreak of violence by the National Organization of Cypriot Fighters (EOKA) on the last night of March 1955. They thus let loose forces which in the end no one could control. The Greeks failed to achieve *enosis*; the British failed to retain their colony; the Turks alone made gains from the mistakes of others.

First reactions to the violence were confused. At the end of June 1955 the British government invited the Greek and Turkish governments to a conference on Cyprus in London. The Turks accepted at once, but the Greeks hesitated. Makarios, who met Papagos in July, urged rejection. In the end, however, Papagos accepted, while renewing the appeal to the United Nations. The conference met for a week at the end of August and early September. It heard Harold Macmillan, the British Foreign Secretary, say that the principle of self-determination was not permanently excluded. This was a small improvement from the Greek point of view. But while the delegates were still in London, the Turks responded to the violence in Cyprus by two days of anti-Greek riots in Istanbul and Izmir. It was later established that both the riots and the specious excuse for them had been contrived by the Turkish government.

September 1955 was a bleak month for the Greeks. On the twenty-fourth the UN General Assembly voted against the inscription of the Greek appeal on its agenda. The next day a new Governor of Cyprus was nominated: Field Marshal Sir John Harding, the retiring Chief of the General Staff. His appointment was assumed to foreshadow a policy of military repression. He arrived in Nicosia on 3 October, the day before

Papagos died. Inter-community relations in Cyprus, which had once been peaceful and tolerant, were now bitter and suspicious. Such was the grave state of affairs which Karamanlis inherited.

Things were perhaps not as bad as they seemed. It was true that the Turks could never again be excluded from the dispute, even though they had renounced all claims over Cyprus in the Treaty of Lausanne in 1923. But the British no longer absolutely rejected self-determination. It was true that Harding was a military governor; but he brought with him a surprisingly conciliatory offer. The Harding plan recognized the right of self-determination in principle, but at an unspecified date. Meanwhile there should be immediate talks on a self-governing constitution. If Karamanlis had been fully in control, a settlement on these lines might have been possible. But the British government would not discuss Cyprus with the Greeks, only with the Cypriots. Karamanlis was new to office, he had many other distractions, and he could do no more than advise Makarios, who was in turn under pressure from Grivas.

Makarios and Grivas had done the Greek cause a great service by forcing the issue on the attention of the world. But they were troublesome allies for the Greek Prime Minister. Though Makarios was an inspiring national leader, he had defects as a politician. He knew little of the world outside Cyprus; he wanted to dictate the policy of the Greek government; and he negotiated in the spirit of the bazaar, always demanding more than his opponent was willing to concede. In Karamanlis' words, 'He wanted to play a greater role than his small country permitted.' He was also conscious of the driving force of Grivas behind him. Grivas had similar limitations, as well as a conviction that the issue could be settled by force. Makarios dared not seem less determined than the guerrilla at his back.

Karamanlis advised Makarios to pursue bilateral talks with Harding in order to exclude the Turks. Meanwhile he himself demanded and received amends for the outrages in Istanbul and Izmir. Turkish troops saluted the Greek flag in Izmir, and the Turkish government agreed to pay damages and to safeguard the Patriarchal residence in Istanbul. It was Karamanlis' first diplomatic success. But the British and the Cypriots were harder to handle.

While Harding and Makarios pursued their talks, the first Greek Cypriot was condemned to death at the end of October. In the last week of November Harding declared a state of emergency. When the condemned Cypriot and another Greek were hanged on 10 May 1956, Karamanlis commented bitterly: 'Whom God wishes to destroy he first drives mad.' The street in Athens in which the British Embassy stands was renamed after the two victims.

In the meantime negotiations in Nicosia had broken down. The positions of Harding and Makarios did not differ by much. Makarios wanted to discuss a date for self-determination before discussing a self-governing constitution. He also disliked a phrase in Harding's formula which mentioned 'the framework of treaties and alliances' as a limitation on the right of self-determination. From habit, he pressed for just a little more than whatever had been conceded.

From London Eden sent a friendly message to Karamanlis on 23 November urging him to support the British formula. He evidently thought the new Prime Minister would be pliant. Karamanlis coolly declined in his reply on the twenty-eighth, not because he opposed the formula but because the British government still treated Cyprus as a matter of 'domestic jurisdiction' in which Greece had no standing. The next message from Eden expressed his surprise in chilly terms. He also claimed to have American support for his policy, which Karamanlis doubted. But Karamanlis sent a conciliatory letter to the British Ambassador on 2 December, saying that the whole subject was being examined afresh and that his government's views would be communicated in a few days.

In fact on 5 December a long memorandum was forwarded by the Greek Foreign Minister, Spyros Theotokis, with Karamanlis' approval. It reasserted the principle of self-determination and expressed satisfaction that it was recognized by the British Government. It also contained an undertaking to offer 'suggestions' to Makarios, subject to a few small amendments to Harding's formula, which were accepted. On the same day Theotokis sent an emissary to Nicosia to advise Makarios not to break off negotiations. This was as far as Karamanlis thought it justifiable to go, so long as the British government would not regard him as a party to the negotiations. But it was not far enough to influence Makarios, who issued a statement almost at once, without consulting Athens, in which he demanded self-determination without qualifications. Meanwhile Makarios and Harding continued to meet, though with less and less hope of agreement.

As the general election in Greece approached, it became more difficult for Karamanlis to say anything that could be construed by the Opposition as failing to support Makarios. Although he was favourably disposed towards the British initiative, he would not be manœuvred into becoming a tool of British policy. Privately, he sent a telegram to President Eisenhower in January 1956, asking him to urge conciliation on the British government. He also sent a message to Makarios advising him not to accept a compromise against his better judgement. This was a necessary precaution at election time, when Papandreou was calling his appointment as Prime Minister a 'plot to bury the Cyprus question'.

No sooner was the election over on 19 February than the crisis in Cyprus came to a head. A week after polling day Lennox-Boyd, the Colonial Secretary, paid a flying visit to Nicosia. Makarios probably saw it as a sign that the British were weakening, but in fact they were losing patience. Twice in the first week of March Makarios put out statements blaming the British for the failure of the negotiations. On 5 March, the same day as Makarios' second statement, Lennox-Boyd in turn made a statement in the House of Commons showing the impossibility of negotiating with him. After an ominous pause of four days, Makarios was arrested on the ninth and deported to the Seychelles. The Greek government was taken by surprise. Tsatsos, the Minister in the Prime Minister's office, heard the news while he was on the way to Athens airport to meet Makarios. Karamanlis was the helpless spectator of the follies of two stubborn men.

His first reaction was scarcely surprising. He recalled the Greek Ambassador in London from his post; he announced another renewal of the appeal to the United Nations; and he privately asked the US government again to intervene. To his satisfaction, the American Ambassador in Athens dissociated his government from the action against Makarios. But the situation in Cyprus became unavoidably worse. The British began recruiting auxiliary police, exclusively from the Turkish population. Worse still, the removal of Makarios left Grivas alone to play the leading role. The danger was now that Karamanlis' careful diplomacy would be dragged off course by a headstrong militarist in place of a turbulent priest.

There was also severe criticism in Athens to be faced. The *Vima*, normally friendly, accused Karamanlis of pressing Makarios to compromise. Papandreou and Venizelos attacked both Karamanlis and Theotokis for having abandoned self-determination. Both charges were untrue, as they made clear in response to a motion of no confidence in Parliament on 24 May. But since Karamanlis could see that in future co-operation between Theotokis and the Cypriots was, in his own words, 'difficult if not impossible', he felt obliged to ask for his Foreign Minister's resignation. A new post was found for Theotokis, and Averoff took his place. It was fortunate that this post was now held by a man who enjoyed Karamanlis' full confidence.

Angry exchanges with London continued. On 1 June Eden accused Athens Radio of inciting terrorism, and he stressed the importance of Cyprus in protecting the oil supplies on which Britain's economy depended. In so arguing, he overlooked the fact that in April 1951 Venizelos, as Prime Minister, with the support of all Greek party leaders, had offered in return for *enosis* to grant Britain the necessary bases not only in Cyprus but elsewhere in Greece. What most offended the Greeks, however, was the appeal to what Karamanlis called 'base material interests'.

For the first time he began to look for support outside the Western alliance. Pandit Nehru was in Athens on 25 June, and Shepilov, the Soviet Foreign Minister, came four days later. Both had private meetings with Karamanlis, and neither would have opposed Greece's claim to Cyprus. Even the right-wing newspaper *Kathimerini*, whose proprietor, Helen Vlakhos, was close to Karamanlis, wrote on 1 July of the need to improve relations with the Soviet Union.

At no time did Karamanlis waver in his opposition to Communism or his loyalty to the Western alliance. When Shepilov proposed to him that he should visit the Soviet Union, he replied that he would accept 'on condition that Russia ceased to interfere in Greece's internal affairs and to encourage the KKE'. Shepilov gave the necessary promise, but it was not kept, so the visit did not take place.

But Karamanlis' hostility to Communism and loyalty to the alliance did not weaken his sense of justice and of national independence. For example, although his enemies called him a lackey of the Americans, he was the first to terminate the status of extraterritorial jurisdiction for American servicemen, which had been conceded in 1947. He declared this intention in 1955, as one of his earliest policies. Equally he would not exploit Greek and American anti-Communism. Another of his early measures in 1955 was to rehabilitate a group of Air Force officers who had been cashiered in 1952 under suspicion of complicity in a left-wing conspiracy. In April 1956 he announced the reprieve of all those still under sentence of death from the time of the civil war.

He still regarded the USA as his chief ally in persuading the British to be reasonable about Cyprus. On 4 July he sent Eisenhower a craftily phrased message on the 180th anniversary of Independence, saying that 'the Greek people of Cyprus reject and renounce all loyalty and subjection to the sovereigns of Great Britain, just as your ancestors did.' A week later he received the US Ambassador, to complain of the lack of support for Greece and the favour shown to Turkey by his government. He also sought the intervention of the Council of Europe; alternatively, he offered to accept arbitration by NATO. To recover control over the movement in Cyprus, he sent a senior official of the Ministry of Foreign Affairs, Angelos Vlakhos, as Consul-General. Vlakhos had the notable qualifications of being half-French and well disposed towards the British.

The British response was cool. Eden and his Foreign Secretary, Selwyn Lloyd, still insisted that there could be no early change of direction towards *enosis*. It was suspected in Athens that they had inspired a proposal by a Conservative MP that Cyprus should be partitioned, which soon became the goal of the Turks. But they also sent Lord Radcliffe to Cyprus as a constitutional adviser, to propose reforms leading to self-government. Karamanlis responded to the idea of partition by reminding the British government of Turkey's disloyalty in two world wars. He continued his soundings among the neutral powers, particularly the Yugoslavs. At the end of July he met Tito on Corfu.

By then a greater crisis had overtaken the world. President Nasser nationalized the Suez Canal on 26 July. Cyprus became the base of operations planned, but not yet launched, by the British and French against Egypt. Karamanlis had no intention of exploiting Britain's embarrassment. On the contrary, through Vlakhos he induced Grivas to declare a cease-fire during July. But he was alone among the Western allies in refusing to join in the attempt to put pressure on Egypt through the Suez Canal Users' Association. Nor did the British government help him to be conciliatory. On 8 August five Cypriots were hanged; and on the twenty-sixth excerpts from the captured diaries of Grivas were published in London. The next day EOKA resumed operations.

A further reference to the United Nations was inevitable. This time the British government took the initiative, accusing the Greeks of terrorism while also claiming that the UN had no competence to intervene in a colonial matter. An effect of this initiative was that the Greek appeal was automatically also accepted on to the agenda. Karamanlis himself led the Greek delegation to the General Assembly, arriving in New York on 9 November.

His reception was strikingly favourable. President Eisenhower received him, alone of the leading delegates, at a private meeting on 15 November, and gave a formal luncheon for him, which was attended by prominent Greek-Americans such as Spyro Skouras and Tom Pappas. Another luncheon was given for him on the twentieth by the Greek-American colony. On the twenty-second his speech to the General Assembly made a notable impression. But the British remained intransigent. On the same day they made the death penalty mandatory, even for carrying arms.

Eisenhower now addressed himself to the problem of Cyprus for the first time. Being poorly briefed at his meeting with Karamanlis, he appeared not even to know that Makarios was in exile in the Seychelles. He noted Karamanlis' request that he should press for the Archbishop's release. He did in fact do so, though not until several months later, for he had other problems on his mind with the simultaneous crises in Hungary and the Middle East.

The major topics which Eisenhower and Karamanlis discussed on 15 November were, in order, NATO, Cyprus, the Balkan Pact, US military aid, and US economic aid to Greece. The crisis in the Middle East was discussed only briefly over lunch. Eisenhower said that if the Russians carried out their threat to send 'volunteers' to Egypt, the United States would react with 'all available means'. They also touched on the danger of the Russians and the Arabs involving themselves in the Cyprus dispute. Karamanlis came away with a strong sense of the President's sympathy, though less of his comprehension.

The debate at the United Nations went less well. As higher priority was given to Egypt and Hungary, the subject of Cyprus was not reached until early February 1957. Much had happened before then. Cyprus had been used as a base for British and French aircraft operating against Egypt. Grivas' attitude had consequently hardened. Karamanlis, returning to Athens early on 25 November, had claimed in Parliament an unqualified success over Cyprus. He denounced equally the Soviet coup against Hungary and the Anglo-French coup against Egypt; and he emphasized the value of the Balkan Pact, by which he meant chiefly the relationship with Yugoslavia. On 3 December he and Averoff visited Belgrade, where Tito publicly affirmed his support for self-determination in Cyprus.

The problem of the British still remained. Lord Radcliffe produced his proposals for a new constitution in early December. Lennox-Boyd flew to Athens on the thirteenth to present the plan to the Greeks before announcing it in public, and then went on to Ankara. The plan would have given the Greeks an elected majority in the Cypriot Assembly, but the Governor would have retained overriding powers. The Greeks suspected that Lennox-Boyd himself favoured partition: not without reason, for he expressly mentioned the possibility of 'double self-determination' when he presented the plan to the House of Commons. His breezy, offhand manner, which might have appealed to African chiefs, offended the Greeks. He had long and fruitless talks with Karamanlis and Averoff. His request for an audience with the King was coldly refused. The Greek government had no hesitation in rejecting the Radcliffe plan.

The concatenation of events at the end of 1956 greatly increased Karamanlis' difficulties. After the Anglo-French failure against Egypt, Harding's rule in Cyprus became more severe, and the Turkish Cypriots began a campaign of retaliation. Even the Americans were less sympathetic to the Greek cause. In the UN debate at the end of February 1957 they gave the Greeks little support. The debate ended with a resolution urging a 'peaceful, just and democratic solution', which could be, and was, variously interpreted. Averoff bravely claimed that it implicitly condemned partition and recognized that the Radcliffe plan was unacceptable. But another motion of no confidence was tabled in Parliament soon after his return. Although it was defeated on 15 March, the government's confidence was not widely shared.

Karamanlis still sought an understanding with the British. Through Vlakhos, he persuaded Grivas to offer another truce if Makarios were released. Grivas made the offer on 14 March, and next day Karamanlis wrote to remind Eisenhower of his undertaking to approach the British government. Eden, with whom Eisenhower was scarcely on speaking terms since the attack on Egypt, had resigned early in January. Macmillan, who suceeded him, was to meet Eisenhower in Bermuda on 22 March. On that date Makarios informed the Governor of the Seychelles that he welcomed Grivas' statement of the fourteenth. This was considered a sufficient concession. Eisenhower put the suggestion of Makarios' release to Macmillan, and privately told Karamanlis that Macmillan had agreed. Makarios was released on 29 March, but not allowed to return to Cyprus.

He came instead to Athens, arriving in triumph on 17 April. If anything, he had become more intransigent in exile. Passing through Nairobi on his way, he made a statement flatly refusing any fresh negotiations unless the state of emergency was ended and he was allowed to return to Cyprus. He neither consulted the Greek government nor offered it a word of thanks. Karamanlis did not attend his welcome at the airport, but the King gave him a formal luncheon and a high decoration.

Averoff and. Vlakhos urgently briefed Makarios on the necessity of persuading Grivas to end the activities of EOKA, because of the growing danger of Turkish retaliation. Makarios agreed without qualification, but merely passed the advice on to Grivas without supporting it. In his reply to Makarios, Grivas violently attacked the Greek government, but said he would cease hostilities if Makarios so ordered. But Makarios dared not give him such an order, in case it was disobeyed, nor would Karamanlis press Makarios to do so.

At this stage Karamanlis' position in Parliament was weak. His majority was small, his own party was not wholly united, and the Opposition was bitterly hostile. During May Parliament was recalled from recess for a debate on foreign policy, which was conducted in an acrimonious spirit. On 24 June both Papandreou and Venizelos made speeches in Salonika accusing Karamanlis of 'undermining the struggle for self-determination'. An attempt to end the deadlock was made by the US Ambassador in Athens, who urged Makarios to end the armed conflict and go to London to renew negotiations. Otherwise, he hinted, the US government would support partition. Makarios wrote to Macmillan on 28 May that he was ready to negotiate, but only on self-determination, which was his interpretation of the UN resolution. Macmillan's reply was naturally negative. So yet another initiative petered out.

Once more the dispute was referred to the United Nations, in the autumn of 1957. But in the meantime two developments had occurred, little noticed at the time, which were to bear fruit later. In February the Secretary-General of NATO, Lord Ismay, offered NATO's services to mediate. Being British, he was unlikely to be acceptable in person, but his successor, Paul Spaak, the former Prime Minister of Belgium, was able to renew the offer later. Then in July Makarios hinted for the first time, in a press interview, that he might accept independence for Cyprus, provided that *enosis* was not excluded in the long run.

As usual, Makarios spoke without consulting the Greek government, but Averoff sounded Grivas on the possibility of independence during the following month. In September Spaak began consultations on the possibility of independence within the Commonwealth, but the Turks rejected it; and so did Makarios, characteristically changing his mind, when Averoff consulted him. The US government, which had supported Spaak's initiative, became impatient. Dulles, the

Secretary of State, turned against the Greeks, and advised them to withdraw their appeal to the United Nations.

Karamanlis had to seek support wherever he could, which meant primarily outside the Western alliance. He visited Cairo in August 1957 as the guest of President Nasser, and obtained his formal support for self-determination. This commitment guaranteed widespread backing from the Arab states, where both Karamanlis and Makarios already enjoyed good standing. In November the Lebanese President visited Athens as the guest of the King. Krishna Menon, the Indian Foreign Minister, was known to be sympathetic.

There were also tempting overtures from behind the Iron Curtain. The Romanian government proposed an agreement on co-operation and non-aggression between Greece and the Balkan states. Tito accepted the proposal, and his Vice-President visited Athens in October. But Karamanlis resisted the temptation and refused. A more satisfactory ally had emerged in the west, when the British Labour Party passed a resolution at its annual conference on 4 October in favour of self-determination for Cyprus within five years.

Less satisfactory, though this had become normal, was the debate at the United Nations in December 1957. The political committee of the General Assembly voted in favour of self-determination, but the majority did not reach the two-thirds required to make it effective. The biggest disappointment was the abstention of the US delegate. The Greeks lost the sympathy even of Krishna Menon, who had offered to propose a motion for independence. Averoff consulted Makarios, who was in New York, but his response was inexplicably negative, although he himself had first launched the idea. Menon commented sardonically: 'I thought the Greeks had a reputation for being clever.'

So the year ended with mixed prospects. On the positive side was the replacement of Harding in December by a new Governor, Sir Hugh Foot, who brought with him a liberal and conciliatory reputation. On the negative side were the familiar factors: the outright hostility of the Turks, the unpredictable conduct of Makarios and Grivas, the neutrality of the USA, and the uncertainty of British intentions. There were also two new and ominous factors: externally, a campaign of threats from the Soviet Union, and internally an intrigue aimed at the downfall of Karamanlis.

The Soviet threats began in a typically indirect way. In July it was rumoured that NATO intended to install 'nuclear artillery' in Greece. In August there came a hint that the Soviet Union was about to revive the Macedonian question. Macedonia, which was Karamanlis' native territory, was one of the areas where it was assumed that missiles might be located. In January 1958 a long letter came from Bulganin, the Soviet Prime Minister, addressed to all the governments in NATO. Among other topics, the letter contained a warning to Greece against allowing American missiles to be located on Greek soil. Averoff denied in Parliament that there was any such intention. Karamanlis wrote to Bulganin on 5 February that Greece would never engage in aggressive war, and that her precautions were directed solely to self-defence. In May Khrushchev, the First Secretary of the Soviet Communist Party, returned to the theme; again Karamanlis parried the threat, implying that no decision had been taken. More was to be heard of it.

The internal threat to his government was maturing at the same time. In July 1957 his Vice-Premier, Andreas Apostolidis, resigned ostensibly over disagreements with his colleagues, but probably in the hope of bringing down the government. In November Theotokis resigned from the Ministry of Agriculture. More resignations followed at the end of February 1958, caused by dissension over a new electoral law, but again probably with more far-reaching motives. Karamanlis was taken by surprise.

New electoral legislation had been requested by Papandreou, who was anxious to break his link with the extreme left. Karamanlis asked his Minister of the Interior, Dimitrios Makris, to discuss it with Papandreou. But as he was not sure whether Venizelos supported Papandreou, he also asked George Rallis, the Minister in the Prime Minister's office, to discuss it with Venizelos. On 27 February Karamanlis told the Council of Ministers that he had reached agreement with Papandreou on reinforced proportional representation. Rallis protested that this would give EDA second place in the next Parliament.

'Don't put the wind up Papandreou!', Karamanlis urged him. Rallis at once resigned from the government. Later he explained that he had no intention of breaking up the party. Others, however, had more damaging intentions. They persuaded Rallis to join them in resigning from ERE, which he later called 'the most childish thing I ever did'. In the event fifteen Deputies resigned from ERE, leaving Karamanlis without an overall majority.

There was undoubtedly a more widespread intrigue against him, involving the Opposition as well as discontented colleagues, and probably the British and American Embassies and the Court as well. Karamanlis believed that the object was to undermine his position, to force him into a coalition, and to bring the Cyprus dispute to a conclusion satisfactory to the allies. As to the participants in the intrigue, he was inclined to acquit Papandreou but not Venizelos. The nominal leader of the Opposition in Parliament, Savvas Papapolitis, actually offered to bring sixteen of his own Deputies to Karamanlis' support. But he refused the offer, saying later: 'I preferred a radical change in the situation, because I believed that such compromises would make it worse.' For the same reason, when the repentant rebels sought to rejoin ERE, he refused to accept them.

Having replaced the defecting ministers, he went to the King on 2 March to offer his resignation and to seek a dissolution. The King summoned the party leaders, but could not bring about a compromise. A 'service government' was then appointed on 12 March. The new electoral law which Karamanlis had agreed with Papandreou was passed on the thirtieth. Parliament was dissolved, to be followed by a general election on 11 May. The result was a triumph for Karamanlis, a considerable advance for the extreme left, and a disaster for Papandreou and Venizelos. ERE increased its majority to 173 seats; EDA came second, as Rallis had forecast, with seventy-eight; the Liberals won only thirty-six, and the rest thirteen. Karamanlis' second administration was sworn in on 17 May. Events in Cyprus had meanwhile not stood still.

Foot, the new governor, had devised a scheme of his own, the details of which were not published. It was known to have commended itself to the British government, though there were reservations about the early return of Makarios to Cyprus as a condition of renewed negotiations on self-government. The Turks, however, began a campaign of violence in the island at the end of January 1958 to mark their disapproval. At that time Selwyn Lloyd was attending a meeting of the members of the Baghdad Pact in Ankara, where he asked Foot to join him. At first the Turks refused to see Foot, and when they did so treated him with studied rudeness. 'They are insane!', Foot told Vlakhos when he returned to Nicosia. Next, Selwyn Lloyd and Foot visited Athens, where Foot saw Makarios and tried to warn him that partition was becoming inevitable. During April Foot proposed a secret meeting with Grivas, who refused. There was deadlock in every direction.

Throughout April and May 1958 Karamanlis was technically no longer responsible for Cyprus policy. Naturally he referred to it often during his electoral tour, beginning as usual in Salonika and ending in Klavthmonos Square in Athens. When he resumed responsibility after polling day, he found a rapidly deteriorating situation. Both EOKA and its Turkish rival, known as TMT, were conducting campaigns of violence. Zorlu, the Turkish Foreign Minister, was demanding partition. Makarios was about to visit Cairo, as usual without consultation, to enlist the help of President Nasser. The British government were devising yet another plan for Cyprus, which would formally acknowledge the right of the Turkish government to play a role there. The US government was seemingly indifferent.

Macmillan outlined his new plan to the House of Commons on 19 June. In addition to a number of familiar features, it included two which were bound to be unacceptable to the Greeks. There were to be separate legislative councils for the Greek and Turkish communities, which looked like a prelude to partition; and the Governor, who would remain responsible for defence and foreign policy, was to be assisted by a Greek and a Turkish representative, nominated by their respective governments. Averoff pointed out in Parliament that the British proposal would infringe the Treaty of Lausanne, signed in 1923, by which Turkey had renounced all interest in Cyprus. The Council of Ministers had no hesitation in rejecting the plan on 21 June.

To make matters worse, the British Labour Party accepted the Macmillan plan as better than nothing, although it was contrary to the resolution passed at the Labour Party Conference in the previous October. President Eisenhower also sent Karamanlis a personal message on 14 June, counselling moderation. This seemed tantamount to advice to accept the plan; but he also expressed approval of the idea that NATO might help to resolve the dispute. Karamanlis promptly summoned the American Ambassador, to complain that his government had failed to understand the problem.

He himself was under pressure in Parliament from the Opposition, which was now led by the Communist Passalidis as a consequence of EDA's success in the general election. They blamed him for having allowed NATO to interest itself at all in Cyprus. The gravity of the crisis was underlined by a conference in the Ministry of Foreign Affairs on 3 July, at which the Greek representative at the United Nations, George Melas, gave his opinion that the Macmillan plan had ended all hope of self-determination. He did not think independence was practicable, and he advised that the dispute be put temporarily in 'cold storage'. A few weeks later Melas resigned his post, having found himself at loggerheads with Averoff. In these grave circumstances a radical review of Greek policy was imperative.

Even Greece's status in the Western alliance was now at issue. In his statement of policy to the new Parliament on 9 June, Karamanlis had not only expressed bitterness towards Britain but stressed the need to establish friendly relations with the Eastern bloc. To do this was to walk a tightrope. It was possible, he believed, to separate functional matters on which co-operation was possible from matters of principle, such as loyalty to the alliance; but the line of division was a narrow one, which the Communists would readily try to break through.

Only a week before his first speech to Parliament, Karamanlis had been chided by the Bulgarian Prime Minister over Greece's unfriendly attitude. He had replied that no improvement was possible before Bulgaria carried out her obligations under the peace treaty. On 16 June he presided at a ministerial committee to discuss trade relations with the Soviet Union.

But there were ambiguous attitudes on both sides, for there was still a Soviet campaign going on against the supposed installation of American missiles in Greece. Karamanlis would not sacrifice his commitment to the alliance, but the Americans must not take it for granted.

On 10 July he summoned the US Ambassador again and spoke to him in strong terms. He asked point-blank if the US government would intervene with the British over Cyprus, and hinted that if it did not there might be a radical shift in Greek policy. He also expressed the suspicion that the US government was yielding to 'blackmail' by the Turks. A few days later came the first hint of what a radical shift might mean.

In May 1957 Greece had formally adhered to the Eisenhower Doctrine, which guaranteed the security of the Middle East; but when a crisis broke out in the Lebanon in July 1958, leading to the intervention of American troops, Karamanlis refused to allow Greek airports to be used for staging the US airlift. Early in August Eisenhower sent an Under-Secretary of State, Robert Murphy, to Athens to appease Karamanlis' feelings. Murphy spoke warmly of Greece's role among the Arab states, but on Cyprus he was evasive.

Despite the coolness of the Americans and the pessimism of his own representative in New York, Karamanlis again renewed the appeal to the United Nations for self-determination in Cyprus. To have done otherwise would have seemed like a surrender. The appeal was lodged on 15 August, and was to be debated in November. Meanwhile Karamanlis continued the quest for support, both within and outside the alliance.

The Spanish Foreign Minister visited Athens in June. It was a timely opportunity, for Spain also had a grievance against Britain, over Gibraltar, and Spain still had influence among the Latin American states. Tito, whom Averoff visited on Brioni in July, was a dependable friend. In September Karamanlis circulated a note to all members of NATO warning them of the risk to the coherence of the alliance. This, he wrote in a covering letter to Spaak, was not a threat but a genuine anxiety. He summoned the United States Ambassador again on 19 September, to hint once more at the possibility of a change in Greek foreign policy. Finally, he and Averoff visited West Germany together in the middle of November. When they met Chancellor Adenauer, Cyprus was the first item on the agenda.

Karamanlis also made other preparations for the impending crisis. To strengthen his case with the USA, he called for an appreciation by the Chief of the General Staff on the relative importance of Greece and Turkey to the strategy of NATO. The appreciation, submitted on 15 July, was a frank and careful document. It outlined the varying circumstances in which each of the two countries was indispensable, and concluded that Greece was the more important in the most probable circumstances of war; but it naturally did not understate the importance of Turkey. Karamanlis seems not to have made any use of the document.

In a more constructive effort, he helped to bring about another cease-fire in Cyprus, by joining in concerted appeals with the Turkish Prime Minister, the British Governor, and the leaders of the two communities in the island. But EOKA held its fire only until 1 September. The primary task still remained: to neutralize the Macmillan plan.

The one merit of the plan was that it brought matters to a head. A stubborn clash of wills was resolved in a wholly unexpected fashion. To Karamanlis belongs the credit of seeing and seizing the opportunity when it occurred. In the last months of 1958 he had to manœuvre nimbly between several incompatible gambits. The Turks were enthusiastically supporting the Macmillan plan. The British government was determined to enforce it with or without Greek co-operation. The Americans were hoping to avert another acrimonious debate at the United Nations. Spaak was again offering NATO's mediation. Makarios and Grivas were as unpredictable as ever.

On 28 July Spaak sent Karamanlis a letter proposing an alternative version of the Macmillan plan. Since it recognized the impracticability of establishing Greek and Turkish advisers alongside the Governor, Karamanlis thought it at least worth discussing, but he wanted certain amendments. Macmillan, on the other hand, was urging Spaak to press the Greeks to accept his plan as it stood. In the second week of August he visited Athens, Nicosia, and Ankara personally to make it clear that he would not yield.

Karamanlis received Macmillan with equal firmness, but

privately he talked with frank good humour. After listening to Macmillan's exposition, he remarked: 'You have spoken so eloquently and persuasively that I would have accepted your point of view, but for the fact that I know the Cyprus problem better than you.' Over dinner he told Macmillan bluntly: 'The initial mistake was yours, because you set on the Turks to bark, and now that they have begun to bite, even you cannot call them off.'

But there was no concealing the dismay caused in the Greek camp by the Macmillan plan. A member of the Cypriot Ethnarchy summed it up in the words of Christ on the Cross: 'It is finished—*tetelestai*!' Makarios began to distance himself further from the Greek government. When Karamanlis learned that he intended to make a statement criticizing the government's handling of the problem, he summoned Makarios and demanded to know whether he had ever dissented from the policy the Greek government pursued. Makarios agreed that he had not, but added that he now thought Greece should withdraw from NATO. When Karamanlis explained the objections to this course, Makarios again agreed that there was no difference between them; but he always evaded saying so in public. Equally characteristically, Grivas issued a denunciation of both Karamanlis and Makarios. His solution was that Greece should join the non-aligned states.

It fell to Spaak, who flew to Athens on 23 September, to try to repair the damage. He had a long talk with Karamanlis, who told him that if the Macmillan plan were enforced, the Greek government must either resign or withdraw from NATO. Spaak returned to Paris to plan a new conference, based on yet another modification of the Macmillan plan. But the Turkish representative at NATO attacked him in violent terms, and the British government insisted that the Macmillan plan would come into effect on 1 October regardless of any objections. The Turkish government appointed its representative to join the Governor of Cyprus, tactfully choosing its own Consul-General, so that no new face appeared on the scene. Karamanlis naturally refused to make any corresponding appointment. Meanwhile the complex exchanges through Spaak continued. They were clearly foredoomed to failure, but unforeseen events also made them irrelevant.

On 15 September Makarios had an interview with Mrs Barbara Castle, who had been Chairman of the Labour Party when it passed its resolution on Cyprus a year earlier. Once more he spoke without consulting the Greek government, nor even Grivas. Because of the imperative need to avert the imposition of the Macmillan plan, he declared himself willing to accept that Cyprus should become independent, both *enosis* and partition being excluded. The following day Mrs Castle saw Karamanlis and passed on this information. Taken by surprise, Karamanlis had to ask Makarios, who confirmed what she said. He then moved rapidly to take advantage of Makarios' change of front before he could change again.

On 19 September the Council of Ministers met with Makarios present. He said he was accepting independence because he saw no prospect of self-determination. For this he accused the government of weakness, suggesting that the most effective policy would have been a threat to leave NATO. Karamanlis retorted that he had taken no step without Makarios' agreement. There could be no thought, he said, of leaving NATO. After further exchanges, in which Makarios alternately withdrew and repeated his complaints, the meeting was adjourned, but only after it had been agreed in principle to settle for independence. Karamanlis so informed Mrs Castle on the twenty-second.

The consequences were not immediate, partly because Karamanlis had had painful experience of Makarios' habit of changing course, and partly because he wanted the British government, or at least the Labour Party, to be the first to declare itself in favour of independence. When Spaak visited Athens on 23 September, he was requested, with Makarios' agreement, to ask the British government if it would negotiate a plan for independence. Makarios actually confirmed his agreement in a letter to Macmillan on the twenty-seventh. But the British government was still set upon the Macmillan plan, and Macmillan replied in that sense to both Spaak and Makarios on 29 September.

Spaak's own proposals therefore still held the field, but they were no more than modifications of the Macmillan plan. As soon as he received Macmillan's reply, he obtained the agreement of the NATO Council to convene a conference on Cyprus.

Karamanlis held another ministerial meeting with Makarios, which spread over 2 and 3 October, to discuss the proposed conference. It was reluctantly agreed that Greece could not refuse to take part, since the only alternative would be to leave NATO. But Makarios pressed for certain conditions: that in addition to Britain, Greece, and Turkey, the conference should include other members of NATO, such as the United States, France, and Italy, and also representatives of the two Cypriot communities; and that independence should be included among the options to be discussed.

Karamanlis wrote to Spaak on 4 October agreeing to attend the conference, but adding Makarios' conditions with his own support. It was in vain, since the British and the Turks between them vetoed all the conditions. Spaak then proposed a new formula on 13 October, but it was already plain that there was insufficient room for compromise between the opposing views. Finally Karamanlis, under bitter attack from the Opposition for abandoning the cause of self-determination, was obliged to end the talks. On 28 October, in his annual message on the anniversary of the outbreak of war in 1940, he spoke only of 'the struggle for the fulfilment of the wishes of our Cypriot brothers', with no reference to self-determination. The next day he issued a statement blaming Britain and Turkey for frustrating Spaak's proposals. On 1 November he confirmed that the appeal to the United Nations would go forward.

The UN debate began in the political committee of the General Assembly on 25 November. Averoff spoke for Greece, Zorlu for Turkey, Selwyn Lloyd for Britain. Makarios was also present, having earlier confirmed his position: he would accept 'after an agreed period of self-government a status of independence within which international guarantees would be given to the Turkish minority'. Grivas had once more declared a cease-fire for the period of debate in New York.

The three Foreign Ministers all spoke with exceptional restraint, but their arguments were familiar. Selwyn Lloyd presented the Macmillan plan in moderate terms; but in a private meeting with Averoff he declined to consider independence. Averoff nevertheless put the case for independence when he came to speak. Zorlu advocated either the Macmillan plan or partition. None of the three proposals could achieve a majority. The usual bargaining between delegates took place, resulting in an anodyne motion proposed by the Iranian delegate. With some slight amendments, it was approved on 4 December by thirty-one votes to twenty-two, with twenty-eight abstentions.

It was an unsatisfactory outcome for all parties. But matters did not end there, for the General Assembly itself had still to consider the resolution. As the delegates left the political committee, Zorlu went out of his way to congratulate Averoff on his speech. The unexpected gesture led to a friendly conversation, in which the two Foreign Ministers agreed that bilateral talks between Athens and Ankara might well unravel the whole unhappy tangle. So encouraging was their conversation that when the General Assembly met on 6 December, it was confronted not with the resolution of its political committee but with a motion recommending, in familiar terms, a 'peaceful, democratic and just solution'. It was passed unanimously, for everyone sensed that the crisis was over.

The Turks' change of heart was genuine, as was quickly shown by the restraint imposed on the Turkish Press. Possibly their government was swayed by the overthrow of the Iraqi dynasty in July, which had gravely weakened the Baghdad Pact. The Greeks had also seen the writing on the wall, for the US representative at the political committee had appeared to favour partition. But not everyone immediately grasped the significance of the *rapprochement* between Averoff and Zorlu.

In Parliament, the Greek government was severely attacked both from the left, by EDA and Venizelos, and from the right, by Markezinis and Stephanopoulos. Karamanlis and Averoff vigorously defended their policy, pointing out that since Makarios himself had originated the idea of independence, they could hardly oppose it. On 13 December Karamanlis addressed Stephanopoulos with unusual heat, saying that he had 'the guilty conscience of a man who bequeathed his blunders to me'.

The British were also slow to understand the changed atmosphere. On 14 December the British Ambassador called on Karamanlis, anxious to renew negotiations between Makarios and the Governor, and to persuade Makarios to restrain EOKA. This was now *vieux jeu*. Negotiations were about to begin on a different plane between different principals. Averoff and Zorlu met again in Paris on the eighteenth, and informed Selwyn Lloyd of their talks. At last the British government agreed to slow down the Macmillan plan. Macmillan himself now welcomed the idea of independence, provided that British bases were retained on the island, which both the Greek and Turkish governments agreed. Subject to that condition, practically anything that those two governments could agree would be acceptable to the British.

Detailed discussions began in Ankara, between Zorlu and the Greek Ambassador, on 28 December. Ten days later Zorlu made a statement on Cyprus to the Turkish Parliament in friendly terms. The talks went on throughout January 1959. There were inevitably difficulties: for example, the Turks wanted a base for themselves on Cyprus, and also separate, autonomous local authorities, both of which were unacceptable to the Greeks. But by the beginning of February matters were sufficiently advanced for a meeting of the two Prime Ministers and their Foreign Ministers in Zurich.

The meeting in Zurich began on 5 February and lasted six days. Again there were difficulties. According to Vlakhos, who was present, they came near to breakdown more than once. But in the end agreement was reached to establish an independent, unitary Republic of Cyprus. On 11 February Karamanlis returned to Athens and declared himself 'satisfied and proud'. Averoff flew to London the next day to report progress to the British government.

Karamanlis' next task was to persuade Makarios to agree with the proposed solution. At first there seemed to be no difficulty, though later Makarios changed his attitude in order to escape responsibility for a possible failure of the settlement. The two men met on the evening of the eleventh, together with Kanellopoulos and Tsatsos. Also present were Bitsios (Secretary-General of the Foreign Office) and Vlakhos (Consul-General in Nicosia). Makarios listened to Karamanlis, thanked him, and went away to draft a statement. His statement, issued on the twelfth, was brief and satisfactory. It declared that 'the agreement reached lays the foundations for an immediate and definitive solution of the Cyprus issue through the establishment of Cyprus as an independent sovereign state.'

No sooner was it published, however, than Makarios had second thoughts. He summoned Vlakhos and said that he could not subscribe to the agreement as it stood. He saw Karamanlis again that evening, and insisted that he must personally negotiate changes with the leader of the Turkish Cypriots, Dr Kütchük. Karamanlis replied that this was impossible. He explained that the British government had invited the Greek and Turkish Ministers, together with Cypriot representatives, to conclude the negotiations in London on the express condition that what had been agreed at Zurich should not be reopened. Makarios then agreed to the condition, and only after that would Karamanlis accept Macmillan's invitation.

As usual, Makarios wanted to claim that his own bargaining skill had gained more than his colleagues. He determined to make his point when the next stage of the negotiations took place in London. When he flew to London on 15 February, two days ahead of Karamanlis, he took with him thirty-five advisers, including both clergy and the Mayors of the five principal towns. Their function was to share the blame with him if he failed. In the interval before Karamanlis left Athens he learned from Averoff that Makarios was still expressing reluctance to attend the conference, and was invoking various excuses.

On the morning of the seventeenth Karamanlis summoned an emergency meeting of the Council of Ministers, which authorized him to handle the crisis at his discretion. He flew to London later in the day, sending instructions in advance that the Greek Embassy in London should bring together Averoff, Makarios, the Mayor of Nicosia, the Bishop of Kition, and the Abbot of Kykkou to meet him. Makarios had seen Dr Kütchük twice during the day, but could not persuade him to make concessions nor even to negotiate at all. On arrival, Karamanlis demanded to know why Makarios was going back on his agreement. The Bishop of Kition and the Mayor of Nicosia both asked if this was true. Makarios admitted that it was, but added: 'For me it is a question of conscience, and I cannot undertake further responsibilities.'

Karamanlis retorted that 'irrespective of what Makarios

does, in order not to leave Greece exposed to ridicule, I will take part in the conference, but at that point I terminate the Cyprus policy of the Greek government.' He added that 'if Makarios wants to continue the struggle, he must find another champion.' He then walked out of the room, leaving Makarios in a state of fury.

By this time Makarios had antagonized several of his own fellow churchmen, some of whom had always distrusted his judgement or regarded him with jealousy. The Bishop of Kition, who had warmly congratulated Karamanlis in a telegram a few days earlier, now asked why Makarios was causing a crisis. At one point, when Makarios threatened resignation, the Abbot of Kykkou, his own spiritual adviser, said: 'All right, resign!' Makarios turned pale at that, and was silent. No doubt he had real anxieties, which he never fully disclosed. Nevertheless, he did in the end attend the conference.

The conference had almost been rendered abortive by a calamity before it began. The aircraft bringing the Turkish delegation crashed on arrival, with many casualties; but Menderes, the Prime Minister, and Zorlu survived. In Rome, on their way, Menderes had offered Karamanlis and Averoff a lift on his aircraft for the last stage, but the offer was prudently refused. Menderes' survival greatly enhanced his prestige among his superstitious countrymen, and perhaps contributed to the speed with which the negotiations were concluded. The British raised no objections to what had been agreed at Zurich, since their own interests were safeguarded by the provision of sovereign bases for the British forces. On 19 February the documents were ready, and Selwyn Lloyd asked Makarios if he was ready to sign them.

Makarios consulted his thirty-five advisers, who were divided: twenty-seven for and eight against. The main objections were to the Treaty of Alliance between Greece, Turkey, and the Republic of Cyprus, and to the Treaty of Guarantee between the United Kingdom, Greece, Turkey, and the Republic, since these seemed to place limitations on independence.[2] Makarios, playing for time, gave his reply to Selwyn Lloyd in English: 'If it is now, it is No!' The meeting thereupon

[2] All the relevant documents are published in the blue book *Cyprus* (HMSO, Cmnd. 1093, July 1960).

adjourned until the late afternoon. By then Makarios was at last ready to sign. After doing so, he enthusiastically embraced Karamanlis.

At a reception that night Makarios said to Karamanlis: 'Did you really imagine that I would not sign?' Karamanlis asked indignantly: 'Then why all the fuss?' With a cryptic smile Makarios replied: 'I had my reasons!' Karamanlis asked what they were. Makarios replied: 'I will tell you later.' But he never did so.

Karamanlis was in little doubt what Makarios' reasons were, and he set them down years later. One was to have the excuse, if the agreements went awry, that he had been put under overwhelming pressure. Another was to attract attention to himself. He had a veritable passion, in Karamanlis' view, for the centre of the stage and for dominating Greek policy. He found it intolerable in London that he was little more than a bystander. Karamanlis looked on his role with cool objectivity: 'Our personal relations were neither friendly nor hostile but simply professional, because our characters were radically different.'

Presumably Makarios also had more serious anxieties than his own self-esteem. One was no doubt the ominous silence of Grivas, who had not been consulted. Makarios had written to Grivas that the agreement was the best obtainable in the circumstances, and Averoff warned him that the only alternative was partition. But it would have been awkward for Makarios, and also for Karamanlis, if EOKA had refused to lay down its arms.

Grivas' silence continued until 10 March, when at last he proclaimed the end of the struggle and called for 'concord, unity, and love'. He came to Athens in triumph a week later. Karamanlis sent him only a brief message of welcome, but Parliament voted him high honours and the King promoted him Lieutenant-General. His later career in politics was inglorious. He and Makarios were never entirely reconciled: they agreed only in blaming Karamanlis for failing to achieve the impossible.

Makarios suggested another reason for his hesitations in a letter to Papandreou, when the latter was Prime Minister five years later. 'In my personal opinion, under the prevailing circumstances, no alternative was possible,' he wrote on 1 March 1964; but he also added: 'I did not believe for a moment that the agreements would constitute a permanent settlement.' He might have been expressing both a fear and a hope: a fear that the settlement would break down completely, a hope that it would lead after all to *enosis*. These were genuine causes for uncertainty.

Karamanlis also had not given up hope of *enosis* in the long run. Even Menderes had admitted to him in private conversation that 'sooner or later the trend of events would lead to *enosis*'. Karamanlis was confident that the agreements would have that result if Makarios played his hand right. In a letter to Kanellopoulos from Paris (written, by coincidence, the day after Makarios' letter to Papandreou, 2 March 1964), he described the tactics which he had recommended to Makarios soon after the agreements were signed.

His advice had been that Makarios should seek to assuage the suspicions of the Turks, to co-ordinate his policy with the Greek government, and to join NATO as an independent state. Thus the Greek nation would have two voices in all international bodies. In more than one later letter Karamanlis argued that if Makarios had followed his advice, 'we should easily arrive one day at *enosis*'. He was confirmed in his optimism in July 1964 when Dean Acheson, the former US Secretary of State, put forward a plan for *enosis* with compensations for the Turks. But whether valid or not, his hopes were frustrated by the conduct of Makarios as President.

All that is certain is that at the end of the London conference, whatever the text of the agreements, neither Karamanlis nor Makarios looked on the settlement as finally excluding *enosis*. Karamanlis' last words to Makarios in London clearly carried this implication: 'Father, take the agreements into thy hands and work patiently upon them. We shall all help.' The ecclesiatical language and the unusual use of the second person singular were both significant. But Makarios was not patient, and would not accept advice.

There were still long negotiations on the details to be conducted before the work begun in Zurich and London could be completed. The Republic of Cyprus did not formally come into existence for another eighteen months. In the interval Karamanlis worked strenuously to remedy the state of international isolation which had so nearly brought disaster to Greece. Links with the Western alliance, particularly with the United States, Britain, and Turkey, had to be reforged. Alternating threats and temptations from behind the Iron Curtain had to be resisted, without provoking violent retaliation. And Greece had to be projected on to a wider stage. The world must know and accept Greece as a modern state, not merely the homeland of industrious emigrants and expatriate shipping magnates.

Karamanlis' international reputation already stood high; from 1959 it rose still higher. He began to receive honorific decorations from many countries, which eventually reached a tally of twenty-three Grand Crosses. They came, during his first premiership, not only from Greece's allies—France, Belgium, the Netherlands, Italy, West Germany—but also from neutrals—Spain, Austria, Yugoslavia, the United Arab Republic, Thailand. Through the person of Karamanlis, Greece too was honoured.

In the exchanges of official visits which took place in the years following the Cyprus settlement, Greece received guests from the uncommitted world (Egypt, Argentina, India, Nigeria) as well as Western Europe. The world's Press also took notice of Karamanlis, though he never adopted the flamboyant manner which attracts publicity. A French newspaper praised his energy, ability, and unblemished character; a German newspaper found him as well dressed as Anthony Eden; the American Press noted his refusal to discuss Greece's internal politics on foreign soil; the Turks commented shrewdly on the value to the USA of his good standing in the Arab world.

In the atmosphere of goodwill which followed the Cyprus settlement it was not difficult to reforge the alliance. Eisenhower sent Karamanlis a telegram of congratulations as soon as the agreements were signed. The Greek Ambassador in Paris reported a significant talk with de Gaulle on 4 March, which led a year later to the much-desired participation of the French in the Salonika Trade Fair. On 25 March, Greece's National Day, the Italians invited Karamanlis to make an official visit to Rome. An even more gratifying invitation arrived the next day, to visit Ankara. The Turkish visit took place in May, and was highly successful. Nothing like it had occurred since Elevtherios Venizelos was invited by Atatürk in 1930.

Later in May 1959 the King and Queen visited Italy, accompanied by Averoff, who stayed on to discuss the possibility of Greece's association with the European Economic Community. At the end of May the British Minister of Defence was in Athens; a month later Spaak came again; at the end of August came Dr Erhardt, the West German Minister of Finance; and in November Karamanlis and Averoff made their visit to Rome. By then it had been agreed in principle to negotiate a Treaty of Association between Greece and the EEC. None of these moves would have been possible while the Cyprus dispute remained unresolved.

But there were still difficulties. The settlement was severely criticized in Parliament, especially by Venizelos. Papandreou held his fire for the time being, because he was anxious to co-operate with Karamanlis in other fields. The negotiations with the Turks met a number of obstacles, needing Karamanlis' personal intervention more than once. The goodwill of the other allies was also not completely solid. The French and British governments were continually pressing for the settlement of pre-war debts. The Americans intended to terminate all economic aid, on the ground that Greece was now strong enough to do without it. Karamanlis bluntly drew the Americans' attention to the fact that Turkey was being aided disproportionately. 'Give the Turks more advice and less money,' he told a Congressman who visited him on his way to Ankara. At the same time there were rumours of pressure from the US government to allow missiles to be installed in Greece. Although they were unfounded, they attracted Soviet wrath.

Relations with the Soviet bloc were also returning to normality, which meant constant tension, in the wake of the Cyprus settlement. Even the Yugoslavs were uneasy about the reconciliation between Greece and Turkey, for their own relations with the Turks were not good. The Yugoslavs were equally under pressure from the Soviet Union, which hindered discussions on Greco-Yugoslav frontier questions. Consequently the Cyprus settlement did not lead to a revival of the Balkan Pact between Yugoslavia, Greece, and Turkey. On

3 March Karamanlis had a meeting in Rhodes with Tito, who was returning from a visit to India. Tito told him that he had agreed with Nehru to adopt a policy of non-alignment. The Balkan Pact was therefore allowed quietly to lapse.

Nor did the Cyprus settlement have a good effect on Greece's relations with the Balkan satellites. The Bulgarians were again pressing Greece to restore diplomatic relations, which Karamanlis again said was impossible until they paid their wartime reparations. In Albania on 24 May Khrushchev made a speech criticizing Italy and Greece for their supposed willingness to accept American missile bases, and the Bulgarians joined in the attack. Pressure was then renewed by the Romanian government, which proposed a 'missile-free' zone in the Balkans. Karamanlis rejected the proposal on 10 June.

These pressures from the Soviet bloc were the natural consequence of Greece's improved relations with the West, which were in turn the consequence of the Cyprus settlement. But it was a price well worth paying for Karamanlis. He had assurances from the US Secretary of State that Greece and Italy would be protected against Soviet threats. He also enjoyed the supreme reward for his loyalty at the end of 1959, when President Eisenhower visited Athens in the course of a tour round eleven nations in sensitive areas. The President arrived from Tehran on 14 December. Apart from public appearances, which stirred great enthusiasm, he had a long talk with Karamanlis on the morning of the fifteenth. Kanellopoulos, Tsatsos, and government officials were also present.

Nothing is more striking about his character than the forthright confidence with which Karamanlis talked to the most powerful man in the world. It was a clear sign that Greece was again conspicuously on the map; and it was one man's achievement. Whereas previous Prime Ministers of Greece had made a personal impact on the world, Karamanlis was creating a country which made an international impact in its own right.

There was no formal agenda between the President and the Prime Minister. Karamanlis spoke of the subjects in the forefront of his mind: the Soviet threat, concealed by the screen of *détente*; the pressures on Greece from her Communist neighbours; the need to confront the world's problems 'in a global way'—a phrase he used in English. Greece, he stressed, 'belongs ideologically to the West, but she is isolated geographically and racially.' He went on to speak of the need for American support—moral, political and economic—adding that this, not the reverse, was the order of priority. He made no reference to Cyprus: that was a closed chapter.

Eisenhower's remarks were characteristically rambling. He said that he would soon be retiring, and he hoped Nixon would succeed him. He criticized de Gaulle as 'myopic', incurably convinced that he alone was right. He emphasized the scale of US overseas aid, reminding Karamanlis that this was never accompanied by pressure. He regretted that the other allies did not do more to help Greece economically. He talked of giving Macmillan, de Gaulle, and Adenauer 'a tongue-lashing' if they failed to see the importance of defending Greece and Turkey. He acknowledged the danger of Soviet penetration into Afghanistan.

On specific topics he was vague or ill-informed. He asked whether the Communist Party was legal in Greece, and was gratified that it was not. When Karamanlis asked if the rumour was true that he intended to withdraw the Sixth Fleet from the Mediterranean, he was evasive. This was curious, because there was no such intention, and he was due to leave the next day for Tunisia on the flagship of the Fleet. On Berlin, however, he was categorical: he would make no concessions.

The lofty *tour d'horizon* ended with a firm hint from Karamanlis that economic aid was still essential. Eisenhower instructed his staff to take note of it. The meeting adjourned, to be followed by more ceremonial occasions: a reception in Parliament, which Eisenhower addressed from the presidential chair; a state banquet; election to honorary membership of the Academy of Athens; and the conferment of the freedom of many towns which Eisenhower never saw. He left Greece the same evening to continue his tour, cruising for two days in the Mediterranean.

It happened that on the day of Eisenhower's arrival in Athens, Archbishop Makarios was elected President of the future Republic of Cyprus by two-thirds of the votes cast, with Dr Kütchük unopposed as his Vice-President. Karamanlis sent Makarios a warm message of congratulation. But there were other less agreeable matters arising in Cyprus. During the same month of December 1959 Karamanlis had to write a severe letter to Menderes about difficulties in the constitutional talks, including a 'clear tendency towards partition' in the Turkish drafts. About the same date Averoff wrote to Makarios complaining of Cypriot hostility towards the settlement and 'a spirit of animosity and criticism towards the Greek government' which was being deliberately stirred up. There were also complaints from the British government of the slow and devious negotiations with Makarios over the British bases. The year ended with another minor irritation: the first rumours of Grivas' intention to become active in politics, which he had expressly forsworn when he arrived in Athens in March.

On the international scene, however, Karamanlis was still reaping the benefits of the settlement. Exchanges of official visits multiplied in 1960. Among many others, the West German Minister of Defence, Franz-Josef Strauss, came in March; the American Secretary of State, Christian Herter, and the Dutch Foreign Minister in May; President Nasser in June. At the end of June Karamanlis and Averoff visited Tito on Brioni. The climax of the season of visits came in July, when Karamanlis went to Paris for meetings with de Gaulle and his Prime Minister, Michel Debré.

But the summer was also beset with anxieties. Khrushchev continued his attacks on Greece over the American missile bases. Averoff had meetings with the US Ambassador on 14 and 19 April to reassure himself of American support; and between the two meetings he summoned the Soviet Ambassador to protest against an article in *Izvestia* extolling the KKE. In May Khrushchev frustrated the proposed Summit Conference in Paris, using the U2 incident as his excuse. Karamanlis expressed his regret at the breakdown, and in reply to a letter of explanation from Eisenhower he sent a warm and loyal message. On 2 June came a letter from Khrushchev containing well-worn proposals for general disarmament, to which Karamanlis sent a polite reply on the eighteenth expressing his reliance on negotiations through the United Nations. In July he had to rebuff another approach from the Bulgarian government, on the familiar ground that the peace treaty must first be fulfilled.

More immediately disturbing was a grave crisis in Turkey. It began, so far as Karamanlis was concerned, in April 1960 with the news that an exchange of visits between Menderes and the Soviet Prime Minister was arranged for July. Averoff sought and received assurances from the US Ambassador that this should not be interpreted as a change in Turkish policy. It was important to be reassured because Menderes and Zorlu were also due to visit Athens during the summer. But none of these visits took place. At the end of April riots broke out in Istanbul and Ankara against the Turkish government. On 23 May military law was proclaimed. The next day a senior official of the Turkish Ministry of Foreign Affairs, Selim Sarper, arrived in Athens to discuss a postponement of Menderes' visit.

The visit had already been postponed twice. In the presence of Averoff, Sarper asked Karamanlis whether a third postponement would embarrass him. If so, the visit would certainly take place. After a moment's reflection, gazing out of the window, Karamanlis turned to Sarper and said emphatically: 'Fly back to Ankara at once—tell Menderes to dissolve Parliament *tonight*, and hold elections—it's the only way out!'

Sarper left at once to return to Ankara, but it was too late. The situation was out of hand already. The Turkish government fell on the twenty-eighth. Menderes and Zorlu were arrested, together with President Bayar and other ministers; and Sarper, though he was not a party to the conspiracy, succeeded as Foreign Minister. After a long and humiliating trial, despite international protests in which Karamanlis joined, Menderes, Zorlu, and another minister were hanged in September 1961.

Although Karamanlis had formed a personal sympathy for Menderes, he could not afford to let the Cyprus settlement be compromised by refusing to recognize the new Turkish government. Recognition came at the end of May 1960, three days after the revolution. Negotiations in Nicosia between the Greeks, the Turks, and the British slowly progressed. Final agreement on all the necessary documents was reached on 1 July. At the end of the month a general election took place in Cyprus, at which Makarios' party triumphed among the Greeks, winning thirty out of thirty-five seats, the remainder going to the Communists. Dr Kütchük's party won all fifteen of the Turkish seats.

Makarios and Karamanlis exchanged formal messages of thanks and congratulations. The Republic of Cyprus came into being on 16 August. Karamanlis' first great aim was achieved, though it saddened him that Makarios never invited him to Cyprus.

Chapter 4

Transforming the Economy

THE second of Karamanlis' major aims was to transform Greece into a modern industrial state. Like the settlement of Cyprus, the task began from the first day he took office, but it was a much longer-term undertaking. His qualifications for it were unusual and not at first sight obvious. His ministerial experience had lain entirely in spending departments: transport, welfare, communications, public works, and—most expensive of all—national defence. He had not held any of the ministries responsible for the generation of wealth to finance public expenditure: agriculture, trade, industry, finance, co-ordination. But he had acquired the experience needed to direct the national economy in a more practical school.

He was the first Prime Minister of Greece, at any rate in the twentieth century, who had known the hardships of village life and had himself worked in the fields with his hands. He had seen in his father's experience the risks of bankruptcy. As an insurance salesman he had had contact with the problems of middle- and working-class Greeks. He had sat through the sterile decade of dictatorship, war, and enemy occupation with far fewer resources than most politicians. He had never been corrupted by the megalopolitan fallacy that Athens is Greece. Life had taught him what every peasant knew, but not every politician or economist, that one cannot reap where one does not sow. He had, in fact, a provincial Greek's grasp on the realities of life.

If there had been any doubt of Karamanlis' intention to direct economic policy himself, it should not have survived his first three months in office. His first speech in Parliament had emphasized economic themes: a balanced budget, suppression of tax evasion, monetary control, a stable currency, reform of the banking and investment system. Banking had never been his field, but it was the scene of his first intervention in November 1955.

Under the previous government, Markezinis had brought about the amalgamation of the National Bank—which was partly state-owned—and the Bank of Athens. The Director-General of the amalgamated bank had been accused of misusing his powers. On 25 November his dismissal was announced, and the banks were divided again. At the same time government commissioners were appointed to control the Commercial Ionian Bank, against which there had been similar accusations. These were bold and stern measures to take a few weeks after entering office.

There was no aspect of economic policy to which Karamanlis' attention did not extend. He was regularly in the chair at ministerial committees. In December 1955, though heavily engaged in the Cyprus problem, he presided at long meetings in the Ministry of Agriculture and the Ministry of Public Works. He supervised the preparation of the budget, which was tabled in Parliament on 16 December, balanced as he had forecast without new taxation. He personally scrutinized and accepted a number of demands from the Union of Civil Servants, which included subsidies for medical treatment, housing, and the cost of living.

The modernization of Greece's industrial economy was launched in December, Karamanlis' third month of office. On the fifteenth he accompanied the King at the foundation of an oil refinery at Aspropyrgos. Three days later, during a short tour of central Greece, he was present at the foundation of a hydroelectric power-station on the River Megdhova. The provinces, not merely Athens, were to be industrialized.

The budget for 1956 reflected the same intention, with a greatly increased provision for public works: roads, bridges, buildings, agricultural improvement. Six months later Karamanlis personally announced the addition of major projects to the list: oil refineries, power-stations, dockyards, asbestos mining, fertilizer production, air communications, tourist hotels. The outstanding characteristic of these projects, unlike so many ambitious plans in the past, was that they all came to fruition.

For Karamanlis was not content to announce them: he supervised them, insisted on progress reports, visited the sites, allowed their executants no rest until they were completed.

Other governments had said that Greece should have an international airline and modern shipbuilding facilities. Karamanlis had agreements to establish them signed with private capitalists within six months. Characteristically, too, he announced on 1 August 1956 that the power-station on the River Megdhova would be in operation by 1962. He was better than his word, for it came into operation in October 1960.

When developing countries launch themselves on a course of industrialization, their leaders often forget that their most fundamental industry is agriculture. Power-stations and factory chimneys have more popular appeal; the fields lie derelict. There was no danger that a Prime Minister born in a Macedonian village would make that mistake. In particular, both his father and his younger brother had harsh experience of the vagaries of the tobacco industry, which was the only branch of agriculture on which a major manufacturing industry had been based. Tobacco was doubly important, both as the country's chief earner of foreign exchange and because the Union of Tobacco-workers had been one of the main bases of the Greek Communist Party among industrial workers. Karamanlis was determined to set the tobacco industry on a stable and productive course.

In March 1956, the month in which he was sworn into office after his first election victory, he announced plans for the rehabilitation of landless peasants and the stabilization of tobacco cultivation. More trained agricultural experts were to be recruited; the capital of the Agricultural Bank was to be increased; loans on easy terms were to be advanced for small-scale improvements; horticulture was to be protected; guaranteed prices for tobacco were to be introduced. The plans for promoting horticulture and tobacco-growing were debated in Parliament on 3 July.

Unusually for a Prime Minister, Karamanlis attended the debate. Still more unusually, he intervened in it. After recapitulating the recent history of the tobacco industry, he took occasion to rebuke a member of the Opposition for 'insulting the government at a time when the state is taking unprecedented measures for the protection of tobacco producers'. It was the voice of the son of the Macedonian village schoolmaster that spoke.

As the year advanced, Karamanlis' plans for the future grew more ambitious. After his agreement with Aristotle Onassis in July to establish what became the Olympic Airways Corporation, he made a further agreement with Onassis' brother-in-law and rival, Stavros Niarkhos, to establish a shipbuilding yard at Skaramanga. This was said to be the largest private investment yet made in Greece. It was followed a few weeks later by an agreement with an American company to develop a number of metallurgical projects in Greece. Foreign capital was essential to exploit Greece's raw materials, but the subject was controversial because of unhappy experience with foreign capitalists in the past. So the legislation ratifying the American agreement was carefully drawn and thoroughly discussed before it was approved on 1 October.

On the following day Karamanlis' government set a new landmark. One of Greece's resources which had never been systematically developed was its combination of climate, physical beauty, and history: the tourist industry was practically non-existent. Inadequate communications and hotels, hindered by ten years of warfare, had kept development at a standstill. Karamanlis recognized from the first that tourism could become the country's main source of foreign exchange. His first step was to introduce legislation on 2 October for the promotion of a tourist area at Vouliagmeni, on the coast near Athens. In token of its importance, the draft law was supported in Parliament by Costa Tsatsos, the eminent scholar who held the office of Minister in the Prime Minister's office. It was the forerunner of a spate of similar schemes all over the mainland and islands.

Ironically, one of the earliest testimonials to Karamanlis' success in economic planning was a cut of twenty-three million dollars in American aid. The testimonial was welcome but the cut was not. Some time passed, owing to the strain of the Cyprus dispute and other priorities, before Karamanlis was able to present effective arguments to the US government on Greece's needs. But in May 1958, immediately after his second election victory, he had a memorandum prepared for submission to the Americans summarizing the economic state of the country. The national income was 240 dollars a head, and a quarter of the population was unemployed or underemployed.

It was imperative to accelerate industrial development, but it was impossible to do so entirely from internal resources. It was proposed to ask the US government for a further ten million dollars in economic aid and thirty-five million in military aid. The Americans were also to be asked for an indication of their intentions over the next four years.

These were perennial themes. The subject was raised again in 1959, when the US Congress reduced the appropriation requested by Eisenhower for overseas aid; and it was raised by Karamanlis with the President during his visit to Athens in December. At the same time he was looking in other directions for help. He approached the Germans and the French for new investment in Greek industry, but not the British because they were still raising difficulties about past debts. In agreement with the Americans he also sought help from NATO in meeting the costs of defence. Linked with both these lines of approach was his determination to secure a Treaty of Association with the European Economic Community, leading eventually to full membership. This prospect was discussed within the Council of Ministers as early as the middle of 1958, less than a year after the signature of the Treaty of Rome. The Minister of Co-ordination also discussed it with his colleagues in Paris during October, by which date the Treaty had not yet come into operation. No time was to be wasted.

Association with the EEC would impose strains on Greece as well as creating opportunities. It would be a complement and not an alternative to domestic development. For Karamanlis it was a challenge, and he presented it to his colleagues as such. The tempo of economic progress must be accelerated; it must not be confined to the vicinity of Athens; and it must be pressed on a broad front. Apart from presiding at committees in different ministries, Karamanlis took advantage of his regional tours to stimulate action. Visiting his native Macedonia in June 1957, he held a meeting of officials to discuss road construction, flood control, irrigation, hospitals, forestry, marketing, electrification, tourism, education, and the fine arts. A month later he was in Epirus to inaugurate an irrigation system, while the King attended the foundation of a lignite plant at Ptolemais. At the end of August Karamanlis opened a new aqueduct to supply the Marathon Dam, and then flew back to Salonika to open the Annual Trade Fair.

The increase in the capacity of the Marathon Dam was a matter of special satisfaction to Karamanlis, because he had initiated the project as Minister of Public Works. He again took the unusual step of speaking himself when questions on the subject were raised in Parliament. In a long review of the history of the capital's water-supply, he remarked that 'everyone who has studied the problem will recall that it came up against such technical and political obstacles that it would have remained unsolved for ever unless someone were found with the practical intelligence and political courage to solve it.' He ended by expressing pride that 'in a matter which had preoccupied Athens ever since it existed as a city, I had the courage to undertake the responsibility and produce the solution.'

Besides pressing individual projects, he also gave close attention to the administrative machinery of economic development. Company law was reformed. Private banks were freed from restrictions on their lending policies. The Agricultural Bank was reorganized in order to expand and simplify investment. A National Tobacco Organization was set up by law to market tobacco abroad and maintain fair prices. Legislation was introduced to provide for the financial as well as administrative devolution of local government. Provision was made for the Army to lend technical assistance in major public works. A Council on social and economic policy was formed, including industrialists as well as government officials.

Karamanlis himself took the chair at a meeting of this Council in July 1958, as a result of which the government announced measures to save foreign currency, to cut luxury expenditure, and to reform the tax system. Other innovations sprang from it. Early in 1959 a new procedure was introduced for allocating public contracts and monitoring them technically and financially. Soon afterwards a reorganization of the Ministry of Co-ordination was announced. Later in the same year the Organization of Industrial Development was set up as a limited company. All these initiatives were closely supervised by Karamanlis.

Not all of them were wholly successful. During a visit to Salonika at the end of July 1959, Karamanlis was obliged to admit, and to complain, that 'the state mechanism is limping'. He censured those locally responsible and urged them to accelerate the construction projects in the city. Without the impetus which he provided, the rate of progress would certainly have been slower. Hence his regular visits in person to areas where new capital projects were in progress. Workers on the tourist development at Vouliagmeni, on the construction projects round Salonika and in Thessaly, on the power-station at Ptolemais, on the harbour-works at Keratsini, on the developments round Ioannina, all became accustomed to seeing the Prime Minister not merely laying foundation-stones and cutting inaugural ribbons but inspecting progress on their sites.

A senior official once urged him to take more time to relax. 'Even Churchill used to relax sometimes at the height of the war,' he told the Prime Minister. Karamanlis thought seriously for a moment on his advice, and replied: 'Churchill only had to govern the British!' His sardonic humour set him apart from his people, whom he wanted to educate as well as to bully. He felt bound to remind them that they had severer problems than the Western democracies. 'In Greece', he would say, 'it is not enough to wind up your watch: to make progress you have to push the hands on with your finger!'

To take the measure of his personal commitment to economic development, it is only necessary to set it alongside his simultaneous preoccupation with the Cyprus problem. The latter reached its point of extreme crisis in the autumn of 1958. During the last week of October and the first week of November that year, Karmanlis was deeply engaged in resisting the Macmillan plan, negotiating with Spaak on the NATO initiative, preparing Greece's case for the United Nations, and trying to persuade Makarios to see reason. He was also preparing for an official visit to Germany, where Cyprus would be top of the agenda and economic questions second. But during the same two weeks he made time to preside at a ministerial committee on the domestic distribution of tobacco, and another on the establishment of a thermoelectric power-station and the purchase of a French ferry-boat; to lay the foundation-stone of a new Polytechnic at Salonika; to inaugurate two newly completed dams on the Vardar and Aliakmon rivers; to discuss a report on the EEC; and to accompany the King at the opening of the Aspropyrgos oil refinery, which had been started three years earlier. Nor was this an exceptional fortnight.

If Greece were to prosper in association with Western Europe, which was Karamanlis' goal, then there were many other respects in which the Greek way of life had to be changed. Not all of them were economic, though all depended on the health of the economy. It was a challenge which demanded an imaginative response on a very wide front comprising welfare, insurance, education, culture, athletics, and much else. The bare statistics give an indication of Karamanlis' response to the challenge: between 1955 and 1963 expenditure on welfare grew by more than 150 per cent, and education expenditure by almost 200 per cent. But statistics are not necessarily a good index of imagination.

One of Karamanlis' earliest aspirations had been to revise the system of social insurance, whose inadequacy he had appreciated both as a young insurance salesman in Macedonia and as Minister of Welfare in 1948. It was on his initiative that legislation was passed in December 1958 to provide hospital and medical care for pensioners. Two years later, when legislation was introduced in November 1960 to provide social insurance for agricultural workers, he spoke himself in the parliamentary debate, urging a speedy passage of the law. It was, for its time, a revolutionary measure, covering forty per cent of the population and providing not only pensions and medical care but also insurance against agricultural damage by 'acts of God'. Unfortunately the Opposition delayed it until May 1961; but a year later, on 10 June 1962, Karamanlis was able to hand over the first fifty pension certificates to agricultural workers, out of 305,000 who would qualify at the end of the month.

The improvement of education was another necessity not less obvious than social insurance. In 1957 an inter-party committee was appointed to study the educational needs of the country. It produced an agreed report, which Karamanlis took as the basis for legislation in the summer of 1959. The first task was to modernize higher education, starting with the technical, professional, and commercial sectors. The two Universities of Athens and Salonika and the Polytechnic of

Athens were greatly expanded. Education at all levels became virtually free. Since the cost of education grew from seven to ten per cent of the budget in eight years, Karamanlis deeply resented the accusation of the Opposition that he had neglected education. He pointed out that the further expansion under his successors was made possible only by the economic growth which he had promoted.

The Europeanization of Greece had other less obvious requirements. Metric weights and measures were introduced early in 1959. An astronomical observatory and a centre of scientific research were established later in the year. A television service, funded from Italian reparations, followed in 1960. The face of Athens was also to be renovated. As Minister of Public Works, Karamanlis had been responsible for a major reconstruction of the highways through the capital. Now he set about further improvements by abolishing the last trams, demolishing the wooden huts which had once housed refugees, and instituting *son et lumière* on the Acropolis.

A Greek Prime Minister so deeply conscious of history, past and future, could not neglect athletics. Karamanlis decided that they must be officially sponsored, to enable young Greeks to enter international competitions on equal terms. A Secretary-General for Athletics was appointed in 1957, and two years later a national football pool was set up to finance sport in general. Stadiums, gymnasia, and swimming-pools were built in most of the principal cities. In August 1961 Karamanlis opened a new athletic stadium at Aghios Kosmas, the first project of its kind completed since the war. The idea of restoring the Olympic Games to Greece was perhaps already in his mind. Apart from his own youthful interest in sport—which was to be revived on the golf-course in later years—he was conscious of the prestige brought to Greece by the gold medal won by the Crown Prince as a yachtsman in the 1960 Olympic Games.

So the imaginative ideas flowed continuously from his mind. But these were no substitute for the hard grind of industrialization, which was the essential basis for innovations. Never allowing his ministers to relax their attention, he intensified the pace of economic growth in 1959-60, both by exhortation and by strict planning. Typical items can be picked almost at random from his diary of official engagements: a ministerial committee on marketing; a speech on the importance of exports; a new programme of public works; a five-year plan for agriculture, manufacture, and tourism; a scheme for co-ordinating cotton production; an exhibition on domestically fed animals; ministerial committees on the budget; the annual opening of the Salonika Trade Fair; a briefing on the progress of the Organization of Industrial Development; the foundation of a dam on the River Nestos; a plan for reconstructing the habour at Salonika; the formation of a limited company to produce and market sugar; a major new hotel at Salonika; a discussion on trade with the Soviet Union; a proposal to supply tobacco to Communist China; a meeting at the Bank of Greece to review the economic situation; compensation for Cretan farmers hit by plant disease; government imports of olive oil and rice to stabilize prices; and much else. These were not simply items of government business but personal activities of the Prime Minister himself.

They were not, however, the main economic burden. Two related requirements outweighed them all in Karamanlis' mind: to attract industrial investment from abroad, and to negotiate a Treaty of Association with the EEC. Work on both had to begin without delay. When Karamanlis and Averoff visited Bonn in November 1958, the main topics of discussion with Adenauer, after Cyprus, were the need to attract German investment and to increase Greek tobacco sales. The first results were seen in March 1959, when Parliament approved a contract with a German firm to set up a nitrogen plant at Ptolemais, followed nine months later by the signing of another German contract for a sugar refinery at Larisa.

There was also welcome news from Paris. In April 1959 it was reported that the French intended to take part in the Salonika Trade Fair, which they did in the following year. Closer relations with the French led to a contract with a French company for oil-prospecting on the borders of Thessaly and Macedonia, and to another for the establishment of an aluminium plant jointly funded by the French and Niarkhos. American and British investment, however, still languished.

Dependence on foreign investment and economic aid must in any case not become total: Karamanlis insisted that domestic

resources should also contribute. The budget which he announced in January 1960 showed the highest figure ever
for capital projects, with an increase of thirty per cent over
1959. He drew attention to the fact that within the total the
allocation to agricultural investment was the highest of all,
followed by communications, industry and energy, local
government projects, and tourism. Tourism, as he pointed out,
now ranked third after agriculture and manufacturing industry
in the national economy. He was also setting ambitious targets
in industry: during the year he announced plans to set up an
iron and steel plant; and he assumed personal control of the
atomic-energy programme, with the result that Greece's first
nuclear reactor was inaugurated in August 1961.

By the beginning of 1961 he was able to issue a statement
declaring his government's intention of 'progressively con-
verting the national economy from intensive agriculture to
industry'. The choice of words was significant: agriculture was
intensive because it had been the first priority, but the con-
version to industry was already in progress. This had been
Karamanlis' aim since 1955, but it would have been too bold
a boast to make at that date. By January 1962 he was able to
go further in his New Year message: 'For the first time steps
are on record towards the definitive emergence of the country
from its status of underdevelopment.' It was ready, in fact,
given reasonable safeguards, to face the challenge of the Common Market.

After soundings among the Germans, the French, and the
Italians in particular, Karamanlis opened formal negotiations
with the EEC in 1959. The ministerial responsibility rested
with the Minister of Co-ordination, but Karamanlis chose as
chief negotiator Professor John Pesmazoglou, who belonged
to a family long eminent in the financial and political world.
It was an inspired choice. Pesmazoglou had a Cambridge
doctorate and held concurrently the posts of Professor of
Economics at the University of Athens and Deputy Governor
of the Bank of Greece. In politics he was a social democrat, a
somewhat rare persuasion in Greece. For Karamanlis, joining the EEC was a political as much as an economic commitment. It was characteristic of him to choose as his agent a
technocrat whose politics were not identical with his own,

and yet were nearer to his own than many people would have supposed.

It happened that Pesmazoglou had been one of the first to urge on Karamanlis, in a memorandum dated 9 April 1959, the importance of negotiating with the EEC as soon as possible. By June the negotiations were in progress. There was initially some reluctance on the part of the six members of the EEC. This was disappointing for Karamanlis, especially as NATO (including the same six) was at the same time failing to provide adequate support for Greece's defence burden. The French and Italians were particularly difficult, because Greece would compete with some of their most valuable products; and even more so would Spain, which would one day follow Greece's example. But agreement in principle was eventually reached, and announced in a joint communiqué on 17 October.

Even after that, difficult questions of detail remained, especially over agricultural products. Reporting on the problems in December, Pesmazoglou urged that strong political pressure should be put on the Foreign Ministers of the Six. Karamanlis responded vigorously, and in some cases went higher. On 4 March 1960 he summoned the Ambassadors of the Six and demanded an early decision. He pressed the Dutch Foreign Minister on a visit to Athens in May. He complained to the Italian Ambassador in July, and wrote personally to his Prime Minister in November. When he visited Paris in July, he pressed de Gaulle and Debré; and while still in Paris, he sent a similar message to the German government through diplomatic channels. In August he sent a further letter to Adenauer, complaining particularly of obstruction by the Italians. In October, hearing of similar obstruction by French officials, he wrote personally to de Gaulle about it. On 26 November he sent an identical letter to the six Prime Ministers, with an extra paragraph addressed to the obstinate Italians.

As a precaution, on 1 December Karamanlis presided at a ministerial committee to consider the consequences if the negotiations failed. It was agreed that a failure would not be disastrous, but it would be advisable to seek a special source of finance from NATO. Later in the same month Averoff informed his colleagues in Paris that Greece would withdraw from negotiations with the EEC if her views were not met.

Gradually, however, the Six began to respond more favourably at the highest level: the Belgian and French Prime Ministers in December, the Italian in January 1961. The Germans, the Dutch, and the Luxemburgers had never been difficult. By 15 January the negotiations were effectively concluded; only matters of drafting remained. Finally on 31 March the Treaty of Association was initialled.

After the removal of a few more obstacles, introduced mainly by the Italians, the Treaty was formally signed in Athens on 9 July 1961, to come into operation in November 1962. At the same time the EEC promised Greece long-term, low-interest loans totalling 125 million dollars. The agreement was warmly welcomed by the industrial community, the ship-owners, and the agricultural producers. Another important aspect of it was emphasized by *Kathimerini* on 4 April: it would relieve Greece of the risk of dependence on exports to Eastern Europe.

A new phase of policy had already been opened. In February, a few weeks before the treaty with the EEC was initialled, Karamanlis had made an official visit to London, accompanied by Averoff, both their wives, and numerous officials. The visit had multiple significance. It set the seal of reconciliation on the Cyprus settlement; it marked the fact that Karamanlis was an acknowledged figure on the high-level circuit of international exchanges; it paved the way for a state visit to London by King Paul and Queen Frederika; and it signalled a fresh initiative in Karamanlis' approach to foreign and economic policy.

The topics of discussion in London were familiar, but there was a new emphasis. Cyprus and the past were to be set aside; negotiations on public debt were to be treated with patience; the EEC was a subject on which Karamanlis had more up-to-date news for Macmillan than vice versa; economic and technical aid were important, but British resources were known to be diminishing; and finally there was the question of what Karamanlis called 'the interdependence of the free nations'.

The natural context for discussing the last point was NATO, on which Karamanlis was now laying increased emphasis. He saw the alliance as a source of financial as well as moral support, now that unilateral aid from the USA was declining.

Thus NATO was taking the place of the EEC in the forefront of his mind for the time being. Two months after his visit to Britain, he flew to Canada for the first time, and then to the USA. Britain, Canada, and the USA were all members of NATO, but none of them was in the EEC.

It was Eisenhower who had first hinted to Karamanlis, in December 1959, that NATO might be a source of economic support. This was one respect in which Karamanlis hoped that NATO could extend its formal commitments. Another, which he suggested both to the Canadian Prime Minister, Diefenbaker, and to Eisenhower's successor, President Kennedy, was to be prepared to act collectively outside the geographical limits of the alliance—for example, in the Middle East or Africa. Diefenbaker was shocked by the idea of NATO acting as a bloc, but Kennedy seemed more receptive. Following a similar line of thought, Karamanlis expressed anxiety to Hamarskjöld, the Secretary-General of the United Nations, about the Soviet bloc's successful use of UN machinery, in contrast with the lack of purpose shown by the Western democracies.

Karamanlis' reception in Washington was highly gratifying. President Kennedy sent his personal aircraft to fetch him from Canada. The two men had several private meetings, during which Kennedy consulted Karamanlis on many international topics, including that perennial enigma of American presidents, the personality of de Gaulle. He also took Karamanlis into his confidence about the disastrous attempt to overthrow Fidel Castro in Cuba, which was launched on 17 April, the very day of Karamanlis' arrival, and immediately proved a fiasco. 'This wretched operation was organized by my predecessors,' Kennedy told him, 'but I had to take the responsibility.' Karamanlis commented openly to the Press that, while he knew nothing about the Cuban affair, 'any country has the right to be concerned over what happens in its immediate neighbourhood'.

Most exceptionally, Kennedy attended a dinner at the Greek Embassy. He told Karamanlis of his desire to visit Greece. His wife paid a visit to Greece, in 1962, but the President's hope was frustrated, first by pressure of business and then by tragedy. Karamanlis corresponded with him until his death, and afterwards with his brothers. Like Macmillan,

Karamanlis valued his friendship with Kennedy more than with any other contemporary statesman.

From his talks in Washington, which included the Secretaries of State, Defence, and the Treasury as well as the President, it was clear that the halcyon days of American aid were over. There was even pressure, as in London, for speedier negotiations on public debt still outstanding.On his return to Greece Karamanlis therefore concentrated his efforts on NATO as a source of greater economic support. He emphasized that his reasons for doing so were political and psychological rather than economic: financial aid was to be the visible sign of moral support.

The subject was raised by Averoff at a meeting of the NATO Council in Paris during May 1961. He reported that the other members had agreed to send a three-man mission to study the needs of Greece and Turkey. He also reported that the US government was willing to make Polaris submarines available to NATO, to be manned by multinational crews. The Greek government agreed to take part in this so-called 'multilateral force', though in the end nothing came of it. Nor did the prospect of NATO aid prove much more fruitful.

It was not until early in 1962 that the three-man mission arrived in Athens. The delay was not wholly the fault of NATO, for in the interval Greece had held another general election. The election, which was mandatory by May 1962, was held early, on 29 October 1961. It once more strengthened Karamanlis' position: he won only three extra seats, making a total of 176, but his popular vote reached fifty per cent, and EDA fell back into third place. But the results deeply embittered Papandreou and Venizelos, the defeated leaders of the new Centre Union, although they came second with 100 seats. This was the beginning of what was called the 'relentless struggle' against Karamanlis' fourth administration.[1]

He had called the election early because of the favourable circumstances resulting from the negotiations with the EEC and his successful journeys abroad. There was also, however, a growing state of international tension, which was the reason for his emphasis on the need for the support of NATO. In the summer of 1961 the Berlin wall was built, and Greece was a

[1] See pp. 131–9 below.

regular target of Soviet hostility. Both the Russian and the Bulgarian Press persistently attacked Karamanlis' foreign policy. The most ominous onslaught came on 12 August, when Khrushchev warned that he would not hesitate to attack American bases in Greece with missiles, which 'will not spare either olive-groves or the Acropolis'. Karamanlis made a cool and dignified reply the following day. His memorable phrase —'the ideals which the rock of the Acropolis symbolizes will prove stronger than Russian rockets'—earned him world-wide admiration and a personal message of congratulation from President Kennedy.

Despite these threats, and despite the reinforced strength of the Greek government after the election, the proceedings of NATO were dilatory and the determination of the US government to reduce its aid to Greece was unyielding. Karamanlis used an unusual channel—his friend Archbishop Iakovos, the head of the Orthodox Church in America—to remonstrate with Kennedy. At the same time Averoff pressed Greece's case with the US Ambassador in Athens. The so-called 'three wise men' from NATO eventually arrived on 19 January 1962.

One of the three was an American, but the Greeks' arguments to him were of no avail. The three reported at the end of March that Greece was now capable of carrying the whole burden of defence costs. Karamanlis reacted indignantly and repeatedly—on his visit to Brussels and Paris in April, at a further meeting with the US Ambassador, and during discussions with the NATO Ministers of Defence and Foreign Affairs, who met in Athens in May.

On that last occasion the American delegation was led by Dean Rusk, the Secretary of State himself. With his agreement the meeting decided to reconsider the Greek case, and to set up a special consortium charged with the task of providing financial aid. Again there were delays, especially on the part of the British government, which demanded fresh negotiations on Greece's pre-war debts as a condition of its participation in the consortium. Karamanlis had a series of difficult meetings with the British and US Ambassadors during July.

He complained to the US Ambassador on 3 July that the American government departments were showing 'a complete lack of understanding of Greek reality and Greek needs'.

Although the formation of the NATO consortium was announced in early August, it was also made clear that the US
government would not increase its contribution. At the end
of August Karamanlis took the unusual step of making his
complaints public, in an interview with the *New York Times*.
He spoke similarly to Vice-President Lyndon Johnson, who
visited Athens early in September.

Disappointed though he was over the reduction in US aid,
Karamanlis would entertain no thought of disloyalty to the
alliance. He showed this clearly in October 1962 during the
Soviet–American confrontation over Cuba. At his request,
Greek shipowners undertook not to lease ships to carry car-
goes to Cuba, and Averoff publicly declared Greece's unqualified support for the USA. Partly in recognition of this loyalty,
and partly because an agreement was at last signed with US
bond-holders of pre-war Greek public debt, the US government reciprocated with a guarantee of support for the NATO
consortium.

This message was conveyed to Karamanlis in a letter from
Lyndon Johnson dated 19 October. The consortium then allo-
cated twenty-three and a half million dollars to Greece, but
the outcome was only partially satisfactory, for US aid was
cut by a further ten million. Averoff, who was at a meeting
of NATO ministers in Paris, considered that they had entirely
failed to understand Greece's needs. A few weeks later, on
15 February 1963, Kennedy sent a warm letter to Karamanlis
thanking him for his support over Cuba, but also warning him
that American resources were limited, so that further cuts in
aid were probable.

Both NATO and the USA thus disappointed Karamanlis'
hopes. Yet his personal standing remained very high, as was
evident from the number of his invitations abroad and of
high-level visitors to Athens. Among the latter, besides Lyndon
Johnson (who came twice in 1961–2), there were Spaak and
his successor Dr Stikker from NATO, the French Prime Minister and Foreign Minister, the US Secretary of State, the
Italian President, and finally President de Gaulle himself in
May 1963. It was gratifying that Karamanlis' advice was now
sought on matters far outside the scope of the alliance. De
Gaulle would consult him about the reliability of Tito and

Nasser, and the difficulties caused by Britain's application to the EEC. Adenauer, Eisenhower, and Kennedy all discussed with him the difficulties caused by de Gaulle. Tito would consult him about the Americans and the Americans about Tito. The Turks were particularly impressed by his international reputation, as Averoff found when he visited Ankara in August 1962.

But respect was no substitute for economic aid. Successive approaches to the Americans were politely rebuffed. Kennedy's forecast of a further reduction proved correct, although he himself pressed Congress to be more generous. Only dollar loans for industrial investment were in future to be available. NATO also was unforthcoming.

Averoff complained to the NATO Council in May 1963 that the first six months' operation of the consortium had produced nothing (though this was not strictly true), 'because we are confronted with the negative stance of the members of NATO'. The repeated representations by the British Ambassador in Athens on the subject of Greece's pre-war debts suggest one reason for the negative stance. The German government, at least, offered eight million dollars towards Greece's defence expenditure in 1963, and then there were also reparations still coming in from Germany and Italy; but all this was not commensurate with Greece's needs.

These were in fact days of serious anxiety for Karamanlis' government. He was under continual attack from the Soviet bloc, while the parliamentary Opposition at home was becoming more and more subservient to EDA, the front of the still outlawed KKE. In March 1962 Karamanlis received the new Soviet Ambassador and bluntly warned him against interference in Greece's affairs. But in October, during the Cuba crisis, there were violent Soviet attacks on Greece for harbouring American missiles. On 26 October Averoff summoned the Soviet Ambassador and told him categorically that there were 'no missile bases in Greece'. But the attacks continued, regularly echoed by the Bulgarians. Even with the Yugoslavs relations deteriorated: rumours of a *rapprochement* with the Soviet Union were followed by a revival of Yugoslav claims to Macedonia.

Whether Soviet interference extended to Greece's internal

problems was uncertain. The year 1962 was marked by serious disturbances, but they probably needed no external stimulus. Strikes and demonstrations began from genuine grievances, only to be converted into violent clashes by the intervention of EDA. Papandreou's 'relentless struggle' gave the Communists easy opportunities to exploit. On 11 April the police dispersed a student demonstration in Athens, which had been banned. On the twentieth the police prevented a public meeting called by Papandreou, who had insisted on holding it in the open although permission had been given only for an indoor meeting. In July a meeting of sultana producers at Iraklion in Crete to discuss their problems ended in violence. In September there were riots in Xeromero at a demonstration by tobacco producers. In October building workers on strike clashed again with the police. In December students were demonstrating once more with demands for more money to be spent on education. Early in 1963 there were strikes by dock-workers, leading to clashes with the police, and by teachers, who were threatened with conscription if they did not return to work. In March the doctors and lawyers went on strike for higher pay. Until the 1961 election, protests over social and economic problems had been relatively muted, and violence was rare. A serious clash between police and Communists during a strike of building workers in December 1960 was exceptional. More typical was a strike in the Agricultural Bank in February 1961 over the cost of living, which was quickly settled on Karamanlis' personal intervention. The rest of that year was quiet, so the deterioration in 1962 was all the more marked.

There were nevertheless reasonable grounds for optimism about the national economy. Karamanlis had presided at two ministerial meetings, in July and November 1961, to review the progress of the economy, which was found to be satisfactory and relatively free from inflation. This conclusion was endorsed by the Bank of Greece, which reported in March 1962 that the national income had grown in real terms by seventy-seven per cent between 1950 and 1961. Owing to a poor harvest, the rate of growth in 1962 was reduced to a little over six per cent, but this was still sufficiently high to show that there were no grounds for discontent in the general state of the economy. When disturbances broke out in that year, it was clear that the causes were political.

Such disturbances could be seen as part of the price of rapid industrialization. But Karamanlis was in no doubt that industrialization must go on if Greece was to benefit from the Treaty of Association with the EEC. The pace accelerated in 1961-2, with a regular alternation of new projects launched and earlier ones coming to completion. The King inaugurated Greece's first nuclear reactor in August 1961. At the end of the same month, before the opening of the Salonika Trade Fair, ministers inaugurated a sugar factory, a new hotel, a new railway station, and an irrigation system, all in the neighbourhood of the northern capital. At the opening of the Trade Fair Karamanlis announced more new projects, one of which was to be a state-funded refrigeration plant. A year later he opened the first stage of a new motorway between Athens and Salonika, and soon afterwards another motorway between Athens and Corinth. In October 1962 he opened two new chemical factories in Macedonia. In November a contract was signed with an American company, owned by the Greek-American millionaire Tom Pappas, for a second oil refinery.

'We are less poor than in the past,' said Karamanlis in a statement on 30 December 1962. 'Our progress is significant, but still insufficient in comparison with our needs and our aims.' A few weeks earlier he had told the ERE group in Parliament that his forecast, made in 1955, that Greece's national income would be doubled in ten years, was well on course to fulfilment; but he made no public boast. His cautious optimism was endorsed by the London *Financial Times*, which praised the financial and economic recovery of Greece in an article on 8 January 1963.

The progress continued in the New Year. In February an international competition was announced for a radio and television station. In April Karamanlis opened an aluminium-smelter on the Gulf of Corinth. In June the King opened a new steel plant at Elevsis. These were not the last fruits of Karamanlis' economic and industrial policies, but from June 1963 onwards he was no longer there to take credit for them.

It was not an economic crisis which led to the resignation of Karamanlis' third administration on 11 June 1963. On the contrary, the economic prospect was bright. The Treaty of Association with the EEC duly came into operation on 1 November 1962. Its initial effect was examined by the Governor of the Bank of Greece in his annual report six months later. The balance of trade had been adversely affected, but there had been an increase in invisible earnings. It was too soon to pass further judgement.

When Karamanlis' first eight years of office ended in mid-1963, however, there were grounds for optimism about the national economy. The national income had nearly doubled in real terms. Income per caput had grown from 305 to 565 dollars a year, whereas the Retail Price Index had risen by only seventeen per cent, a lower percentage than in most of the industrialized countries of Europe. Whichever indicator were chosen, the rate of growth was impressive. Fixed capital investment, agricultural and industrial production, energy consumption, all grew by nearly 100 per cent. Since agriculture was still the major industry, the growth of mechanization was particularly important: there were nearly four times as many tractors in use by 1963 as in 1955, and there was a similar expansion of other agricultural equipment. The growth of agriculture and industry, together with that of tourism, substantially relieved the balance of payments: reserves of foreign currency were more than doubled. Both public and private investment were also more than doubled; and most striking of all, private savings deposits were multiplied nearly ten times.

On the basis of this economic growth, government expenditure was directed to capital needs rather than current consumption. The improvement of roads, harbours, and housing, the expansion of the merchant marine, telecommunications, and air transport, and the creation of basic industries, all combined into a revolution in the history of Greece. But contrary to the view propagated by Karamanlis' critics, the social sector was not neglected. While the national income grew by ninety-six per cent in eight years, expenditure on welfare grew by over 150 per cent and educational expenditure by nearly 200 per cent. For the first time hospitals, schools, and athletic facilities became virtually free. Agricultural workers in particular benefited from free medical treatment, social insurance, pensions, subsidies on marginal land, land distribution to poor peasants, and the rebuilding of houses destroyed by war and other disasters.

No one would deny that this progress was initially made possible by American aid. But equally no one could deny that the aid had been efficiently used. Moreover, apart from military support, American aid was already coming to an end by 1955; and if Karamanlis pressed for its continuation on a limited scale, it was primarily for psychological reasons. To him the important thing was that Greece should achieve what American economists called 'take-off'. He wrote a revealing note, after he had left the premiership for the Presidency, to explain his passionate dedication to economic development:

I believed that the defects of our race were due to its age-old poverty, from which even ancient Greece was not free. And the worst thing was that these weaknesses manifested themselves principally in our political life, which was permanently unstable and erratic for precisely that reason. So my political philosophy was based on the view that for Greece to become a serious modern power, the Greeks must become good responsible citizens. But in order to become good citizens they must be freed from their weaknesses; and to be freed from their weaknesses they must first be freed from their poverty.

By 1963 Karamanlis could nearly claim that Greece was a modern European state. There was still some way to go, but he had achieved the first objective of accelerating economic growth by promoting capital investment without reducing the level of current consumption in the process. His determination to secure full membership of the EEC was unshaken but not yet achieved. The second of the major aims with which he took office was therefore not yet accomplished, though a major and irreversible step had been taken towards it. The third and most difficult aim remained.

Chapter 5

Cleaning up Public Life

IN one important respect Karamanlis set a personal example of a new kind. He was one of the least ceremonious of Prime Ministers. He treated public occasions with a light touch which did not in the least detract from their dignity. Unlike most of his predecessors, he might often be seen walking across the street from his office to Parliament without even asking the police to hold up the traffic. At midday, when he had no official engagement, he would ring up Rallis or Averoff and propose to meet for lunch at an unpretentious restaurant. His meals were extremely simple: the time was taken up with conversation rather than eating. He never ceased to be a politician, even at mealtime. If one of his colleagues suggested that he ought to go home to lunch with his wife, he would reply: 'Women are to wait!'

Such informal habits could be social faults. A close friend described him in a slang phrase as *monokhnotos*, which means literally 'of one breath'. It might be translated 'blunt' or even 'boorish'; at any rate, the opposite of 'urbane'. Another, who knew him even better, said that 'he treats people badly because they let him treat them badly.' His judgement of himself was frank: 'I have dried up my soul to keep myself where I am.' The world found him a hard man, but Tsatsos qualified the verdict: it was a hardness of the will, not of the soul. A woman friend called him the sweetest of men, but political rivals found him aloof and haughty. He knew when to be secretive and silent. He was also capable of calculated outbursts of rage. If these were social faults, they were also political assets for a man who had set out to clean up public life in Greece, which sorely needed it.

He had often spoken of this task. What he meant was that Greece must develop the habits and conventions of a Western democracy. Politics meant more to him than the party system.

It comprised the whole scope of organized life in a human community, as it had done indeed since Aristotle, the tutor of an earlier Macedonian leader, Alexander the Great, had written that 'man is a political animal'. What was needed, he saw, was not simply a reform of the party system but a modernization of Greek society. It was a psychological as well as an economic task.

His main target lay in Parliament, so that an account of his efforts at 'cleaning up political life' must be concentrated on that area. But he had also both narrower and broader fields in view. The narrower fields included local government, the civil service, and the armed forces. The broader fields included the Church, the monarchy, and the constitution itself. Most of these demanded his attention only intermittently, but sometimes—especially in the case of the last two—they could be crucially important.

With the Church Karamanlis' relations were, in his own words, 'rather formal'. There were even occasions of conflict. But the Church was too fundamental an element in Greek life to be regarded as a subject for political interference. No Prime Minister—least of all one who had had to deal with Archbishop Makarios—could be unaware of the irresistible influence of the Church. It was also valuable as a channel of communication with Greek communities abroad, through such notable leaders as the Patriarch of Alexandria and Archbishop Iakovos, the head of the Church in the USA, with whom Karamanlis' relations were particularly intimate. His many honours included crosses presented by the Patriarchs of Constantinople, Alexandria, Antioch, and Jerusalem, as well as the autonomous communities of Mount Athos. He regularly took the appropriate part in all the Church's formal occasions. When he had occasion to visit Patras, it was no accident that he was there on the day sacred to the city's patron, St. Andrew. The Church was his ally, not one of his targets, in the task of cleaning up public life.

There were, however, sometimes unavoidable occasions when the state had to intervene in ecclesiastical affairs. The most disagreeable case occurred in January 1962, when the newly elected Archbishop of Athens was accused of immorality. He was pressed to resign, but refused. Finally Karamanlis was obliged to resort to the threat of legislation to depose him; and fortunately the threat sufficed.

Other occasions when the government had to take an initiative were always agreed in advance with the Orthodox hierarchy, as is the way between the Church of England and Parliament. In 1958 Karamanlis thus made provision to harmonize the stipends of the clergy. A year later legislation was introduced on the constitution of the Church. Kanellopoulos, in presenting the draft law, made the point that the Greeks were virtually unique in the degree to which their nationality and their religion coincided. That was precisely why no government could contemplate an unwanted interference in Church affairs.

In narrower fields of public life the Prime Minister's interventions could be, and had to be, more radical. Like many of his predecessors, Karamanlis was exasperated by the unsatisfactory workings of Greek bureaucracy; but exasperation was not enough. He insisted that civil servants must be approachable and more conscious of their duties and loyalties. A number of senior administrators and even ambassadors were removed for failing to meet his requirements. He considered opening an office to receive complaints from the public, on the model of the Scandinavian Ombudsman. In 1959 he introduced legislation aimed at the improvement of public administration. The codification of existing legislation was a subject on which he would himself take the chair at ministerial committees.

In the end it became plain to him that the defects of bureaucracy could not be cured by legislation, since it was the excess of legislation which nourished the bureaucracy. It annoyed him that quite minor matters could only be put into effect by legislation, not by administrative action. Since his objective was to strengthen the executive, it was bound to be resisted not only by the civil service but by the Opposition in Parliament.

By the end of his first period of office, he had concluded that the constitution itself would have to be amended, at least in what were called the non-fundamental articles—that is to say, those which could be altered by a two-thirds majority in Parliament. By that time, however, much wider problems had emerged in the government's relations both with the

Opposition and with the Palace, so the necessary legislation was never introduced.

Although in dealing with the problems of central government Karamanlis' aim was to strengthen the executive, in the field of local government his aim was to devolve power. He wanted to make local authorities more responsive to local needs by decentralizing financial control and by segregating local from national politics. His intention was not to disinterest himself from local government: no son of a village schoolmaster could do that. He paid close attention to the advice of the elected representatives of local communities, inviting them to meet him when they held their conferences in Athens and meeting them on their own ground during his provincial tours, which he made much more frequently than previous Prime Ministers. He might have to suffer in silence from an occasional ineptitude—a Mayor of Ioannina, for example, holding forth on his hopes for an early liberation of northern Epirus from the Albanians—but this did not discourage him from wanting local leaders to act responsibly and independently.

To the surprise of his party, he refused to endorse candidates for local office with a party label. The logic was simple: every region had different interests, and no one party could have a monopoly of wisdom about all of them. But in national politics he was unreservedly a party man. He believed in homogeneous parties possessing continuity and coherence. He wished them to be united by policies, not simply by personalities. He disliked coalitions. Even more, he disliked combinations formed merely for electoral purposes, with no common policy and no intention of forming a united government. He hoped that in due course these principles would also be adopted by his opponents. For a start, however, all he could do was to set them an example in his own party.

He formed ERE as soon as he came into office, and it survived intact not only through his eight years in power but through the eleven years of his self-imposed exile. He gained important recruits to his party: Tsatsos and Averoff from the Liberals; Kanellopoulos when the Populists broke up, and a number of lesser figures. He was friendly with political opponents outside as well as in Parliament: Dimitrios Lambrakis, the proprietor of the liberal *Vima*, never attacked him: George

1. Karamanlis as a child with his father.   2. Karamanlis as a student.

3. Karamanlis on a shooting expedition.

4. Karamanlis as Prime Minister.

5. Karamanlis with Archbishop Makarios.

6. Karamanlis at an election meeting, 15 November 1974.

7. Karamanlis signing the Treaty of Accession to the EEC, 28 April 1979. Seated on his right is George Rallis, his Foreign Minister and successor as Prime Minister.

8. Karamanlis taking the oath as President of the Republic, 15 May 1980.

Papandreou's son Andreas (also a future Prime Minister) owed to Karamanlis his appointment as special adviser to the Bank of Greece. He suffered few defections from ERE and bore the defectors no malice. George Rallis and Panayotis Papaligouras, whose resignations precipitated the 1958 election, were taken back into the government after the 1961 election. There were other resignations, but ERE was unmistakably the same party when Karamanlis left office as when he came into it.

It was quite otherwise with the Opposition, which was perpetually reshuffling and re-forming coalitions and alliances. The Liberal leadership was disputed between Papandreou and Venizelos, who had nominally united their two parties in February 1957. Because of their rivalry, there were times when the initiative slipped into the hands of the extreme left. Typical tactics of both centre and left were an interminable series of votes of censure in Parliament, which were invariably defeated, and repeated attempts to uncover political and financial scandals culminating in Papandreou's 'relentless struggle'.

The one notable success of the centre was to gain support from the Palace in 1963, though for divided reasons: from the King because he sincerely believed in an alternating two-party system, but from the Queen out of personal antagonism towards Karamanlis. This climax was in remarkable contrast with 1955, when the Palace was directly responsible for Karamanlis' appointment in the teeth of oppositon from the centre and left.

The pattern of opposition had been set as soon as he was appointed, with denunciations of the 'government of favouritism' and threats to abstain from the general election of 1956 unless a 'service government' were appointed to conduct it. There was nothing in the constitution to require such a procedure, which Karamanlis later called scornfully 'a Greek invention'. At his first election the one concession he made was to replace the men in the more sensitive posts with neutral ministers. The Liberals retaliated, instead of abstaining, by forming a coalition with EDA. They were to regret it in later years, when they became virtually prisoners of the Communists. In his final speech before polling day Karamanlis denounced the 'formation of the new EAM', and called once more for 'the renovation of political life'.

Soon after his first victory, Karmanlis spoke to the ERE Deputies in Parliament about the 'permanent political crisis which cripples Greece', attributing it to 'the lack of parties with consistent principles'. Such a party was what he was determined to make of ERE. He also took the opportunity of assuring his supporters that ministers would in future be more accessible to Deputies. He himself was exceptionally conscientious in attending debates, and even intervening on quite minor issues.

But Papandreou and Venizelos would not conform to Karamanlis' ideas of responsible opposition. Whatever the government did, they were against it, even in a national crisis such as that of Cyprus. They were against the new initiative which led to Grivas' cease-fire in August 1956; they accused Karamanlis of abandoning self-determination; they criticized the UN motion urging a 'peaceful, democratic and just solution' in February 1957; they blamed the government for 'lack of aggressiveness'. Their first motion of no confidence over Cyprus was tabled in March 1957. Though it was defeated by 161 votes to 135, they were soon to be delighted by the support of a violent tirade against the government from Grivas. 'The temptation of the Opposition', as a later historian wrote, 'to use the Cyprus crisis, even at the nation's peril, to try to regain power was overriding.'[1]

Tempers became increasingly frayed in 1957, and bitter words were exchanged in Parliament, but not by Karamanlis. During a debate on 22 May he heard one Deputy call another 'traitor'. He rose to deliver a rebuke: 'The use of this word has become a deplorable tradition in our country—a tradition of which all politicians in the past have been victims. . . . It is time we became more careful both in our actions and in our language, for this is a blight on the history and often on the honour of the nation.' The thought remained in the forefront of his mind. Speaking in Macedonia two weeks later he reaffirmed his guiding principle: 'I shall continue inflexibly my efforts to clean up public life.'

Still the Opposition refused to reciprocate. Towards the end of June 1957 Papandreou and Venizelos were both speaking in Salonika. They attacked Karamanlis for 'undermining

[1] Nancy Crawshaw, *The Cyprus Revolt* (London, 1978), p. 230.

self-determination' and demanded new elections. Venizelos added a personal accusation against Karamanlis of dishonesty in the purchase of a plot of land in the Athens suburb of Philothei. The charge was repudiated as 'baseless and malicious' by officials of the bank concerned in the transaction, but it was not withdrawn. Before long even Papandreou was trying to find some way of disengaging himself from the incubus of Venizelos and his humiliating dependence on EDA; but in public the campaign of vilification continued.

On 1 September 1957 Karamanlis was again in Macedonia. In a speech at Drama he said: 'Eighteen months ago, on this spot, I had the honour of seeking your confidence and of declaring to you that I would strive for the creation of a new political life, freed from the passions and prejudices of the past.' The rest of his speech was an impressive account of achievements in many sectors; but progress in 'cleaning up public life' was not among them. On the contrary, the passions and prejudices of the past were already launching an intrigue to bring about his downfall. It was this intrigue which precipitated the premature general election of May 1958, which in turn led to the collapse of the Liberal Opposition and the emergence of EDA as the second party in Parliament.

Soon after that election, Karamanlis expressed the hope to his Deputies that Papandreou and Venizelos would 'abandon the slogans which promoted the revival of Communism'. But in fact the Liberals, with only thirty-six seats, were little better than acolytes of EDA. For the first time ever it was a Communist, Passalidis, who made the opening speech as leader of the official Opposition in Parliament.

Throughout the first year of Karamanlis' new government, the main target of criticism was his policy over Cyprus. Being led by a Communist, the criticism was invariably destructive, and the Liberals followed suit. First Passalidis, and then Venizelos, attacked the introduction of NATO into the affair. It was a natural point for a Communist to make, but hardly for Venizelos, who had been head of the government which negotiated Greece's adherence to the North Atlantic Treaty. In October EDA again attacked the government for failing to consult Parliament about Cyprus, and again the Liberals followed suit. In December the same complaints were raised again after the debate at the United Nations. But Nemesis was overtaking at least the non-Communist opposition.

The upheaval of the 1958 election forced the defeated parties to reconsider their positions, especially as the Cyprus dispute was reaching its most acute phase. The first party to recognize the consequences was that of the Populists, whose joint leader with Tsaldaris was Kanellopoulos. He declared on 10 October that his party, which had been reduced to four seats, would offer the government a free hand for a month. The Populists virtually ceased to exist as a party, and it was only a short step for Kanellopoulos to join the government himself, which he did as Vice-Premier in January 1959.

For the Liberals the consequences of defeat were more traumatic. On 3 November 1958 Papandreou and Venizelos resigned from the joint leadership of the party, and a temporary leader was elected. But this arrangement lasted only a month. In December Papandreou declared himself an 'independent Liberal', and in April 1959 he announced the formation of a new 'Liberal Democratic Party'. Venizelos resumed the leadership of the original Liberal Party on his own. Many similar reshuffles, of a similarly impermanent character, took place in the following two years.

A 'New Political Movement' was launched early in 1959 by a group of dissident Liberals, including Papaligouras and George Rallis, but it did not survive long. A 'Party of National Reconstruction' was formed by General Grivas in 1960, with the support of Venizelos and Stephanopoulos, but this too was short-lived. Both Papandreou and Venizelos then turned their thoughts independently to the possibility of a coalition with Karamanlis.

It was characteristic of Karamanlis that he took no pleasure in the disarray of the non-Communist Opposition. He actively encouraged its various leaders to come together in a new political group, but he frowned on the idea of admitting them to a coalition with his own government. In April 1960 he remarked publicly that 'if we look back over our history, we shall see that the destruction of democracies was invariably the sequel to a period of demagogy and confusion.' But it was also characteristic of the Opposition that it could unite on nothing except abuse and censure.

A typical attempt to embarrass Karamanlis was made in January 1959, shortly before his historic meeting with the Turks in Zurich. A debate was initiated by Markezinis, who was supported by Venizelos, about a letter published in a Patras newspaper by a former Deputy. It quoted a memorandum that Panayotis Pipinelis (now a Deputy) had written in September 1955, which was alleged to state that Karamanlis had committed himself to a compromise on Cyprus as a condition of his appointment as Prime Minister. It was not difficult for Karamanlis to show that he had made no such commitment. He had merely been consulted by Pipinelis, on behalf of the King, like other political leaders from various parties. But the embarrassment was achieved.

The Opposition continued to find grounds for criticizing Karamanlis over Cyprus, helped by the doubts raised by Makarios and Grivas, and by the resignation of the Greek representative at the United Nations. The Zurich-London agreements were the subject of motions of no confidence by both EDA and Venizelos, which were defeated by 170 votes to 118 on 27 February 1959. But Venizelos declared that if he came to power he would repudiate the agreements. Papandreou was also critical but reluctantly accepted them. The sequel was paradoxical: when the two men came to power together at the end of 1963, it was Papandreou as Prime Minister who wanted to overturn the settlement and Venizelos as Foreign Minister who preferred to maintain it.

Venizelos in opposition was a very different character from Venizelos in government. He had a weakness for attacking his opponents not only in Parliament but on journeys abroad. In April 1959, when he visited Ankara, he was reported by the Greek Embassy to be predicting that the Cyprus settlement would create future friction—which was true, but tactless at that time and place. In later years he committed many similar indiscretions: when in Rome in November 1961 he attacked the recent Greek elections as fraudulent; in Bucharest in 1962 he supported the Romanian plan for a missile-free zone in the Balkans; and in Moscow he spoke in favour of legalizing the KKE. It was noticed, on the other hand, that when Karamanlis went abroad, he rigorously abstained from discussing his country's internal politics.

Between 1958 and 1961 Venizelos rather than Papandreou was the more aggressive force in the Liberal Opposition, and the closer of the two to EDA. He even criticized Papandreou as a 'fellow-traveller' with Karamanlis, while missing no opportunity of embarrassing the latter. A trivial but tiresome example arose from an agreement negotiated on frontier issues with the Yugoslavs. Venizelos wrote to Karamanlis on 4 August 1959 complaining that it had conferred recognition on the Slavomacedonian language. Karamanlis replied on the twentieth that it did no such thing: it merely stated that documents would be drafted in the official languages of the respective countries. Venizelos persisted in a second letter, to which Karamanlis replied on 1 September that the Macedonian language had already been designated as one of the official languages of Yugoslavia when Venizelos had himself signed the first post-war agreement between the two countries as Prime Minister in 1951.

The pointless correspondence lapsed, and the Opposition turned to other ploys. President Eisenhower was due in Athens in December 1959. It was therefore planned to table a motion of no confidence in the government during his visit. But Karamanlis ingeniously turned the tables by putting down a motion of confidence himself on 23 November, three weeks before the President's visit. His motion gave him the right to speak first, and precluded a no-confidence motion immediately afterwards as a manifest absurdity.

He spoke only briefly, leaving it to his colleagues to amplify his government's claim to the country's confidence. Almost all the leaders on all sides joined in the debate: Protopapadakis, the Minister of Co-ordination, and Averoff, the Foreign Minister; Passalidis and Venizelos, to both of whom Karamanlis replied; Tsirimokos, leader of the Democratic Union, to whom Kanellopoulos replied; Markezinis, leader of the Progressive Party, to whom Karamanlis replied again; and several others over several days, to whom Karamanlis exercised his right of reply again and again. Finally his motion of confidence was carried on 4 December by 169 votes to 117.

The most notable absentee from the debate was Papandreou, who was seeking a way out of the confusion besetting the Liberals and an escape from the association with EDA. In

November 1959 he set himself at a distance from Venizelos and EDA by rejecting the Romanian proposal for a missile-free zone in the Balkans. When EDA tabled another motion of no confidence in April 1960, he persuaded his colleagues not to take part in the debate, but characteristically this did not prevent them from voting on it against the government. Later in the year Papandreou declared himself against the legalization of the KKE, which had been advocated by both Tsirimokos and Venizelos. So the confusion continued throughout 1960.

The attacks of EDA on Karamanlis were now being switched from political to personal topics. In December 1960 an EDA Deputy tabled a lengthy question in Parliament insinuating corruption on the part of Karamanlis' brother Aleko and his wife. Aleko replied vigorously in a letter to the Press. But Karamanlis, having been similarly attacked himself in the past, proposed that Parliament should set up a special court to examine accusations against party leaders and past or present Prime Ministers. He castigated the 'disease of lying' which had affected every political leader from the earliest times. The principle was approved, but no legislation was ever introduced, apparently in deference to the Opposition, which did not want to see its grievance removed. Karamanlis was to suffer again from the consequences.

The Opposition had now found another scandal to exploit. In 1959 Karamanlis had agreed to end the trials of Germans for war crimes in Greece, and to hand over the responsibility for prosecutions to the West German government. Among the first beneficiaries was a Nazi official, Dr Max Merten, who had been sentenced to twenty-four years' imprisonment in March 1959, but was released and deported in November. He took advantage of his liberty to publish libellous stories in the German Press, beginning in September 1960.

The substance of his stories deserves no detailed comment, for they were easily shown to consist entirely of falsehoods. The falsehoods were directed at Karamanlis, at two of his ministers (Makris and Themelis), at Makris' wife, and at other minor characters. As an example of his vicious fantasies, it may be mentioned that he accused Karamanlis of having betrayed to the Germans the date and the hour of the attack on the Gorgopotamos railway viaduct in November 1942; but he did not explain why, in that case, the Germans did nothing to prevent it.

Absurd as most of Merten's fictions were, some of the victims naturally took action to vindicate themselves in court. Karamanlis scorned to do so, but he made it clear that no obstacle would be put in Merten's way to prevent him from coming to Athens to give evidence in court, nor would he be arrested. Merten chose not to come. The left-wing Press and EDA, however, sought to embarrass Karamanlis by urging him to sue Merten in a German court, where he would have to go to give evidence in person.

A debate on the Merten case took place in Parliament on 12 October 1960. It was not difficult to dispose of Merten's lies. It was shown, for example, that he had confused Karamanlis' minister, Dimitrios Makris, with a well-known collaborator of the same surname; his claim that a photograph of Karamanlis with himself in Salonika was in the possession of the British authorities drew a categorical denial from the Foreign Office; the allegation that Makris' wife was Karamanlis' niece, or that she had known either of them during the occupation, was a fabrication; and so on. Karamanlis and his two ministers all spoke convincingly in the debate. But EDA, undeterred by overwhelming evidence, still demanded the government's resignation. Papandreou took no position on the allegations, but supported the demand on other grounds.

Although the government came through the debate successfully, the matter was not allowed to rest. In January 1961 a letter was published in a German newspaper from an official of the Foreign Ministry in Bonn, hinting that pressure had been exercised by the Greek government on the German government to repudiate Merten's stories. The letter was reproduced in the Athens Press, and Merten took the opportunity to repeat his falsehoods. To embarrass Karamanlis on the eve of his departure for an official visit to London, the Opposition insisted on another debate on 26 January. Averoff assured Parliament that the German government knew nothing of the letter, which was unauthorized.

Still the affair went on, for the Opposition had not finished with it. They noted with glee that the Greek Ambassador in Bonn resigned in June 1961, and disbelieved Averoff's statement that his resignation had nothing to do with the case of Merten. Meanwhile the libel actions against Merten were proceeding very slowly, because several witnesses called by Makris were accused of perjury. The charges of perjury were dismissed in August but the affair did not reach a final conclusion until the Athens criminal court convicted Merten and the two German publishers of libel on 10 November. Sentences of imprisonment and heavy fines were imposed, naturally without effect.

At last the Opposition gave up the hunt. With no further scandals to fasten on for the time being, and with a general election not far away, the fragments of the Liberal Party resumed their efforts to reorganize themselves. Papandreou had been the first to approach Karamanlis, with a proposal that he should nominate two junior ministers in the government and that an electoral system should be devised which would frustrate both EDA and Venizelos. Karamanlis refused the offer of co-operation, but agreed to make amendments to the electoral law which would facilitate Papandreou's wish to break free from EDA. Later Venizelos also approached Karamanlis with a proposal to nominate a minister from his party, implying that he himself intended to withdraw from politics and leave Greece. Karamanlis suspected his motives, and rebuffed the approach.

It was now left to the ex-Liberal leaders to settle their own problems. At first they only succeeded in aggravating their confusion. One suggestion, which was improbably attributed to Karamanlis himself, was that they should accept the leadership of Markezinis; another was that they should turn to Grivas. Venizelos, however, advised his followers to join Tsirimokos' Democratic Union. Many of them preferred to rally to Papandreou instead; and a few even deserted Venizelos to join ERE. Their minds were at last concentrated on first priorities when Karamanlis introduced the draft of a new electoral law in May 1961.

His proposal was a novel extension of the principle of reinforced proportional representation. The novelty was a provision that any party winning less than seventeen per cent of the votes in the first count would drop out of the second count, so that the stronger parties would be further strengthened. Papandreou welcomed the provision, but Venizelos and Tsirimokos objected to it and refused to take part in the debate. The latter two were in process of merging their parties and attracting new recruits, but by the beginning of August their efforts had broken down. They suffered a further blow early in September, when Grivas withdrew his support from Venizelos.

In the end it was Papandreou who came to the rescue of the Opposition. He negotiated an alliance which brought together not only Venizelos and the Liberals but also the Democratic Union of Tsirimokos, the Progressive Party of Markezinis, and the Popular Social Party of Stephanopoulos. The grand alliance was called the Centre Union, but its only unifying bond was hostility to Karamanlis. At the same time the Communist-led EDA formed an alliance with other small parties of the left, to be collectively known as the Pan-Democratic Agrarian Front of Greece (PAME).

All these manœuvres were in marked contrast with the more straightforward conduct of ERE's affairs. The voters drew their own conclusions in the election of 29 October, the outcome of which has been described in the previous chapter.[2] This was the only election at which, in Karamanlis' own later judgement, he faced no danger of defeat. Speaking immediately afterwards, he declared that: 'The victory is not mine: it is the victory of the Greek people, whose political maturity has been confirmed by the result of the election. The condemnation of EDA in particular has demonstrated the will of the people to protect democracy and the fundamental interests of the nation against any attack.' But in fact it was the Centre Union rather than EDA which reacted most bitterly to its defeat, even though it had pushed EDA back into third place. Papandreou now launched the 'relentless struggle'.

Karamanlis was confident that the election had not been in any way irregular. This was shown by many indications, not least an explicit recognition by the liberal *Vima* on 31 October. The election had been held under a 'service government', which ensured neutrality; and the electoral system had been agreed

[2] See p. 109 above.

in advance with Papandreou. Karamanlis had deliberately avoided gestures aimed at personal popularity: for example, having a surplus on the 1961 budget, he had devoted it to investment rather than to gratifying the 'demands of the people'. He had personally addressed both the military leadership and the election officials, urging them to ensure fair conduct. Finally he argued that his victory had been so decisive that falsification on the requisite scale could not have been concealed.

Papandreou claimed, however, that the election had been fraudulent owing to interference by the armed forces. He alleged that they had put into operation what was called the 'Pericles Plan' in order to manipulate the results. After prolonged investigation, the charge was eventually rejected by the courts in 1966, when Karamanlis was out of office. It was established that the Pericles Plan was concerned solely with the contingency of a war or a Communist rebellion, that it had no relevance to election procedures, that it was never communicated to anyone outside the Ministry of Defence, and that it was simply retained on file in draft form.

If there had been any truth in the allegation of fraud, the responsibility would have rested with the 'service government'. Karamanlis had himself proposed the appointment of such a government by the King, and had suggested that the Prime Minister should be General Tsakalotos, whose background was Venizelist and therefore presumably acceptable to the Opposition. The King agreed, and Karamanlis informed Tsakalotos accordingly.But the King also wished to appoint to the Ministry of Defence one of his own courtiers, Air Marshal Potamianos, who was unacceptable to Tsakalotos. The latter therefore withdrew, and the King then appointed General Dovas as Prime Minister with Potamianos as Minister of Defence. The third key figure was the Chief of the General Staff, General Kardamakis, who alone of the three was personally close to Karamanlis.

All three denied any irregularities on the part of the armed forces. But some years later Karamanlis learned (in part from a letter written by Kardamakis on 25 September 1966, in reply to an enquiry by Karamanlis) that Potamianos had played a part in promoting the interests of Papandreou. There had been a campaign of propaganda within the armed forces, after the success of EDA in the 1958 election, to indoctrinate the services with a strong dose of anti-Communist sentiments. These 'senseless plans', as Karamanlis later called them, were carried out by the 'secret services' without his knowledge. But they were known to Potamianos, who suggested to Papandreou that he should take advantage of them in the 1961 election. The suggestion was that servicemen, with their strongly anti-Communist prejudices, should be used to persuade voters to support the Centre Union rather than EDA. Some inkling of this plan came to Karamanlis' knowledge at the time, from Deputies of the Centre Union who were aware of it. It was more fully revealed by the left-of-centre newspaper *Elevtheria* on 7 September 1965.

It is hardly surprising that so ludicrous a plan failed to have any effect on the election at all. The only point of interest is that it shows, in Karamanlis' words, that 'The plans for the notorious "force and fraud" were known to my opponents but not to myself.' Kardamakis' letter reported that there were practically no cases of interference by the armed forces. If there were isolated cases of force, particularly in one or two places near the Bulgarian frontier, they were no more numerous than in any previous election. Kardamakis added the significant point that the election of 1961 was the first in which the Court intervened deliberately, though without any significant effect, against Karamanlis himself. He believed that this was done with the knowledge of the Queen, but not of the King.

Such intrigues and accusations play a part in all Greek elections. There was no reason at the time to suppose that they would play any more part in the future course of events than they had on previous occasions; but they were a troublesome element in that sickness of Greek public life which Karamanlis wanted to 'clean up'. When the ERE Deputies met for the first time after the election, Karamanlis spoke to them of his regret at the disarray of the Opposition, and especially at the accusations which were being made against the armed forces. Dovas was astonished at the accusations, but Karamanlis was not: he attributed them to the necessity for the Centre Union to find excuses for their defeat.

On 5 November Papandreou denounced the new government as 'illegal'. Ten days later the Deputies of the Centre

Union met and proclaimed a 'relentless struggle' against it. On the eighteenth Papandreou held a press conference which lasted for four hours, entirely devoted to attacks on the conduct of the election. After Karamanlis had presented his programme to Parliament on 5 December, Papandreou renewed the attack in a public statement. Both the Centre Union and EDA at first refused to attend Parliament.

With the help of General Dovas, Karamanlis tried to mitigate the quarrel. Dovas said that he had at once replaced any election officials about whom Papandreou complained. A few cases of double voting were sent for trial. Other misdemeanours were admitted, the culprits identified, and sent for trial; but they were not confined to supporters of ERE. The courts invalidated the poll in only eight out of some 9,700 polling stations. Clearly there had been no massive fraud.

The Opposition eventually took their seats on 9 January 1962 in order to attend a debate on the ratification of the EEC Treaty of Association. But they seized the opportunity to reaffirm the 'relentless struggle' and to demand the impeachment of Dovas' ministers. On 18 January Papandreou tabled a motion of no confidence, and on the twenty-third a series of impeachment motions. EDA supported all of them, but inevitably they were all defeated.

Papandreou addressed his parliamentary party on 6 March in terms disquietingly similar to the EDA line. Two days later a group of ERE Deputies who had formerly been Liberals, including Averoff and other ministers, issued a statement severely criticizing Papandreou, who seemed to be virtually a prisoner of EDA. Violent demonstrations, strikes, and public meetings which often led to bloodshed, were beginning to escape Papandreou's control. At the same time the Opposition was turning its hostility against a new target: the Royal Family.

Karamanlis was anxious to protect the Crown from both isolation and criticism. He never attempted to exploit the alleged 'favouritism' to which his original appointment was attributed. He deferred to the King as head of state at both formal and informal occasions. It was the King who inaugurated new industrial projects and laid foundation-stones, with the Prime Minister at his side. Apart from regular audiences to keep the King informed, Karamanlis invariably called at the Palace after every journey abroad. When Lyndon Johnson visited Greece in September 1962, he politely insisted that the Vice-President should fly up to Corfu to pay his respects to the King. But despite Karamanlis' solicitude, it proved impossible to shelter the Crown entirely.

The first overt attack was made in October 1956, when the Opposition voted against an increase in the King's revenue. The activities of certain courtiers were particularly criticized. As a result, although the increase was approved by Parliament, the King refused to accept it. Writing to Karamanlis on 12 October 1956, the King noted that 'trouble has been stirred up about the participation of officials of the Court in various committees.' and commented that 'the practice has been going on for many years, and took place with the knowledge of every post-war government, without anyone raising any question of its acceptability until now.' He briefly defended the integrity of his courtiers, and ended the letter on a chilly note which did not disguise his resentment.

No one could legitimately complain about the constitutional role played by the King during the next few years. He performed his sometimes delicate functions with tact and propriety: for example, in consulting the leaders of the parties before granting Karamanlis' request for a dissolution of Parliament in March 1958; and in refusing to be drawn by the Greek Cypriots into personal involvement in the *enosis* campaign behind his government's back. Nevertheless attacks on the monarchy began again in 1959. Again the ostensible cause was money: it arose from a rumour about negotiations on a dowry for Princess Sophia, though she did not in fact even become engaged to be married until two years later. On 20 October 1959 Karamanlis issued a forceful statement deploring the abuse of this 'fictitious issue' as an excuse for attacks on the Crown. He described the campaign as deliberately aimed at 'undermining the foundations of the state'.

For a time criticism relapsed into silence, at least so far as the Press and Parliament were concerned, until after the general election of 1961. Then it began again as one element in the 'relentless struggle'. In February 1962 a member of EDA moved for a reduction of payments to Deputies, ministers, and the Palace; but the motion was quickly dismissed as 'untimely and pointless'. The question of a dowry for Princess Sophia, however, was raised again, this time officially, when she became engaged to Don Juan Carlos, the future King of Spain.

When the dowry was debated on 14 March 1962, Papandreou and EDA were predictably opposed to it. The Minister of Finance pointed out that there were five precedents for such a dowry since Greece became an independent monarchy, and that the sum now proposed was by far the smallest of all. In the end the proposal was carried without difficulty, but a more serious controversy arose a few months later, when a fresh proposal to increase the royal revenues was made in September.

This time the Opposition's grievance was that it had not been consulted in advance. As there was no doubt that the motion would be carried, the Centre Union and EDA contented themselves by leaving the Chamber before the vote. But Papandreou and Venizelos further emphasized their displeasure by declining invitations to a state dinner given by the King in honour of Archbishop Makarios. Papandreou also began to hint that the King was under an obligation to dissolve the 'unconstitutional' Parliament.

It was plain to Karamanlis that Papandreou was not trying to subvert the monarchy, as EDA was, but to bend it to his will. There was a certain irony in the relations of both men with the Palace, for Karamanlis already had difficulties with the Queen, whereas the King was not personally hostile to him but sympathized with the idea that an alternation of the parties in power was desirable for the health of Greek democracy. Thus the Palace was leaning towards Papandreou's side even while he belaboured it. But his 'relentless struggle' made it difficult for the King to maintain his constitutional balance. By the end of 1962 the battle was joined by the extremists, who sought to widen it beyond possibility of compromise.

In early December a prison sentence was passed on an EDA Deputy for publishing an insulting article about the Queen. The leaders of the Centre Union protested at the severity of the sentence. Two weeks later two journalists were arrested for publishing further insults to the Queen. In March 1963 another EDA Deputy made a derogatory reference to Greece's 'foreign King'. At the same time other members of EDA chose different lines of attack on the government; a minister was accused of having served in the German SS, an under-secretary of other forms of collaboration with the Germans.

Another indirect attack was launched early in the New Year, when the left-of-centre newspaper *Elevtheria* published an article accusing General Kardamakis of political partisanship during the 1961 election, when he was Chief of the General Staff. The proprietor, Panos Kokkas, was put under arrest on the grounds that the article was subversive. Papandreou and Venizelos both gave evidence for the defence at his trial, which ended in his acquittal on 7 March. Although the verdict was in no way a condemnation of the General, it was naturally exploited by Papandreou in the 'relentless struggle'.

The Opposition increased its pressure on the King to dissolve Parliament: in other words, to dismiss Karamanlis. During January 1963 Venizelos, who had close personal relations with the King, visited the Palace to press this advice. The King informed Karamanlis of this meeting, after which Karamanlis issued a statement praising the King's devotion to the constitution and his refusal to become involved in party quarrels. His statement was the occasion of an angry exchange between Venizelos and Karamanlis in March. Karamanlis had observed that Venizelos had been accompanied to the Palace by Tsirimokos but not by Papandreou. He inferred that the latter was not in complete control of the Centre Union, which Papandreou virtually confirmed by threatening to expel both Venizelos and Tsirimokos from the party—naturally without effect.

The chaotic state of public life at this time convinced Karamanlis that more radical measures were needed to clean it up. He had hinted before the election at a project to revise the non-fundamental articles of the constitution, which he now decided to revive. This intention was known and reported in the Press as early as October 1962, but it was not until the following February that it was ready for discussion with the Opposition and his own followers. By then Venizelos was tired of the 'relentless struggle', though Papandreou was not. At Venizelos' request, a series of secret meetings was arranged between him and Pipinelis, who was acting for Karamanlis, on 16, 19, and 21 February. Papandreou was deliberately excluded on the assumption that he was out of the effective leadership. But Venizelos insisted that he must consult Papandreou, and did so between the second and third meetings, despite the objections of Pipinelis.

The proposed amendments to the constitution affected many aspects of public life: the rights of civil servants, the Press, education, security, legislative procedure, taxation, the responsibilities of Deputies, and much else. Venizelos asked for political concessions in return for his party's support. Karamanlis was willing to concede some of his requests but rejected two in particular: that the electoral system of simple proportional representation should be reintroduced, and that the Army should lose the right to vote. When Venizelos told Pipinelis on 21 February that Papandreou insisted on these conditions, the talks broke down. But Karamanlis tabled his proposals, totalling twenty-three, before Parliament on the same day, though not yet as legislation.

He would need 200 votes to carry his amendments, but he could not rely on more than 176. Only Markezinis offered support, but with qualifications. EDA was at first non-committal. The Centre Union refused co-operation, though some of Papandreou's supporters openly criticized his attitude. When the President of the Assembly invited all the parties on 28 February to nominate members of a constitutional commission, both EDA and the Centre Union refused outright. Nevertheless the President nominated members of the Centre Union, at which Papandreou protested in Parliament on 6 March. An angry scene followed, aggravated by the reaction of Deputies of EDA.

Orderly government seemed to be on the edge of breakdown. On 24 March, the eve of Greece's National Day, Karamanlis issued a statement declaring that his government would protect the freedom, unity, and tranquillity of the country 'provided that passion is subordinated to reason, interest to duty, demagogy to truth'. The question of constitutional reform was now submerged in wider issues, among which the most serious was the growing boldness of the outlawed KKE.

The extreme left in Parliament had effectively seized the

initiative from the Centre Union. After a violent clash between police and striking dock-workers on 1 February, EDA tabled a motion of censure on the government's policy of strike-breaking. In the debate on the eleventh, Papandreou spoke first and reaffirmed the 'relentless struggle', but his party abstained from voting with EDA. Karamanlis showed his contempt for this half-hearted performance by taking no part in the debate himself.

Members of the Centre Union, though not Papandreou, joined EDA in campaigning for the legalization of KKE, the release of 'political prisoners', and the return of expatriate Communists from abroad. These demands were pressed in many debates during March and April 1963. Other themes, such as American 'missile bases' and the 'illegality' of the government, were interwoven with them. Support was sought from abroad, especially from Italy, France, and Britain. A 'peace march' was planned from Marathon to Athens, with the participation of eminent foreigners, including Bertrand Russell. It was banned by the government, but an attempt to carry it out led to more clashes with the police.

At the end of March a left-wing congress was held in Paris to urge an amnesty for the Greek Communists. It was attended by Deputies from the Centre Union as well as EDA, but Papandreou declared their presence 'unofficial'. At the end of April another group of foreign supporters of the campaign arrived in Athens. One of their leaders, a French Socialist, addressed an aggressive letter to the King, which Averoff advised him to return as unacceptable.

The campaign had now outgrown any interest in facts. When the abortive 'peace march' was debated in Parliament on 3 April, the government spokesman pointed out that only 975 alleged Communists were held in prison, all of whom had been convicted by due process of law. It was true, however, that many of them had been sentenced by military courts during the civil war. But Papandreou and Venizelos could hardly make a case against the government over these cases, since many of them had been sentenced under coalition governments including Liberal ministers.

In a further debate on 2 May, it was shown that a policy of progressive release had been going on for some time. This news did not suffice to prevent yet another motion of no confidence, which was defeated on 6 May. The Centre Union abstained on this occasion, but continued the 'relentless struggle' against the 'illegal government', even after the courts had dismissed all but nine of their ninety-three specific complaints about the 1961 election.

Events were now moving towards a final crisis; but when it came, it took an unexpected form. Two names stood in the centre of the left-wing campaign. One was Grigorios Lambrakis, a doctor and a distinguished athlete, who was a Deputy of EDA and had played a leading role in planning the 'peace march'. The other was Tony Ambatielos, a leading member of the Seamen's Union, who had been condemned to death during the civil war. He had been reprieved but was still in prison.

As Ambatielos had an English wife, and his union had been active in British ports, the campaign for his release was easily stimulated in Britain. A golden opportunity for the purpose would be provided by the royal visit to London, which was planned for July 1963. The personality of the Queen was sufficient guarantee that the opportunity would be fully exploited. That, and the tragedy of Lambrakis in May, ensured a crisis which frustrated for many years Karamanlis' efforts to clean up public life in Greece. Even after he had retired from politics, nearly twenty years later, he wrote: 'I doubt if I achieved it.'

Chapter 6

The Royal Crisis

As so often in Greek history, the crisis of 1963 flowed from the personal relations of the Royal Family and the Prime Minister. Relations between an elected Prime Minister and a constitutional monarch rest as much on customs and conventions as on the text of the constitution. The Greek constitution gave powers to the King which it was not always wise to enforce to the limit; but the line which it was unwise to cross was ill-defined. Customs can vary, and conventions can be differently interpreted. The consequent disagreements had been painful in the past, and were to be so again. Karamanlis' relations with the Court, which had been excellent in 1955, became strained in 1962. But when he spoke critically of the Court, he had in mind not so much the King as some of those around him, including Queen Frederika, certain courtiers, and even the young Crown Prince.

His proposals to amend the constitution had not been aimed against the King. On the contrary, his purpose was, he said, 'to protect the Crown by eliminating constitutional crises'. He warmly admired the King, but he was less at ease with the Queen, although she had been his strong supporter when he was first appointed. The Crown Prince remained an inexperienced boy in Karamanlis' eyes, even though he had legally come of age at eighteen in 1958 and regularly attended royal audiences. About some of the officials at Court Karamanlis had serious misgivings, and he regretted the fact that he had no permanent representative of his own in the Palace.

The disagreements began over relatively small matters, such as the cost of the royal yacht and the provision of royal aircraft. Soon personal friction followed. One year the Queen wanted to take the whole family on holiday in Austria. Karamanlis insisted that the Crown Prince must stay in Greece if the King left. An angry dispute ended with the Queen exclaiming: 'You want to get rid of us and make Constantine King!'.

There was a more serious dispute when the Queen tried to alter the Speech from the Throne at the Opening of Parliament, which was well known to be a statement of government policy. The King also asserted his right to prepare his own speeches on less formal occasions, even when the subject might be regarded as political. Speaking to Army officers in Salonika early in 1962, he declared: 'God has united us—I belong to you and you belong to me.' It was true that he was Commander-in-Chief of the armed forces, but his words could be taken as asserting a special relationship which excluded the elected government. This time it was George Papandreou who publicly rebuked him.

Although Karamanlis maintained a tactful silence whenever he could, he felt obliged later in the year to remonstrate with the King in writing. His letter, dated 3 October 1962, began with a long and respectful preamble which nevertheless hinted as 'a different assessment of certain matters'. This, he said, had led to difficulties and misunderstandings. He wished to protect the acknowledged popularity of the King and the security of the Throne 'not from political or moral mishaps but from a lack of sufficient attention to matters which, though insignificant in themselves, could be damaging, especially in our country, with unhappy consequences'. Having thus gently prepared the ground, he proceeded to make six complaints.

First, there was a mistaken notion that ostentation strengthened the Throne. On the contrary, its chief asset should be simplicity, which also suited the King's personality. Secondly, frequent visits abroad, especially if the King and the Crown Prince went together, created a bad impression. Thirdly, it was wrong for the King to make speeches whose content was unknown to the government. It should be possible, by consultation, to give his speeches 'the seal of his personality' without prejudicing the government's responsibility for their political content. Fourthly—in effect, a repetition of the first point—royal expenditure which entailed extra cost to the taxpayer should be avoided. Fifthly, the absence of a political adviser in the Palace with authority to speak for the government was a serious matter. Sixthly, although the Fund for the Northern Provinces, founded by the Queen, had done valuable service, it was time to reconstitute it on a legal basis.

He concluded by warning the King that the changes which he advised would be desirable even in normal circumstances: all the more so at a time when a campaign was in progress aimed at 'the destruction of the Crown'.

The King's reply, dated 14 October, showed that he was deeply hurt. In contrast with earlier letters addressed to 'Dear Mr Prime Minister', his letter opened abruptly: 'Mr Prime Minister'. He began with a personal reminder: 'Seven years ago I chose you as Prime Minister, and my choice as well as my confidence in your person have been fully justified.' He had known that his decision would attract criticism, but he took the risk because he wanted a stable government; and stable government 'presupposes the full protection of the Crown'. But recently a campaign of vilification had been stirred up 'not only against my person but also against my wife, my children, and my late parents'. The state (meaning the government) had failed to find any satisfactory way of protecting the Crown against it. The Prime Minister's letter appeared actually to adopt some of the Opposition's arguments instead of refuting them.

He gave some examples that might have been used to restore the 'true picture of the Throne'. He had recently made a present to the state of his private estate at Polydendri. The necessity of an increase in the royal revenue had been recognized, but the matter had been handled 'without serious preparation or enlightenment of public opinion'. He wished to remind Karamanlis that he had himself been on the throne more than eight years longer than Karamanlis had been Prime Minister, and he had worked with sixteen different governments. Then he proceeded to answer Karamanlis' six points.

First, he pointed out that the Greek monarchy had always been the least ostentatious in the world, and he himself had restricted it even further than his parents. Secondly, 'My journeys abroad are entirely my own affair.' No previous Prime Minister had ever suggested otherwise. In any case, modern communications made it easy to return immediately in any emergency. Thirdly, 'Royal speeches are made by me.' He always sent drafts in advance to the government, but he would not give up his right to speak his own mind 'on the moral, religious, or philosophical level', and to address to the armed forces 'such words as I think appropriate'. On the fourth point, he accepted in principle what Karamanlis said, but rebutted charges of extravagance at public expense.

The last two points were the most embarrassing. On the fifth one, the King replied that the Prime Minister himself was his political adviser, but he added a hint that it was not his own fault if the post of director of his political office was vacant. In fact Air Marshal Potamianos had recently been removed from this post on Karamanlis' insistence, and this had been resented by the Queen; but Potamianos could not in any case have been regarded as a political adviser in the Palace with the authority to speak for the government.

On the sixth point, the King agreed to reconsider the status of the Queen's Fund, but insisted that the criticisms of it were politically inspired. He concluded with three brief comments: 'Your letter has not in the least caused me displeasure.'; 'No Greek understands the Greek people better than I do myself.'; 'I do not understand what you mean by the expression 'destruction of the Crown.' All that was necessary, he implied, was greater determination by the government to enlighten public opinion.

Karamanlis considered that it was not his responsibility to engage in publicity on behalf of the monarchy. That, he argued, would only make it the subject of more political controversy, and so damage it further. As soon as he received the King's letter he requested an audience. When it took place a few days later, he submitted his resignation on the ground of 'fundamental disagreements on the method of our collaboration'. The King was astounded, and said there was no more than 'a different assessment of certain situations'. The argument ended on an inconclusive note, and Karamanlis did not press his resignation; but inevitably a degree of tension remained. A few weeks later the King offered Karamanlis the Grand Cross of the Order of the Redeemer, which he declined. 'It is too soon,' was his reply: 'I have not yet completed my mission.'

Unfortunately a new crisis was at hand, with the Crown at the centre of it. For several reasons, publicity was concentrated on the Royal Family in 1963. The centenary of the dynasty fell in that year, and celebrations began in March. The King and Queen of Denmark arrived on the twenty-third, representing the family from which the dynasty descended. A state banquet, at which both King Paul and Karamanlis spoke, was held on the twenty-fifth, Greece's National Day. Other major events were also approaching: President de Gaulle was due on a state visit in May; the millennium of the monastic colony on Mount Athos was to be celebrated in the same month; and in July King Paul and Queen Frederika were to make a state visit to London.

But the Opposition, especially EDA, was determined that these events should be exploited for hostile propaganda. At the beginning of the centenary celebrations, Papandreou addressed a long letter to the King on 20 March calling on him to do his duty: in other words, to dissolve Parliament and proclaim a general election. Soon afterwards newspapers supporting the Centre Union suggested that the Americans were intervening with the King to keep the government in office. Another cause of criticism was the ban on the 'peace march'. The first climax on the way to catastrophe came in April, when the affair of Tony Ambatielos was the centre of the storm. It arose from an incident in London involving his wife with Queen Frederika.

The Queen had been invited to London on a private visit to attend the wedding of Princess Alexandra. Karamanlis advised against the visit, arguing that the left in Britain would use it for propaganda purposes which would prejudice the more important state visit in July. But the Queen insisted, and flew to London with her daughter, Princess Irene, on 20 April. The same evening, as they were leaving Claridge's Hotel by a side-door, they were approached in an aggressive manner by a group of demonstrators for political amnesty, among them Mrs Ambatielos. They ran down a cul-de-sac and took refuge in a private house. Although they were naturally frightened, they suffered no violence.

When Karamanlis heard of the incident, he hoped to pass over it in silence, but this was no longer possible because the Queen had already appeared on television. She also expected an apology from the British government. Lord Home, the Foreign Secretary, duly sent an apology on 28 April, which led to left-wing protests in the House of Commons. By then, after consulting the Council of Ministers, Karamanlis had decided to recommend the postponement of the state visit in July.

The Queen returned to Greece on 1 May. She and the King were on tour in the Peloponnese when Karamanlis' decision was conveyed to the King's private secretary, Khoidas. It was Karamanlis' intention to announce the postponement at once, but when the King was informed by telephone he refused to agree. He asked that the matter should be left in suspense until he returned to Athens.

The first opportunity to discuss the matter face to face came only when Karamanlis had an audience with the King on 13 May. In fact little was said about it, because there was the more urgent business of discussing the arrangements for a state visit by President de Gaulle, who was due to arrive in Athens on the sixteenth. Naturally both the King and Karamanlis were deeply involved in this long-sought occasion. But it was interrupted by another drama.

Late at night on the eighteenth, after a banquet at the French Embassy, the King was taken ill with appendicitis. He was operated on early on the nineteenth, and the Crown Prince took over the duties of host for de Gaulle's final day in Greece. Unfortunately there was an unhappy scene at the hospital, when the Queen and Karamanlis met in an ante-room. A dispute arose between them over the celebration of the millennium of Mount Athos, which was due in a few days' time. The Queen insisted that it must be postponed, but Karamanlis would only undertake to examine whether this was possible, and pointed out that it was for the government to decide. After some heated exchanges, the Queen went in to complain to the King. In the event, the Patriarch of Constantinople was consulted. He said that the presence of the King was most desirable, and he was confident that the Turkish government would allow him to leave Istanbul in June as readily as in May. Since none of the guests had yet arrived, Karamanlis took the decision: the celebration was postponed for a month.

Meanwhile he and de Gaulle had met for formal discussions on the morning of the nineteenth. De Gaulle began by congratulating him on the economic progress achieved by Greece in recent years. Karamanlis gave his reasons for anxiety about the future: low national income, lack of capital investment, and 'one of the most aggressive Communist parties in Europe'. The next three or four years would be decisive, he said, for by then 'either stability will be assured or there will be a total collapse'. It was a prescient remark, for the Colonels' *coup d'état* came just under four years later.

De Gaulle then gave an optimistic account of French prospects. He defined his defence policy in terms of an independent nuclear capacity with a dual purpose: to defend the Western alliance in cases where the USA would not intervene, but also to make it more likely that the USA would be forced to intervene. Karamanlis asked whether the USA might agree to the creation of allied nuclear forces whose use would be determined by a vote. De Gaulle replied that neither the Americans nor he himself would ever agree to 'subordinate their forces to the judgement of others'. He showed his distrust of the Americans in discussing other topics, such as tariff reductions. On the other hand, he had a friendly word for the Germans: 'They do not inconvenience us in the slightest.' The conversation revealed nothing new, but it was a refreshing change for Karamanlis from the sterile wrangles of domestic politics.

De Gaulle, the Crown Prince, and Karamanlis flew to Salonika on the twentieth. After inspecting a parade of troops, visiting a French military cemetery, and attending a banquet in his honour, de Gaulle flew back to Paris direct from Salonika. The Crown Prince and Karamanlis flew back to Athens the same evening. Two days later, on 22 May, Salonika was the scene of a major tragedy which inflamed the internal crisis to the point of explosion.

At the end of a left-wing demonstration, the EDA Deputy Grigorios Lambrakis was deliberately run down by a three-wheeled vehicle and critically injured. Karamanlis at once appreciated the gravity of the crime. He sent Papakonstantinou, his Minister of Justice, to the northern capital on the twenty-third, followed by George Rallis, his Minister of the Interior, two days later. He also sent a special aircraft to fetch doctors from London. But in spite of every effort, Lambrakis died on the twenty-sixth. The sequel was a concerted outcry from the left blaming Karamanlis' government. Papandreou denounced him as 'not only morally but legally' guilty of Lambrakis' death. Karamanlis retorted that these were words which he would be ashamed of for the rest of his life.

There was no conceivable advantage to Karamanlis in the

elimination of Lambrakis. Two judicial enquiries, conducted during the premiership of Papandreou, established beyond doubt that no political responsibility lay behind the crime. This was further confirmed when two men were eventually convicted, not of murder but of manslaughter, and sentenced to ten and eight years' imprisonment. But myths die hard in the ancestral home of mythology. Seventeen years after the crime, it was still necessary to repudiate once more the fictitious version of the Lambrakis tragedy, as well as that of the 1961 General Election.[1]

If it had not been for the ugly episode in London and the tragedy in Salonika, the months of May and June would have been very encouraging for Karamanlis. Apart from the success of de Gaulle's visit, there was also better news about aid from the United States. On 1 May the Chairman of the US Chiefs of Staff was in Athens, and took note of Greece's needs. At the beginning of June Papaligouras, the Minister of Co-ordination, met President Kennedy in Washington. A few days later he also met Dean Rusk, the Secretary of State, and Macnamara, the Secretary for Defence. On 7 June he sent an encouraging report to Athens on the possibility of Greece's needs being more generously met. It was a pleasant coincidence that on 29 May Karamanlis had the task of unveiling a bust of President Truman, whose initiative had saved Greece in 1947. But this was to be his last public function for many years; nor did the future of the talks in Washington concern him, for his days in office were numbered.

At the beginning of June, in entirely new circumstances, Karamanlis once more discussed the state visit to London with his closest colleagues, who again agreed that it must be postponed. This conclusion was communicated on 4 June through Khoidas to the King, who was away on a convalescent cruise in the Aegean. The next day the King replied that he did not agree. On the sixth and seventh Karamanlis discussed the subject further with his colleagues, who were still of the same opinion. Karamanlis then asked for an audience, which took

---

[1] Letter in *Ta Nea*, 15 February 1980, written by Constantine Papakonstantinou, who was then Vice-Premier.

place on the eighth at the royal residence in Athens. The Crown Prince was also present.

Karamanlis explained his objections to the visit because of the recent disturbance in London, which was likely to be repeated. He added that the British government could not guarantee the prevention of 'insults to the Crown and the country'. The King dissented on the ground that a postponement would be a victory for the Communists and a discourtesy to Queen Elizabeth. Karamanlis replied that the reactions of 'anarchists' could be ignored, but there had also been offensive attacks in the House of Commons, where the question of the royal visit was raised on 14 May, and in the British Press. There was, he added, no question of discourtesy to Queen Elizabeth, because the matter was 'not personal but political', and responsibility for the decision would rest with the government.

The King asked him if he was pressing his views 'to the point of a dispute', which would imply an intention to resign. Karamanlis replied that in the interests of the Crown and the country he was obliged to insist. The discussion ended with a request by the King that they should meet again two days later, on 10 June.

By that date Karamanlis was deeply disturbed about his relations with the Palace. Five years later he wrote about his feelings at the time: 'My relations with the King were good until my resignation, and I believe he accepted it with regret. But it is impossible to say the same about the Queen and the Crown Prince, whose hostile attitude towards me began to be unmistakable from about 1961, as was evident from many typical instances.' Senior colleagues also confirmed Karamanlis' impression. As for the King, his conduct sometimes puzzled Karamanlis. Once when he returned from an audience, he told his wife that the King appeared to be drunk. But it was certainly impossible that this could be true. It was simply a sympton of a state of affairs which Karamanlis found inexplicable.

His disquiet was shared, in a more general way, by others in positions of responsibility. Senior Generals, led by Kardamakis, approached Karamanlis to ask if they should make representations to the King about the dispute. He told them to mind their own business and not to interfere. Rumour had it, however, that they would willingly have undertaken a coup on his behalf if he had given them the slightest encouragement.

But he would not in any case deviate from the path of persuasion. On the morning of 10 June he went to the royal residence at Tatoi to see the King and the Crown Prince again. The King said that the problem had caused him great anxiety, and he saw the arguments on both sides. He was now chiefly concerned about the impression that would be caused at Buckingham Palace, especially as a previously planned visit had been cancelled under Papagos owing to the Cyprus dispute. He knew that the British government wished the visit to be made, and was confident that any attempt to disrupt it by demonstrations could be successfully contained.

Karamanlis explained again that the responsibility for a postponement would rest with his own government. A far worse impression would be caused if it became known that the King had ignored the advice of his Prime Minister—something which would be unthinkable in Britain. Their disagreement would then be not simply a political but a constitutional matter. He felt obliged to insist on his advice to the point of resignation.

The King begged Karamanlis not to insist upon resignation. But he added that if a final disagreement and breach were inevitable, he hoped that Karamanlis would 'make it easy for him to confront the subsequent developments'. To this Karamanlis replied that he would do his best, but he feared that the country would be 'moving into a dangerous vicissitude', which would damage the Crown. He had the impression that his arguments had prevailed.

The discussion turned to the question, how should Queen Elizabeth be informed if the visit were postponed? It would be natural to send an emissary at the highest level, with a letter and an oral message. The Crown Prince, who evidently thought, like Karamanlis, that his father had agreed to the postponement, offered to go himself. But he quickly realized that, although Karamanlis welcomed the suggestion, his father was offended. The King asked Karamanlis to return later in the day to receive his final decision. But at midday, while Karamanlis was reporting to his Council of Ministers, Khoidas telephoned him to postpone the meeting till the next morning.

The next day, 11 June, was decisive. When Karamanlis arrived at Tatoi, the King told him, with regret, that he had decided not to accept his advice. Karamanlis also expressed regret, and submitted his resignation. He advised that a 'service government' should be appointed, which would not present itself to Parliament; that Parliament should be dissolved, and that the general election should take place under the majority system, as had been provided in the electoral law of 1961.

Karamanlis also advised, subject to the agreement of the Opposition, that the new Parliament should have powers to revise the constitution. On this the King reserved judgement. For the second time, he offered Karamanlis the Grand Cross of the Order of the Redeemer. As on the first occasion, Karamanlis refused, saying with a smile that the Order was usually conferred on Prime Ministers who had been dismissed.

On leaving the King, Karamanlis convened the Council of Ministers again to tell them of his resignation and of the advice he had given the King. All of them supported his decision, though Kanellopoulos questioned whether he should have insisted to the point of resignation. Karamanlis pointed out that his resignation was inevitable on grounds both of principle and of substance: on principle because the sovereign was obliged to act on the advice of his Prime Minister in a political matter; in substance because a postponement of the royal visit was imperative for 'the dignity and interests of the country'.

It was not known what prompted the King's decision at the last moment, but Khoidas told Karamanlis that he had been annoyed by reports of the disagreement in the press, and saw the issue as one of personal prestige. Most people thought the Queen had been a more powerful influence than the Press. Her hand was also seen in the issue of a statement by the King before any was made by the government, which Karamanlis called 'a new blunder'.

On 12 June the King summoned the party leaders to hear their advice. It appeared that the Opposition, which had been clamouring for fresh elections since 1961, now did not want them. That evening Karamanlis summoned his colleagues

again, and afterwards issued a statement repeating the advice
he had given the King.

The next day Khoidas came to tell him that the King had
decided to appoint a government which would present itself
to Parliament, for two reasons: first, he wanted the royal visit
to London to take place with the support of a government
enjoying the confidence of Parliament; secondly, he wanted
the electoral system to be changed to simple proportional
representation. Karamanlis replied that he disagreed on both
points: a 'service government' would be adequate for the
period of the royal visit; and a reversion to simple proportional
representation would only encourage the multiplicity of parties
which had done damage in the past.

Khoidas said that the King feared that if the electoral system
were not changed, the Opposition would abstain from the
election or form a new popular front. Karamanlis replied that
it would be disastrous to yield to such blackmail. He begged
the King to think again. He also reminded Khoidas that since
he still held the majority in Parliament, it would be wrong to
ignore his advice. If the King did so, Karamanlis would have
to 'consider whether he could help him'.

After Khoidas left, he held another meeting of his colleagues
to explain why he insisted on his advice. There was general
agreement, but this time a minority shared the King's fear that
the Opposition might abstain from the election if the system
were not changed. Karamanlis repeated that he would not
yield to blackmail, and that if the new government were to
present itself to Parliament the political uncertainty would be
prolonged indefinitely. It would end in 'total disintegration'.
In view of the rumours already circulating of dissension within
ERE, he obtained his colleagues' agreement that there would
be no 'disruptive activities' among them, however freely they
might discuss the crisis in private. A brief statement was issued
to the Press, denying the rumours. But Karamanlis was already
aware that a group of dissidents, led by Theotokis, was in-
triguing against him and had assured the King of their support.

The next day Khoidas telephoned Karamanlis to tell him
that the King wanted to see him again before finally deciding.
As it was Friday, the audience was arranged for the following
Monday, 17 June. But on the Sunday evening Khoidas visited

Karamanlis at home to brief him on the King's latest thoughts. He still wished the new government to present itself to Parliament and to introduce a change in the electoral law, but he now wished to include four or five members of ERE in the government.

Once more Karamanlis disagreed. He pointed out that the new suggestion would confirm the rumours of dissension within ERE. Khoidas said that naturally the ERE members would seek Karamanlis' consent first, to which Karamanlis replied that equally naturally he would refuse, since he would be regarded as a fool if he agreed. Khoidas hastily assured him that there was no intention of 'creating issues to the detriment of the solidarity of the ERE leadership'. Karamanlis had his doubts about that.

He asked Khoidas whether the King had appreciated that he still held the majority in Parliament. What would the King do if ERE voted against the new government? Khoidas replied that in that case the king feared that 'we shall find ourselves in an anomalous situation'. Karamanlis expressed astonishment at this reply, because his impression was that 'they (the Court) are rather reckoning—mistakenly, of course—on splitting the majority.'

Khoidas changed the subject and asked Karamanlis whether he would have any new and different proposal to make to the King next day. Karamanlis replied that he had not 'accepted the audience on conditions'. He still intended to persuade the King to do the right thing; and failing that, to see whether and how he could help him. The present discussion, he said, had convinced him that the King had not yet appreciated that the majority in Parliament was still held by himself. Khoidas protested that the King regarded him as the only political adviser on whom he and the country could rely. He asked if Karamanlis would object to his own presence at the audience next day. Karamanlis said he saw no need for it.

This chilly interview convinced Karamanlis that there was no prospect of changing the King's mind. He was faced by a clear dilemma: either to give way himself, against his better judgement; or to overthrow the new government, by his party's votes, as soon as it was appointed. Since both alternatives were unacceptable, he decided to withdraw from the political scene. With this in mind, he went again to Tatoi on the morning of 17 June.

He told the King that he would do his best to be helpful, but he could not alter his advice. He reminded the King of many occasions when he had urged that the political situation required bold and radical remedies, which could only be achieved by the majority system of election and a revision of the constitution. He emphasized that it would be a mistake to miss the present opportunity of guiding the country into 'a new and healthier period of politics'. He reaffirmed the rest of his advice.

The King replied that he preferred simple proportional representation because it would show the true strength of the parties, and especially the weakness of the Communists. Karamanlis disagreed, but did not prolong the discussion because he wished at once to declare his intention of withdrawing from politics and leaving Greece. Much shocked by this statement, the King stressed the harmful effect it would have. On further consideration of the consequences, Karamanlis said he would leave Greece temporarily and make his final decision later; and he would advise his party to help the King through the present crisis.

The tension then noticeably relaxed, Karamanlis agreed without difficulty to the King's proposal that the new Prime Minister should be a member of ERE, provided that the man chosen would declare his intention of playing no further part in politics. Karamanlis proposed the name of Pipinelis, which the King somewhat reluctantly accepted. After exchanging expressions of mutual respect, the King and his former Prime Minister parted.

That afternoon Karamanlis called his colleagues together for the last time, to tell them of his decision. He appointed a three-man commission—Rodopoulos, Kanellopoulos, and Papaligouras—to take over the leadership of ERE. The next day, 18 June, the new government was sworn in under Pipinelis. On that day also Karamanlis and his wife flew from Athens to Zurich. It was announced on the twenty-first that ERE would support the new government in Parliament, but Papandreou refused to do the same. Pipinelis announced that the royal visit to London would take place, and a general election would follow it. On 25 June he received a vote of confidence by 172 votes to fourteen, the Centre Union abstaining. The King and Queen, with their new Prime Minister, set out for London on 8 July.

The expected demonstrations took place during the royal visit, but the police were able to keep them under control: seventy-five people were arrested. Subsequently serious criticisms were made of the Metropolitan Police, not without justification in one or two cases. There were unhappy echoes, on a minor scale, of the tragedy of Salonika, where criminal charges were brought against police-officers in connection with the murder of Lambrakis. The one small concession to the agitation which accompanied the royal visit was that Pipinelis privately received Mrs Ambatielos; but the release of her husband was left to the next government.

Altogether, the royal crisis of 1963 was a disastrous affair from start to finish. Clearly it did not end when the King and Queen returned to Athens on 12 July, though the King could not do otherwise than express his satisfaction. The unhappy consequences of the crisis afflicted Greece for more than ten years. Karamanlis could have said: 'I told you so!' But when he was approached by journalists in Zurich to comment on the demonstrations in London, he declined to do so.

PART III

Withdrawal and Return
1963–1974

Chapter 7

Warnings from Abroad

KARAMANLIS' withdrawal in June 1963 turned out to be of brief duration. His definitive withdrawal took place only in December. But the period of rest and reflection in Zurich did not alter his intention to withdraw, which he regarded as merely postponed. He saw it as the only way to resolve the dilemma between two alternatives: 'either an open struggle with the Crown or a deviation from legality, with the inevitable consequence in either case of a renewal of the national schism'. But the King did not so see the matter: he expressed amazement at Karamanlis' withdrawal, and begged him to return.

His closest colleagues also refused to accept that his intention was irrevocable. They continued to write to him as the effective leader of ERE, and he replied as such. Correspondence between Athens and Zurich began within a fortnight of Karamanlis' departure. He wrote himself to the directing committee of ERE on 1 July, recapitulating the views which he had already expressed orally and emphasizing three requirments: that although the electoral system of reinforced proportional representation should be accepted for the present occasion, in future the majority system should be restored; that the revision of the constitution should be pursued, even if it meant prolonging the present Parliament; and that if necessary, to achieve these objects, 'reasonable concessions' should be made to the Opposition to guarantee the integrity of the elections.

It happened that on the same day Pipinelis and Papandreou met to discuss the question of a new electoral law. The law passed before the election of 1961 had prescribed a variant of reinforced proportional representation for that occasion; but it had also prescribed the majority system for the subsequent election. The question was therefore whether that provision should stand or be amended. Pipinelis made the proposal indicated by Karamanlis, but Papandreou preferred simple proportional representation. Thus Papandreou and the King were at one on this issue, against both Karamanlis and the new government.

A draft law prescribing reinforced proportional representation was introduced in Parliament on 17 July, a few days after Pipinelis' return from London with the royal party. It had a stormy passage. On 20 August Ilias Iliou, the leader of EDA, tabled a motion denouncing the 'electoral *coup d'état*' of 1961 and the 'bastard government' of Pipinelis, and his party then withdrew from Parliament. The next day, after a similar denunciation by Papandreou, the Centre Union also withdrew. On the twenty-ninth, after an attack on the electoral system by Markezinis, his progressive Party also withdrew.

In the absence of the Opposition, the bill was passed on 3 September. It did not necessarily follow that a general election was imminent, since Parliament had not yet completed half its term. The next step was therefore the subject of voluminous exchanges between Karamanlis and his party, as well as between the King and party leaders.

On learning that the King was inclined to make concessions to Papandreou, Karamanlis wrote to his directing committee on 9 September to ask if there was any chance, even at such a late stage, of winning the King back to his own original policy, including the majority system. He saw this as a way of eliminating Papandreou, leading to a regeneration of the Centre Union, to the creation of 'a new, healthy Opposition through electoral co-operation with another party', and finally to the 'indispensable revision of the constitution'.

He asked that these ideas should be put to the King through Pipinelis. He also posed a number of questions to his colleagues, the first of which concerned the Progressive Party. He had already put on paper (but not circulated) a note dated 4 September on a proposal for electoral co-operation with Markezinis. The proposal had come from Markezinis through the director of the central office of ERE, Dionysios Verros. Karamanlis was willing to discuss it only if no conditions were attached in advance, but Markezinis wanted proportional representation reintroduced; so the discussion lapsed.

Two letters from Athens crossed his own letter of 9 September. One was from Pipinelis, dated the eighth, which reported on the political situation and expressed the opinion that Papandreou's efforts to overthrow the government would not succeed. The other, more alarming, was from Averoff, dated 10 September. Averoff wrote that although he had every confidence in Pipinelis himself, he thought that he ought to be replaced as Prime Minister in order to satisfy Papandreou's demands.

Karamanlis replied at once to Averoff on the eleventh, rejecting his suggestion. In a letter to Pipinelis the next day he expressed his confidence in him. He added some advice on the way to deal with Papandreou's tactics. He also assured Pipinelis that there was no necessity for any attempt, as Pipinelis had suggested, to 'dissipate the prevailing atmosphere' between the King and himself, since he had 'no personal quarrel' with the King. Finally he hinted once more at a final withdrawal from politics, but with a qualification—'if I could do it without damage to the country'.

On the same date, 12 September, a long letter was sent to Karamanlis over the signatures of all three members of the directing committee of ERE. It answered in great detail the questions which he had put to them in his letter of the ninth. More important, it explained that Karamanlis' suggestion of altering the electoral system again at that late stage was quite impossible, since neither the King nor the non-party members of Pipinelis' government would agree. The latter would resign, thus causing a major new crisis. The letter also explained the impossibility of reopening the question of constitutional amendments in the present Parliament, since that would require a two-thirds majority, which ERE could not secure. One of the three signatories, Constantine Rodopoulos, added that the King, whom he had seen recently in Corfu, was very disturbed at the mere possibility of this suggestion being revived.

All the evidence indicated that the King was desperately anxious to secure the co-operation of Papandreou in the forthcoming election, whenever it might take place. He spoke of the need to 'reduce tension', which in effect meant making substantial concessions to Papandreou. This was made plain in a letter from Pipinelis on 15 September, which reported the King's determination to avoid at all costs the abstention of 'at least a section of the Opposition parties'. Consequently Papandreou would be in a strong position, which could be weakened only by detaching Venizelos from him. The election was now scheduled to be held on 3 November, but Papandreou was demanding the dismissal of Pipinelis and the appointment of a new government, many of its members to be nominated by himself.

On the same date, 15 September, another letter was sent to Karamanlis by Dionysios Verros, the staunchest of his extra-parliamentary supporters. In it he described a meeting which he had just had with the King and the Crown Prince, joined towards the end by Khoidas. The King, Verros wrote, appeared to favour the replacement of Pipinelis and the reintroduction of simple proportional representation. Thus, in other words, he was yielding fully to Papandreou's demands. The King had asked Verros to go to Zurich and seek Karamanlis' consent, to which Verros said he 'replied appropriately': in other words, he refused. He further reported a state of great uneasiness among the officer corps in Salonika, where warrants had been issued for the arrest of a number of Army officers in the Lambrakis case.

Karamanlis' reply to Pipinelis on 18 September was accompanied by a memorandum containing a new proposal: that Pipinelis should form a political government, with Kanellopoulos and Venizelos as Vice-Premiers. His assumption was that Venizelos would welcome the opportunity to be rid of Papandreou. If Venizelos made difficulties, then Pipinelis should form a government drawn exclusively from ERE. As a last resort, if this too proved impracticable, then 'it would be possible, by satisfying even the latest demands of the Opposition, to proceed to a general election by the end of November'. More important still was Karamanlis' covering letter, in which he asked Pipinelis to inform the King that he had now finally decided to withdraw from politics in order to facilitate the restoration of normality and the relaxation of tension.

Verros on the eighteenth, and Pipinelis on the nineteenth, both wrote imploring Karamanlis to reverse his decision, and both quoted the King as being of the same mind. Karamanlis replied by telephone to Verros on the evening of the nineteenth, insisting that his decision was final. He pointed out that his presence in Greece would be incompatible with the policy of relaxing tension—in other words, of making concessions to Papandreou.

On the morning of 20 September Pipinelis sent a message by telephone through Verros. He said that neither the King nor he himself thought Karamanlis' memorandum of the eighteenth was practicable, especially since Venizelos was unwilling to co-operate and was now proposing that the present government should stay in office until May 1964. But Pipinelis still thought that Karamanlis' return to Greece could only be beneficial. Verros added that the Crown Prince had confirmed that this was also the King's view, and his own as well. 'It is absolutely essential', the Crown Prince had said, 'that he should return, and the sooner the better'.

Karamanlis telephoned Verros the same evening. He said that since it was the King's opinion that his absence from Greece might be harmful to the country's interests, he would reconsider his decision on three conditions: first, that the general election should be held on the scheduled date, 3 November, with no further alteration of the electoral law; secondly, that the Pipinelis government should remain in office until then; thirdly, that the foregoing conditions should be resolutely maintained, regardless of the reactions of the Opposition. In reply the King accepted all three conditions. Karamanlis therefore decided to return at once to Greece, after a short visit to Paris to say goodbye to friends. He flew to Paris on 23 September; but while he was there, events took an unexpected course.

The King received Papandreou in audience on 22 September. Papandreou presented his requirements both orally and in writing. He distinguished two hypothetical cases, one presupposing elections within two months, the other presupposing their postponement. He did not define, at least in his written memorandum, which of the two alternatives he preferred, but on the first hypothesis he laid down only two requirements: a modification of the electoral law and a reconstruction of the government to include Ministers 'enjoying the full confidence of the Centre Union' in certain politically sensitive posts. On the second hypothesis, both these requirements were repeated, but the second one was strengthened: the government was not simply to be reconstructed but replaced by a 'service government' of non-political personalities. Several other requirements were also added on the second hypothesis, one of which was that the postponement of the elections should 'not exceed the time necessary for the completion of the Salonika trial'.

Pipinelis received a copy of Papandreou's memorandum on the same day, and sent it at once to Karamanlis. He commented in a covering letter that the only point which the King thought worth discussing was the requirement of a 'service government', and that only subject to Karamanlis' consent. Pipinelis added his own opinion that if Karamanlis agreed to the change of government, a conference of party leaders could perhaps be convened, under the King's chairmanship or even his own, which might have the result of averting any abstention from the elections and ending the 'relentless struggle'.

Karamanlis telephoned his reply to Pipinelis through Verros the next morning. He was indignant that Papandreou's proposals, 'more uncompromising and outrageous than before', should be given a moment's consideration. He asked for an assurance that the King still firmly intended to hold the general election on 3 November. In a further message to the directing committee of ERE, he sharply criticized the King and opposed the idea of a conference of party leaders.

Pipinelis, however, was aware of the precariousness of his position, and had reason to doubt whether Karamanlis would continue to support him in office. He submitted his resignation on the twenty-fifth. The King convened a conference of the party leaders on the same day, but could find no agreement on the best solution. So on the twenty-sixth he accepted Pipinelis' resignation and dissolved Parliament. Two days later he appointed a 'service government' under the President of the Supreme Court, with a mandate to hold a general election on 3 November. His motives were clear: he wanted to end the suspense and to establish a political government as soon as possible; but he believed it was time for power to change hands in the interests of a healthy democracy.

Karamanlis, who was still in Paris, regarded the King's decision as a surrender to Papandreou. Still, he decided reluctantly to continue his journey home. But he told his friends not to organize a massive welcome for him at the airport, in order not to create the impression of a repudiation of the King's action. 'I genuinely prayed', he wrote later, 'that I would lose the election, so that I would have sufficient justification for withdrawing from political life.' In this mood he flew from Paris on 29 September, to resume the leadership of ERE.

In a statement on his arrival in Athens, he declared that democracy, 'in theory the best of all constitutions', was in danger of destroying itself. 'Communism is lying in wait to ambush it', he warned, 'and there exists no political leadership with a high enough sense of responsibility'. His motives were just as clear as the King's: the King believed that democracy would be in danger (though not from Karamanlis) if ERE won a fourth consecutive election; and Karamanlis believed it would be in danger if he were defeated.

A week after his return Karamanlis began his electoral tour. The route was familiar: first Salonika, then eastern Macedonia and Thrace; south through the Aegean islands, then west to Crete; north through the Peloponnese to Roumeli and Epirus; south again to Thessaly, and finally to Athens for a major rally in Klavthmonos Square on 1 November. In his speeches he emphasized the achievements of his last eight years in foreign policy and defence, in promoting industrialization and public works, in raising the national income and stabilizing the currency. Looking forward to the next decade, he outlined a programme of regional development and a radical reform of the educational system. He castigated the Centre Union for acting in virtual alliance with EDA. He frankly expressed a fear that a victory for his opponents would be followed soon afterwards by a dictatorship; 'but it will not be myself who imposes it'.

The Opposition, apart from propounding the theme of a new deal after eight years of misrule, found new items of scandal to use against Karamanlis. On 13 October four police-officers, under arrest in connection with the death of Lambrakis, were acquitted for want of evidence. Although this carried no implications against ERE, it was a reminder of a damaging episode for which the left still held Karamanlis responsible. Later in the month Venizelos alleged, without a shred of evidence, that Karamanlis had agreed with the Americans to give Bulgaria access to the Aegean. Next, the former Ambassador in Bonn, whom Averoff had dismissed, circulated some disparaging rumours about relations with West Germany. Finally Dr Merten, the notorious Nazi war criminal, produced a few more of his fabrications on 1 November, too late to be rebutted before polling day. Probably none of these manœuvres had any effect on the voting.

Despite his wish to withdraw from politics, Karamanlis believed up to the last minute that ERE would win. The poll on 3 November was extremely close, but when the next day's newspapers went to press, before the completion of the count, it was clear that the Centre Union would have a small majority over ERE. The final result gave Papandreou 138 seats and Karamanlis 132; the balance was held by EDA with twenty-eight.

The King, accompanied by the Crown Prince, began receiving the party leaders on the fifth. Karamanlis advised him not to make a hasty decision. He thought the best course would be a coalition under a Prime Minister other than Papandreou or himself. But if the King thought of entrusting a mandate to Papandreou, Karamanlis urged him not to do so without first seeing himself again; and he advised that it should be only an exploratory mandate, not one to form a government. The outcome of their meeting was shrouded in controversy. Karamanlis was convinced that the King had given him an undertaking based on his advice; the Crown Prince was in no doubt that his father had not done so.

In fact the King invited Papandreou to form a government on 6 November, but without the right of dissolution if he were defeated in Parliament. He also allowed Papandreou an exceptionally long period before he had to face Parliament— again contrary to Karamanlis' advice—which enabled him to manœuvre for wider support. On 8 November the ERE Deputies agreed unanimously to vote against Papandreou's government. But even if he could not subvert the ranks of ERE, Papandreou could still win a vote of confidence with the support of EDA.

Karamanlis therefore had to face for the first time the

prospect of becoming the leader of the Parliamentary Opposition. Rumours were circulating in Athens as early as 4 November that he would withdraw again rather than do so. But at first he seemed ready to continue the struggle. On 10 November he even called on Markezinis to discuss the possibility of co-operation in Parliament. This was a forlorn hope, however, for the Progressive Party held only two seats, and Markezinis himself had been defeated.

On 5 November the editor of *Kathimerini*, normally a faithful supporter, published a leading article urging Karamanlis to overcome his disappointment and remain in politics: 'Karamanlis has not the moral right to treat with contempt those who voted for him nor to leave his party without leadership. They voted for him to represent them whether in government or in opposition. If they were voting for him only to be the government, there would be no point in elections . . . '. It was an argument which his closest friends knew he could not accept.

He explained to his parliamentary group that he had two reasons for rejecting such arguments. The first was that if he stayed, his presence would lead to another 'national schism'. The second was his disappointment with the way the political system was working. Privately, though much later, he admitted that 'the function of opposition does not suit my character, both because I am a man of action and because opposition inevitably presupposes an element of demagogy'. He maintained that events proved him right. Certainly there was early evidence of the bitterness he expected.

Papandreou announced on 15 November that he intended to sell what he called Karamanlis' 'luxury armour-plated Chrysler' and build schools with the proceeds. He instructed his officials to seek out evidence of scandals under the previous administration. Without further ado, Karamanlis left Greece on 9 December, handing over the leadership to Kanellopoulos. With him went Amalia. Only her father (Kanellopoulos' brother) and Kanellopoulos himself, with two senior officials of ERE (Kondas and Verros), accompanied them to the airport. No other members of his family were present—not even his youngest brother Akhilleas, who had just been elected to Parliament for the first time, and was to be one of his regular political correspondents. To preserve secrecy, their tickets were booked in the name of a friendly journalist. They went this time straight to Paris, where an apartment was found for them by friends. It was to be Karamanlis' home for the next ten years.

He left a letter in the hands of Kanellopoulos, addressed to his friends in ERE. It was published in *Kathimerini* on 10 December. In it he told them that his decision 'to withdraw from politics' had been taken in June and made known then 'in the proper quarter'. He had come back in September only because he was begged not to carry out his decision before the election. 'It follows', he wrote, 'that my withdrawal from politics is not a consequence of personal bitterness'. It was due to the absence of conditions which would make it possible 'to fulfil my mission, as I at least understood it'. He continued with familiar criticisms of the political system. As he could not reform it in the way he saw to be necessary, it was better to withdraw than to compromise. He hoped that his withdrawal would make the King's task easier, even though his opponents were making it more difficult.

He was departing, he said, without recriminations and with a clear conscience. He stressed his affection and gratitude towards his colleagues, and urged them to maintain their unity and devotion to democracy. Then he recommended to them a course which was not in fact to be taken until after his return: that they should review their organization and draw up a charter for the party 'on the model of parties in other countries, whose durability is due to the renewal of their leadership'. Such a charter would show the strength of the party even in the absence of its founder. It should prescribe a method of electing the leader; but in the meantime he bequeathed the leadership to Kanellopoulos 'in the certainty that you will approve my choice'. Finally, he undertook to help them in their efforts, 'as a private citizen and loyal member of ERE'.

Those closest to Karamanlis were divided in their views of his real intentions. To his wife he spoke at first of 'going away for three months', as if he had no further plan. He seemed to be 'playing for time', she said, deliberately delaying decision. At first he thought of settling in London rather than Paris, for he knew English better than French. Some of his political associates thought that he really had given up public life, and believed that he believed it himself. Others accepted his intention to retire but foresaw that his return would be inevitable. He himself said long afterwards that his decision to end his public career had been definite at the time, 'but it was my intention to return as a private citizen after a few months'. In that case he could not long have remained private.

Tsatsos wrote a prophetic letter to him on the day after his departure, expressing the fear that circumstances would very soon arise in which 'even your enemies will want you back'. The King was simply baffled: he said so to Kanellopoulos, to Averoff, and to his own son. Kanellopoulos reported this to Karamanlis, who replied in January placing the blame on 'the policy of the Crown over the last six months'. It was not long before Papandreou in his turn was placing the blame for his own problems on the Crown.

Looking back on his career during his self-imposed exile (probably in 1967), Karamanlis summarized it under three heads. In foreign policy, he had inherited the problem of Cyprus, the quarrel with Turkey and Britain, the breakdown of the Balkan Pact, and uncertainty about Greece's future in NATO. By settling the Cyprus problem, he had 'averted war and restored the traditional ties of Greece with the West'; and he had formed a link with the EEC. At home, the state of the political parties had been critical when he took office; but he had established a strong new party with a realistic programme, he had turned his back on old divisions, he had pursued a democratic course and avoided extremism. Between 1955 and 1963 there had been eight years of stability, in contrast with fifteen governments during the previous eleven years and nine during the following four years, culminating in a military dictatorship. In the economic field, he claimed that the work of his government had been 'difficult but impressive'. He had inherited a backward country with a budget deficit and huge debts. He illustrated the reversal of these defects with statistics of public finance and economic growth.

Two accusations, however, still rankled: that he had tyrannically oppressed the left, and that he had neglected social welfare and education. Both were answered more effectively in a later letter to an American professor, who had asked for material to defend Karamanlis' record in 1971. He pointed out that all the measures against the left—the imprisonment and exile of Communists, the security laws and outlawry of the KKE, the introduction of 'certificates of political relia- bility', and so on—had taken place before 1951, and most of them had been relaxed under his own government. 'I found 4,498 Communists in prison and reduced them to 937 . . . I found 898 Communists in exile and reduced them to six.' On the second charge, among other points, he replied that under his government annual expenditure on welfare had increased by over 150 per cent, and educational expenditure had in- creased from seven to ten per cent of the budget. He concluded that 'this does not of course mean that in my time the state of Greece was idyllic, but it shows that there was a serious and honest effort to develop the country in a democratic framework'.

Sometimes he was tempted to go further, 'There are', he wrote in 1967, 'governments which do harm, governments which do neither harm nor good, and governments which promote the life of the nation'. His government, he believed, fell into the third category. In 1971 he wrote that there had been only three periods when Greece was effectively governed as a democracy: under Trikoupis in the nineteenth century, under Venizelos in his first period (1910-15), and under himself. These were bold claims, but they could hardly be challenged.

What then caused these achievements to break down? Karamanlis repeatedly denied that his resignation had been caused either by a deterioration of the economic prospect or by the Lambrakis tragedy, as had often been suggested. It had been caused solely by the dispute with the Crown. There had been four specific points of disagreement: the King's rejection of his advice to postpone the visit to London; the King's refusal to dissolve Parliament after Karamanlis' resignation; the King's rejection of his advice to limit Papandreou's man- date in November 1963 to one of 'exploration'; and the King's reluctance to summon the newly elected Parliament immedi- ately in order to clarify the political situation. In several instances the King had simply surrendered to Papandreou's pressure, because he knew that it was only from Papandreou, not from Karamanlis, that his throne might be in danger.

Karamanlis never ceased to be convinced that his withdrawal in December 1963 had been the right course. 'If I had stayed', he wrote in 1980, 'we should have ended in a new schism, perhaps even in a civil war, as happened with Venizelos when he lost the elections in 1933. Furthermore, I should have been destroyed in the period that followed, and I should not have been able to return as the Comforter (*Paraklitos*)[1] at the critical moment in 1974.' In effect he was arguing that in 1963 Greece's fate lay between two catastrophes, for which the blame rested with the demagogy of Papandreou and the weakness of the King. His opponents naturally thought otherwise, but no one would deny that the outcome was catastrophic.

Everything seemed set on a downhill course after the election of 1963. Promising negotiations with the Americans were thrown off course, like everything else in the world, by the assassination of President Kennedy on 22 November. Makarios was provoking a new crisis in Cyprus by demanding changes in the constitution. The new Greek government was precarious, depending on the support of EDA and two defectors from ERE for its vote of confidence on 24 December. Papandreou promptly resigned, saying that he would not lead a government dependent on the Communists. Kanellopoulos was unable to form an alternative government, so Parliament was once more dissolved.

The new election took place on 16 February 1964. This time Papandreou won an absolute majority with 171 seats; but he lost Venizelos, who died during the campaign. King Paul also died, only a few days after swearing in the new government. What should have been a stable situation thus became very uncertain, and eventually fatal to Greece's system of constitutional monarchy.

If Karamanlis had really retired from public life, none of

---

[1] To the Greeks *Paraklitos* means the Holy Spirit. On the other hand, their hope that a Messiah would come to save them was vain, as Karamanlis told his French biographer: 'In our day there are no Messiahs!' (M. Genevoix, *The Greece of Karamanlis* (London, 1973), p. 187.)

these things concerned him. But his correspondence shows that they did, however often he denied any intention of returning. Some of his correspondents deliberately set out to keep alive his interest. One example was a letter from Verros on 11 February, telling him of the hostility towards him of 'those on high', and of their fear that he might return. In his reply on 23 February Karamanlis wrote of his sorrow over the terminal illness of the King, for whom 'I always cherish feelings of love and admiration, aside from our disagreements'. But he added that 'having constantly disagreed with them, I preferred withdrawal to a breach . . . My withdrawal from politics is for good and all'.

A week later, however, he wrote less categorically to Kanellopoulos that he did not intend to return to Greece for a year or eighteen months. At the same time he gave Kanellopoulos the benefit of wide-ranging comments on the political situation. He had nothing to say about the election of 16 February, for which 'there is simply no logical explanation'; but he had hoped that his departure would have the advantage of making people think seriously, which evidently it had not.

He also castigated Makarios, who had infuriated the Turks, appealed to the Soviet Union for support, and brought about an intervention of UN peace-keeping forces in Cyprus. Karamanlis argued that the Zurich-London agreements had 'created the prerequisites, in my opinion, for the definitive outcome: *enosis*'. But Makarios had thrown all his advantages away. Once again it seemed that Karamanlis was beginning to recognize that he was indispensable.

In the same letter he also gave Kanellopoulos general advice on party policy, which was a recurrent theme of his correspondence. But before he settled down to direct ERE from afar, he undertook an extensive world tour in March and April 1964, travelling through the Middle East, India, and the Far East, and returning across America. His wife did not accompany him. He returned to Paris, as he wrote to Tsatsos on 10 May, disappointed with his trip and convinced that he had seen 'one area which in my opinion will become one day a focus of international anxieties'. He had in mind the poverty which he had seen in such potentially rich countries as Iran.

Tsatsos had written on 3 May reporting on the continued devotion of the party to him, and the growing pressure for his return. But Karamanlis in reply reaffirmed his 'definite withdrawal'. He also re-emphasized the need for more vigorous opposition. It was all the more necessary because a new issue had been raised by Papandreou which made it impossible for him to disengage himself entirely from domestic politics.

Papandreou's efforts to uncover scandals had not, in his own judgement at least, been wholly fruitless. He claimed that there had been irregularities in the use of secret funds by the Ministry of Foreign Affairs. He again accused Karamanlis of dishonesty in his purchase of a plot of land. He alleged that Karamanlis' wife had given a present worth £1,000 to President Kennedy's wife during her private visit to Athens in 1962. Finally he introduced legislation to deal with political corruption.

In letters to his friends Karamanlis pointed out that he had proposed similar legislation in 1961, but had dropped it in deference to the Opposition. So he had no objection to his party now supporting it. The specific accusations against Amalia and himself were soon disproved, but the vendetta went on. It extended to a further attempt to hold him morally responsible for the death of Lambrakis.

All these themes were indignantly rebutted in Karamanlis' letters to his friends. 'Lambrakis was never of the slightest interest to the government', he wrote to Kanellopoulos on 27 May, 'nor could the place of the tragedy have been chosen by anyone in his senses'. As he put it later, the crime had been the work of 'a few right-wing scoundrels with the connivance of certain elements in the police, motivated by anti-Communist vindictiveness'. But all this had nothing to do with his party or government.

His letter to Kanellopoulos also repeated his intention to withdraw, with one modification: he would not return within a year, and never to politics. But the letter was full of political advice. He urged Kanellopoulos to pay particular attention to the Army and the judiciary, because the damage inflicted on them by the new government would be 'impossible to cure by normal means, as we know from the past'. He dilated upon the follies of Makarios, whose attempts to amend the 1959 agreement and to obtain support from the Soviet bloc were 'making the eventual solution of *enosis* more remote'. The government, he wrote, had 'let itself be towed along by Makarios'. To make matters worse, Grivas returned openly to Cyprus in June, proclaiming himself 'the Apostle of *enosis*'.

On the charges of personal corruption, Karamanlis wrote to Verros on 6 June that 'as all my colleagues know, my one personal characteristic is not genius or wisdom but strict integrity'. Even Papandreou was having second thoughts about scandalmongering, having discovered that Karamanlis' supposedly 'luxury armour-plated Chrysler' had no armour-plating and had been bought second-hand. He resisted a proposal by EDA to appoint a commission of enquiry directed at Karamanlis personally, but instead he passed legislation 'On the protection of the honour of the political world', which required all politicians and senior officials to declare their assets. Karamanlis was among the first to do so, in *Kathimerini* on 15 December.

His declaration showed that his assets amounted to one sixth of an area of forty *stremmata* (ten acres) near the village of Proti; an old house in the same area; and the building-site of 6,088 square metres at Philothei, which he had bought in 1957 for 365,000 *drachmae* (roughly £4,400) and about which much had already been heard. He also had an option, as a member of a consortium of Deputies, to buy two sites at Kiphissia, near Athens, measuring 1,213 and 1,279 square metres respectively. He listed three small properties which he had sold since 1946. He had no shipping interests and no stocks or shares. His one other material asset was a ten-horse-power German car. The joint income of his wife and himself in 1963 amounted to 269,355 *drachmae* (roughly £3,200) of which his share consisted entirely of his salary as a Deputy and Prime Minister. He had also enjoyed three months' hospitality in Zurich at a friend's expense. That was all.

He authorized his friend and lawyer, Costa Papakonstantinou, himself also a Deputy and former minister, to submit the declaration on his behalf. There was no obligation to publish it, but Papakonstantinou did so because other leading politicians, including Papandreou, Stephanopoulos, and Kanellopoulos, were publishing their declarations on the same day. He wrote to Karamanlis on 24 December that he had not consulted him because he feared the telephone was tapped. He added that the public impression was excellent; but Verros wrote that publication had done him harm, and Tsatsos reported that it had stimulated new speculation about the possibility of his return.

Writing to Verros on 7 January 1965, Karamanlis asked rather anxiously why it had done harm? He himself thought it had done good, for it showed 'with what honesty and self-sacrifice I served my country'. The anxiety behind his question might have suggested again that he had not finally forsworn political life. But to Tsatsos he replied on the eighth that to return 'is not among my intentions'.

For a time, after the publication of the declaration of assets, the government's search for scandals lost impetus. The problem of Cyprus again preoccupied Papandreou, watched by Karamanlis with sardonic sympathy. Makarios and Grivas between them had come near to provoking a Turkish invasion 1964, and Papandreou secretly reinforced the Greek units on the island beyond the numbers allowed by the treaty. He was learning by experience that Makarios and Grivas were irresponsible partners. 'We agree on one thing and you do another', he wrote to them on 8 August 1964, 'and disastrous consequences follow'. President Johnson had sent out Dean Acheson, the former Secretary of State, to devise a solution. His proposal was *enosis* with compensations for the Turks, which at first Papandreou warmly welcomed. But Makarios at once rejected it, and accordingly, under the influence of his son, Papandreou felt obliged to retreat and follow Makarios.

Still each of them was convinced that *enosis* was about to be achieved, by different but equally reckless expedients. Makarios signed a trade agreement with the Soviet Union in June and sent his Foreign Minister to Moscow in September. In the same month Papandreou declared with characteristic rhetoric, in a speech at the Officers' Club in Salonika: '*Enosis* is coming, and with Cyprus as a stepping-stone Hellenism will continue its advance into the Middle East in the steps of Alexander the Great'. Karamanlis might well wonder which of them would precipitate disaster first.

In a letter of 20 October 1964, Kanellopoulos wrote that

Papandreou was claiming credit for the progress in Cyprus which was in fact due to Karamanlis' own policies, 'without which Makarios would not today be head of state and of a government which is now wholly Greek owing to the removal of the Turks from it'. His letter was, however, apologetic in tone, for Karamanlis had been complaining in his own letters to others that Kanellopoulos was proving an ineffective leader of ERE and had been out of touch with him for six months. Kanellopoulos apologized for failing to write earlier, because of pressure of work. Rumours of dissension within ERE had also reached the Press and led to fresh speculation on the possibility of Karamanlis' return.

In the New Year the scandalmongering began again, giving Kanellopoulos and his colleagues a new burden to shoulder on Karamanlis' behalf. An investigation of the Electricity Corporation had produced a severely critical report in September 1964. Although the criticisms were not directed at Karamanlis' government, the opportunity was taken to turn them against him personally. Early in February 1965, on a motion proposed by EDA, Parliament voted in a secret ballot to impeach Karamanlis and two of his colleagues, Papaligouras and Martis, on charges of corruption. A parliamentary commission of investigation was appointed, with members drawn from ERE as well as the Centre Union and EDA. Then towards the end of February Papandreou uncovered another scandal— the 'Pericles Plan', which he called 'the plan for the electoral *coup d'état*' of 1961.

This time Kanellopoulos reacted vigorously. On 19 February he made a public speech in Klavthmonos Square denouncing the government's motives for impeaching Karamanlis and his colleagues. On the twenty-seventh he spoke again, explaining that the Pericles Plan had been aimed solely against Communist subversion, and was in any case never put into operation. On 15 March he wrote at length to Karamanlis on the agony he was suffering over the Pericles affair, and the waste of his time and energy in attending the commission of investigation into the Electricity Corporation affair, which occupied himself and three colleagues up to midnight on three or four days a week.

His only hope, he wrote, was a change of government. 'At

all costs we must split the Centre Union', he added. There could then be a new government based on a section of that party, 'with our support but without our participation'. But he no doubt knew that several of his colleagues, including Verros and Papaligouras as well as Karamanlis himself, thought that he was being insufficiently aggressive.

'The reactions of the party do not correspond to the necessities of present circumstances,' wrote Karamanlis to Verros on 10 April. But he would not lay all the blame on Kanellopoulos. Writing to Kondas on 8 May, he deplored the attacks being made on Kanellopoulos. There was also a curious passage in his letter which again hinted that his political career was not ended. He regretted the attempts being made to promote Mitsotakis, who was Papandreou's Minister of Economic Affairs, as a national leader in 'an anti-Karamanlist spirit'. Mitsotakis, like other Liberals, was later to become a close friend and colleague of his own.

The same letter also contained detailed advice on the tactics to be pursued by ERE. They should show more systematic aggressiveness; they should override the theme of alleged scandals by forcing the government to bring out 'everything it has or doesn't have' for public discussion; and they should divide policy matters under four or five heads, each to be covered by two ex-ministers who would be 'responsible for dealing both with Parliament and with the Press, on their own absolute initiative'. His conclusion was a reassertion of his own authority: 'As you know, I do not want to interfere directly in the affairs of the party, but since the preservation of ERE as the only strong, sound political organization is a national necessity, I shall not hesitate to disown, even in public, those who oppose the above line'.

Meanwhile the initiative still seemed to lie with the Centre Union and EDA. In April 1965 EDA tabled a motion to set up yet another commission of investigation, this time into the management of public works under Karamanlis. They named many specific projects in which, they claimed, excessive costs had been incurred, the construction had been defective, and so on. In May they added still more items to the list. With support from the Centre Union, they carried their motion to set up a twenty-man commission of investigation. It seemed that the Centre Union, even in power, was following the lead of the Communists. On 24 June Iliou, the leader of EDA openly boasted to Papandreou in Parliament: 'We brought you to power!'

Papandreou was already conscious of the damage done by his subservience to EDA. The earlier commission, investigating the affair of the Electricity Corporation, had recommended by a majority on 3 June that Karamanlis and his two colleagues should be put on trial. But later in the month Papandreou decided to drop the matter, and also to abandon the investigation into the misuse of secret funds by the Ministry of Foreign Affairs. His motives were transparent, for his own administration was now on the brink of a crisis.

As long ago as 2 March 1964 Karamanlis had written to Kanellopoulos that the party's dignified silence under attack had not benefited them. A chance to counter-attack in kind began to emerge a year later, when Verros reported on 26 March 1965 the first rumours of a left-wing conspiracy in the Army known as the Shield (*Aspida*). Karamanlis had repeatedly warned his colleagues to watch carefully what was happening in the Army, and Pipinelis had written to him on 10 March about the 'explosive situation' among the officer corps.

Papandreou's son Andreas, who was now a Deputy of the Centre Union and Minister in the Prime Minister's office, was suspected of complicity in the *Aspida* affair. A correspondence between King Constantine and Papandreou on this and other delicate matters began on 8 July. Papandreou wanted to make changes in the upper ranks of the Army, which were naturally dominated by officers appointed under Karamanlis. When his Minister of Defence demurred, Papandreou dismissed him and proposed to take the portfolio himself. This the King refused to sanction, in view of the suspicion hanging over the Prime Minister's son. On 15 July Papandreou resigned and demanded a dissolution of Parliament; but the King contrived, by a series of subterfuges, to form a new government without him.

Once more the cry went up of a 'royal *coup d'état*', to which Papandreou added a new slogan: 'The King reigns, the People rule!' Parliament refused votes of confidence to two governments during August: others failed even to be formed.

Karamanlis wrote to Pipinelis on 22 August regretting that ERE had missed the opportunity to eliminate Papandreou. He thought the best hope was a national government, and he suggested that the Chiefs of Staff should be advised to recommend it to the King. But in September the King succeeded at last in forming a coalition under Stephanopoulos.

When Karamanlis first heard of Papandreou's dismissal, he was uncertain whether to call it fortunate or unfortunate. But whatever the merits of the King's first reaction, 'his subsequent handling was lamentable'. Once the first government after Papandreou had failed, Karamanlis considered that the King should have dissolved Parliament. What he actually did was 'constitutionally legitimate but not above criticism in political terms'. Karamanlis was convinced that without the crisis of 1965 the Centre Union would soon have broken up and the government would have fallen: instead, events 'practically made heroes of them'.

In fact Stephanopoulos' government survived surprisingly long. It had the support of both ERE and the Progressive Party, each of which nominated a 'token minister' of no political significance to serve in it. It was also supported by forty-five former members of the Centre Union, who became known as the 'apostates'. Stephanopoulos won a vote of confidence on 17 September. Kanellopoulos wrote to Karamanlis on 23 October of his 'mental agonies' over the compromise. He was not satisfied with his own handling of the crisis, and wondered gloomily: 'What will happen tomorrow?'

Tomorrow took more than a year to come. The new government did little governing, and the lack of activity is reflected in the comparative dearth of Karamanlis' correspondence. Early in January 1966 Tsatsos wrote to congratulate him on the tenth anniversary of the foundation of ERE. He replied on the seventh, thanking Tsatsos for his good wishes, which had helped to mitigate the bitterness of his 'ill-treatment by the Greeks'. A month later he heard of the final judgement of the high court on the Lambrakis affair, which showed that there was no case against his government or himself. But this did little to raise his spirits. In a letter written during May he forecast the inevitability of a 'deviation' (*ektropi*) from constitutional democracy in Greece.

During March 1966 Karamanlis took a holiday in the Bahamas and the USA. In New York he replied to speculation about his plans by saying: 'If Greece needs me, I will not refuse my services'. But he half withdrew the hint by adding that 'so long as I do not believe that I have a mission, I do not intend to return even if the Greeks invite me unanimously'. Since these words left a confusing impression, he wrote to Tsatsos on 5 May, summarizing his reasons for not returning to Greece.

He spoke of the ill-treatment he had experienced and the investigation of his supposed misdeeds; of the way he had almost been turned into a symbol of national division; and of his temperamental unfitness for this kind of politics. He expressed his conviction that truly democratic government would only become possible in Greece after major changes in the country's life. The first step would have to be a new Parliament with a mandate for constitutional reform, and a government with extraordinary powers, such as the French had had in 1958. It was because there was no prospect of such a change that he chose to remain abroad.

Apart from his trip to America, the first half of 1966 was a time of little activity. He read extensively, including the Greek classics, Shakespeare, Goethe, and Kanellopoulos' monumental *History of the European Spirit*. He improved his French; he took up golf. He was pleased by the attentions of de Gaulle and his ministers. The success of the French in restoring political stability greatly impressed him. French sophistication broadened his intellectual horizon. He had enjoyable conversations with Maurice Genevoix, the novelist and Academician, who published *La Grèce de Caramanlis* in 1972. Still, he did not find Paris altogether congenial.

Later he described his time in France as 'the worst years of my life', but that was no fault of the French. He had little contact with his family in Greece, while they were suffering from the vendetta against him. His youngest brother, Akhilleas, contributed much to his political correspondence, and his sister Olga sent him regular consignments of *spanakopitta* to remind him of their younger days in Serres. None of his immediate family was able to join him in Paris, until a nephew came to stay near the end of his self-imposed exile.

His marriage also was giving way to the strains of exile.

Amalia was a social asset, but they had no children. His natural affection for children was concentrated on nephews and nieces a thousand miles away, and even on Akhilleas, who was young enough to be his son. Women found him attractive, but he was not an ideal husband, having still something of the male chauvinism which dominates the Greek provinces. That Amalia was Kanellopoulos' niece made things no easier, though it never caused personal friction. If his relations with Kanellopoulos were occasionally uneasy, it was for other reasons.

In the latter half of 1966 it became obvious that the 'government of the apostates' could not survive much longer. Kanellopoulos was talking of withdrawing his support.Pipinelis reported on 17 June that there was a growing demand for the return of 'the strong man'. In August the King sent Bitsios, who was now director of his political office, to ask for Karamanlis' advice. Bitsios reported that the King was dissatisfied with Stephanopoulos, but did not want elections and did not think Kanellopoulos could form a government. Karamanlis advised a dissolution once the present government had created the conditions necessary for 'elections without risk'. Failing that, Kanellopoulos should be appointed to replace Stephanopoulos, with the right to a dissolution. Six months were to pass before the King acted on this last piece of advice.

Towards the end of September Karamanlis received important letters from three of his colleagues. Kanellopoulos wrote on the twentieth that the government could not last long. Tsatsos wrote on the twenty-first that he was now doubtful whether to urge Karamanlis' return; but he was attacking the left-wing intellectuals in the Press, with all the vigour of an intellectual, for saying that he should not return. Pipinelis wrote on the twenty-third about the *Aspida* case and its dangers. The gravity of the case became still plainer in October, when twenty-eight officers were committed for trial and the prosecutor said that some civilians might also be involved. He added that if they were Deputies, he would request that their parliamentary immunity be lifted. The reference to Andreas Papandreou was unmistakable.

A still more startling communication reached Karamanlis at the end of September. It was an oral message from the

King, again conveyed by Bitsios. After listening to Karamanlis' proposals for reform under a new government with extraordinary powers, Bitsios told him that the King was opposed to a revision of the constitution; but that if Karamanlis came back to form a government, the King would in certain circumstances support him in a 'deviation' (*ektropi*). This clearly meant at least a partial suspension of the constitution.

Karamanlis pointed out that if he returned as Prime Minister, he would first have to face Parliament, which would reject him; and then he would be compelled to 'turn a temporary deviation into an unconcealed dictatorship'. The subject was therefore dropped. But when Karamanlis wrote again to Tsatsos on 25 October, repeating his reasons for not returning to Greece, he also expressed the fear that 'at the stage matters have reached, the possibility cannot be excluded that you will be led, sooner or later and against your will, into some kind of deviation.' It went without saying that the 'deviation' would not be by himself.

This was a time when Karamanlis had a bitter sense that all he had achieved was falling apart. In the same letter to Tsatsos, he spoke of his father's attempts to dissuade him from politics. He had nevertheless persisted 'because I had the satisfaction of creation, and also because I believed I was improving the political climate of our country'. Now he had doubts: 'Instead of that, our political life has recently degenerated to such an extent that any adjustment is impossible'. He asked Tsatsos whether the situation did not remind him of 1928, when Elevtherios Venizelos returned from self-imposed exile; and whether Venizelos had not made a mistake in returning?

Apart from the follies of Athens, there were also the follies of Nicosia. Karamanlis vented his feelings against Makarios in another letter to Tsatsos on 8 November. The occasion was furnished by Makarios himself, who passed through Paris on the sixth, returning from Latin America. In advance he had asked to see Karamanlis, who agreed very reluctantly. Then Makarios failed to make an appointment, and offered no apology. Karamanlis recalled in his letter that he had not received a word of thanks from Makarios for working out a solution in 1959 'which would have inevitably led to *enosis* if there had been a little sense'. Now, he added, Makarios was treated as a hero, while he himself was abused. Karamanlis was convinced that things would have to get worse before they got better, both in Cyprus and in Greece. In both cases he was right.

There were renewed whispers of a military conspiracy. Stephanopoulos claimed that there was no risk of a coup succeeding, but Karamanlis was less optimistic. He wrote to Pipinelis on 23 November, emphasizing the extreme importance of the *Aspida* trial. He implied that ERE was not vigorous enough in attacking the government, which he severely criticized for having created an even more dangerous situation than it inherited.

The principal danger lay, he wrote, with Andreas Papandreou and his 'revolutionary pronouncements'. Even George Papandreou now recognized that his son's public threats to the constitution were damaging; so too were his own links with the extreme left. To restore a more normal atmosphere, the elder Papandreou entered into an agreement with the King and Kanellopoulos to support a 'service government' in place of Stephanopoulos, and undertook to control his son. Consequently on 20 December Kanellopoulos withdrew ERE's support from Stephanopoulos' government, which duly resigned. The King at last agreed that elections were unavoidable, and appointed a 'service government' with a mandate to conduct them by the end of May 1967.

Rumours were reported in *Elevtheria* on 21 December that the fall of Stephanopoulos' government had been due to an intrigue between Kanellopoulos, Papandreou, and the King. In later reports, culminating on 1 January 1967, the alleged plot was extended to include Helen Vlakhos, the proprietor of *Kathimerini*, and Bitsios, the King's principal adviser. A memorandum was said to exist embodying their agreement with Kanellopoulos and Papandreou. The indirect object of the plot was said, by a train of argument which seemed perverse even for an Athenian rumour, to be to forestall the return of Karamanlis. Naturally, as Akhilleas wrote to him on New Year's day, Kanellopoulos entirely denied the rumour; and Mrs Vlakhos issued a writ for libel. The peculiar episode was characteristic of the current atmosphere of tension.

. Tsatsos wrote to Karamanlis on 9 January 1967 that 'if we

lose these elections, very probably they will be the last free elections for very many years'. What actually happened was worse even than his foreboding. The 'service government' won a vote of confidence on 13 January with the support of the Centre Union and ERE, but the shadow of the *Aspida* case hung over it. Once Parliament was dissolved, Andreas Papandreou would no longer enjoy immunity from arrest and trial.

On 24 February the court trying the twenty-eight officers asked that his immunity be lifted. At George Papandreou's request, the government tried to introduce a clause into its electoral law extending parliamentary immunity to the period of the election. But the ERE Deputies objected. Failing to carry its amendment, the 'service government' resigned on 30 March. The King then tried to form an all-party coalition, but George Papandreou refused his co-operation. Faced with this deadlock, the King then appointed Kanellopoulos on 3 April, at the head of a government drawn exclusively from ERE. Since he did not have a majority in Parliament, the King granted him the right of dissolution. Papandreou thereupon denounced the King, calling him the 'leader of ERE', and proclaiming that the election would also decide the fate of the monarchy.

During these early months of 1967, the political tension became intolerable. Effects of the tension reached Karamanlis in Paris. He learned of disagreements within ERE and of fears that the Centre Union and EDA would co-operate in the elections, leading in effect to the victory of the latter. 'Papandreou will surrender to EDA and the left Centrists,' wrote Tsatsos on 22 January; 'and the armed forces and security units will make no move after the elections to support the King nor to preserve order.' Pressure for Karamanlis' return revived. The King told Averoff and Tsatsos, according to the latter on 24 January, that Karamanlis was 'the only sure solution'. But at that time Karamanlis was away on another visit to the Bahamas and the USA. He told journalists in New York on the twenty-sixth that he had no comments on the speculation about his return. Even after his brother Akhilleas wrote to him on the twenty-eighth that Stephanopoulos, Markezinis, and Mitsotakis were all prepared to serve under him, he maintained the same position.

Kanellopoulos was talking of 'imminent dictatorship', according to a letter from Kondas on 1 March. Archbishop Iakovos told Karamanlis on the second, after a visit to Athens, that 'clearly we shall have a deviation either of the left or of the right if elections take place'. The term 'deviation' was now in standard use for a *coup d'état* leading to dictatorship. Most people thought it would come after the elections, and so it probably would have if the Generals instead of the Colonels had had their way.

Tsatsos visited Karamanlis in Paris on 8 March, but reported on his return to Athens that Karamanlis regarded his return to active politics as 'unlikely to prove helpful'. On the tenth Bitsios visited him again, and asked him what solution he would recommend to the King if he would not return himself. 'Off the cuff', he replied, 'I would suggest a combination of Markezinis and Tsakalotos, if I could convince you of their ability to succeed in such a mission'. Tsakalotos, as a retired General who had played a distinguished role in the civil war, could presumably control the Army. But Bitsios told Karamanlis that the King distrusted both men. He repeated that the King urgently desired his return.

The trial of the twenty-eight officers in the *Aspida* case ended on 16 March with fifteen convictions and thirteen acquittals. The case of Andreas Papandreou was now acutely urgent. Not only was there no chance of extending his immunity into the electoral period, but also that period could no longer be delayed, since Kanellopoulos had no prospect of winning a vote of confidence and must therefore exercise his right to dissolve Parliament. Additionally, serious disorders were breaking out in Athens, which would certainly be aggravated if Andreas Papandreou were arrested.

Karamanlis wrote to Tsatsos on 10 April advising against an immediate dissolution even if Kanellopoulos were defeated in a vote of confidence. He was doubtful whether it was wise of Kanellopoulos to have accepted office in any case. His letter concluded ominously: 'I hear you have all gone mad!' He repeated his fears of a 'deviation' unless his own advice were followed. Ten days later he was proved right.

Chapter 8

Confronting the Colonels

KANELLOPOULOS decided on 14 April 1967 to dissolve Parliament and hold elections on 28 May. But during the night of 20–21 April a group of middle-rank officers led by Colonel George Papadopoulos seized power with the support of key units of the Army. Kanellopoulos and George Papandreou were placed under house arrest; Andreas Papandreou, along with many leading figures of the left, was taken to prison, threatened with trial on charges of complicity in a Communist plot. He was later released and allowed to go into exile, but others were less mercifully treated.

The King reluctantly acquiesced in the coup and in the suspension of parts of the constitution. He agreed to swear in the revolutionary government on condition that a civilian Prime Minister was appointed. The senior public prosecutor, Constantine Kollias, agreed to serve; and the Chief of the General Staff, General Spandidakis, also joined the new government. But effective power rested with Papadopoulos and his two military colleagues, Colonel Makarezos and Brigadier Pattakos, with other shadowy figures behind them: notably Brigadier Ioannidis, their expert in secret intelligence.

Karamanlis' first instinct was to say: 'I told you so!' He issued a statement in Paris which was not published in Athens, but soon became known. In it he said that he had 'foreseen these developments and tried to save Greece's unstable democracy by the enlightenment of our political habits and the modernization of our country's political system'. He had withdrawn because he saw that he was wasting his time. Since then there had been many blunders, for which everyone was to blame, but most of all the leader of the Centre Union. He went on: 'If Papandreou had conducted his policy with elementary intelligence, the country would never have arrived at the present perilous contingency. Instead he made the blunder of letting loose a storm of passions, threatening individuals and institutions, and creating the climate which nourished yesterday's *coup d'état*.' This was to be his last public statement for seven months.

Behind the scenes, however, correspondence and contacts went on. Archbishop Iakovos, who could travel freely between Athens, Paris, and New York, was a useful intermediary. On 29 May Karamanlis wrote to him about his fear that the military dictatorship, already known as the Junta, would prove permanent, whatever its professions. 'Dictatorship is a dangerous experiment,' he wrote. 'That is why I refused it even when it was offered to me by the Army and the Crown.'

Soon afterwards he received a letter from Kollias, the puppet Prime Minister, containing proposals for constitutional reform. He replied on 20 June welcoming this indication of a recognition that the revolution could only be a temporary expedient. He accepted that it was a reaction to an anomalous situation, but its mission must be 'the early restoration of democracy on securer foundations'. He hoped that was the intention, but if there were any delay, 'then it must leave the initiative to the Arbiter of the constitution, giving him its own support'. Kollias sent him what Karamanlis later called 'a more or less reassuring reply'. News of Karamanlis' message also reached the King, who communicated his thanks through Archbishop Iakovos on 25 September.

By the same channel Karamanlis learned of reactions in the USA, which the King visited in early September. The King met President Johnson and the Secretaries of State and Defence, Rusk and Macnamara, as well as a number of senators. They promised him moral and material support and undertook to press the revolutionaries 'to restore the country to parliamentary normality'. A report which reached Karamanlis in the following month, based on conversations with the Greek military attaché in Washington, was less encouraging. It suggested that although the Americans disapproved of the Junta, they were giving it 'the support of toleration' in the hope that it would weaken Communist influences in Greece. They hoped for an eventual return to normality as a result. This optimism was not shared by the King, still less by Karamanlis.

At the end of October the King sent an ADC to tell Karamanlis of his conviction that 'whatever the revolutionaries may say, they are determined to make the present state of things permanent'. The ADC indicated that the King was ready for a clash with them. He asked whether Karamanlis would be ready to lead a transitional government if they were removed. Karamanlis categorically refused, but added that although he did not want to return to politics, he would be prepared to take part in subsequent elections 'if that is judged to be a national duty'.

He also asked the ADC what forces the King could rely on. The answer was that the revolutionaries were too strong in the capital, where they completely dominated the Army, but 'in Macedonia the King could easily lead a counter-revolution, especially as he controls the Navy and most of the Air Force.' Karamanlis warned the King to be very careful in making thorough preparations, 'for possible failure would be a calamity'.

On 9 November Karamanlis sent a long letter to the King by hand of his ADC. After stressing his doubts—despite Kollias' reassurances in response to his letter of 20 June—about the intentions of the revolutionaries, he reminded the King of his reasons for refusing to return: 'The most fundamental was my belief that democracy could not function in Greece without a cleaning-up and modernization of our public life, beginning with the constitution.' Democracy had since collapsed: the Colonels only gave it the *coup de grâce*. It was unfortunate that the political parties had not followed the French precedent, even at the last minute. The consequence was the 'harsh reality' of the dictatorship. The problem of removing the revolutionaries could therefore not be separated from that of removing the conditions which led to their 'deviation'. He believed that a well-conceived plan for eliminating these conditions in advance would either persuade the revolutionaries to relinquish power of their own accord or enable others to compel them to do so.

The actual overthrow of the Junta, he continued, could be achieved in one of two ways: either by the sudden resignation of Kollias and the simultaneous appointment of a strong and determined government; or by the establishment of a legitimate government at Salonika or elsewhere. The new government would have to be carefully chosen in advance by the

King, excluding all the failed politicians of the last three years. He defined its functions thus: to assuage passions and create the psychological conditions for the reconstruction and modernization of political life; to draft a new constitution, which must be 'strict but not undemocratic'; to reform the the administration and educational system; to clean up the national economy by 'radical and unpopular measures'; to restore discipline in the armed forces; and to settle the Cyprus problem, about which he reaffirmed his belief that 'through independence we should easily be on the way to *enosis* if in the meantime we had created the right psychological and diplomatic conditions.' Lastly, the government should conduct a plebiscite and elections.

Karamanlis ended his letter by saying that he could elaborate his views in greater detail if the King would nominate 'the man who is to execute the proposed plan'. Clearly it was not to be himself: he had already refused to lead a transitional government. But the King never replied. Later he explained that his reply had been overtaken by events.

It was a new crisis in Cyprus that brought events to a climax. On 15 November Grivas launched a vicious attack on a Turkish village, which led the Turkish government to retaliate with air strikes and threats of an invasion. Under pressure from the King, Papadopoulos recalled Grivas to Athens, and withdrew some ten thousand Greek troops from the island. In an effort to forestall disaster, Pipinelis agreed to serve the Junta as Foreign Minister. At the same time Makarezos, one of the three military leaders of the Junta, sent an emissary to Karamanlis with an oral message seeking his advice. Karamanlis replied on 24 November that he could give no advice because he had no confidence in the Colonels; 'and besides, it is too late'.

For the first time since April, Karamanlis expressed his views in public on 29 November, by giving an interview with *Le Monde*. He spoke of Cyprus, where he said the natural solution was *enosis*, with concessions to the Turks. He insisted on 'the departure of the revolutionary government, before it is too late'. He described the conditions which led to the coup, but added that it could nevertheless have been averted. He was sceptical about the alleged threat from the Communists, which in any case was less serious than the threat of 'political and moral anarchy'.

When he was asked who was responsible for the abolition of democracy, he replied: 'None and all.' He explained his refusal to return to Greece in his customary terms. The present situation, he said, was 'dangerous and difficult'. He disbelieved the revolutionaries' claim that they intended to restore democracy. He repeatedly insisted that they must resign and restore authority to the King. He defined the conditions necessary for the restoration of democracy in terms identical with his recent letter to the King; and he also separately emphasized the need for constitutional reform.

On the day after this interview was published, Karamanlis was visited by a senior American Ambassador, who told him that the US government was pressing the Junta to hold elections. Karamanlis commented that he would prefer that the Greeks should 'find their own course without the intervention of the Americans'. He also impressed on the Ambassador the need to restrain the Turks, because if a humiliation were inflicted on Greece 'no one can save the situation'. The Colonels were in fact losing control over themselves and preparing to face a war with Turkey over Cyprus, which they could not possibly win. They published a frenzied retort to Karamanlis' interview with *Le Monde*, accusing him of supporting the line of the KKE. To this foolish outburst Karamanlis made a brief and dignified reply. Before the Junta could retort again, a new crisis had been precipitated.

The King had for some time been planning, with a small group of loyal officers, an attempt to overthrow the Junta. Unfortunately he and Karamanlis were now at cross purposes. Karamanlis' public demand that the Colonels should restore power to the King caused them to watch the King's activities more closely than ever. Although the crisis over Cyprus shook their confidence, it also sharpened their alertness. But the King could not delay his plan of action for long if it were not to be betrayed. He launched it, with inadequate preparation, on 13 December.

He flew to the north, where he expected support, and declared the government dismissed. But his appeal to the armed forces to support him had very limited success. The Junta was already well informed of his intentions, and had no difficulty in reasserting their own control. On the following day the King recognized that his plan had failed, and flew out of Greece from Kavalla, with the tacit consent of the Colonels. He was accompanied by his wife and family, including the Queen Mother. Karamanlis was taken by suprise. His first comment to his wife, on hearing the news by telephone, was: 'I told him seven times not to do it!'

Constantine settled in Rome, and from there he telephoned Karamanlis on 19 and 20 December. Karamanlis formed the impression that the King would probably return to Greece, but on humiliating conditions. The failure of his counter-revolution caused the US government to become less hostile to the Junta, which itself became more arrogant. On 14 February 1968 Papadopoulos wrote the King an insolent letter, to which he prepared a somewhat feeble reply.

Before sending it, he telephoned Karamanlis again on 28 February, asking him to receive Leonidas Papagos, the late Field Marshal's son, on his behalf. Papagos showed him the King's draft, which Karamanlis advised him not to send. He also refused to take any initiative himself. On 4 April he saw Papagos again, and declined his proposal of a meeting with the King in Zurich. He refused again to take office if the Junta fell.

When Papagos came a third time on 23 July, to show Karamanlis a draft letter from the King commenting on the new constitution drawn up by the Junta, he merely remarked that it was 'brief and feeble', and advised against sending it. Again he refused to meet the King. But he gave Papagos his own comments on the Colonels' constitution, which he called 'a camouflaged dictatorship'. He also sent his advice to the King to make contact with Pipinelis and the Americans. His contempt for the young King was barely disguised. They had not met since Constantine came to the throne, and to Karamanlis, in his wife's words, Constantine remained simply 'Paul's naughty little boy'.

As the year 1968 progressed, the pressures on Karamanlis to resume a political role came from other directions. Mitsotakis, who was also living in self-imposed exile in Paris, made a statement to *Le Monde* on 1 August suggesting the possibility of a union of the political parties under Karamanlis. The Greek

Ambassador in Washington, Xanthopoulos-Palamas, broached
the possibility of Karamanlis' return in the same month; but
his reply on 28 August was that he would only return if he
were 'unanimously invited' and only after the removal of 'all
those men', which clearly they would not accept.

His brother Akhilleas also wrote to him in the same month,
saying that his silence was being misinterpreted. He replied
on 1 September that he was silent because he had nothing to
add to his statement in the previous November. It was unusual
for a Greek politician to regard a previous statement as a sufficient reason for silence, so misinterpretation was natural.
But when the Colonels asked him indirectly for his comments
on their constitution, which was ratified by a plebiscite on
29 September, he again repeated that he had nothing to say.

Some of his colleagues thought his attitude too negative,
Averoff wrote to him on 14 October about the possibility of
talks with the Colonels, with whom he had indirect contact.
Before Karamanlis could reply, there came the news that
George Papandreou had died. His funeral, to which Karamanlis
sent a wreath, was the occasion of a massive demonstration of
hostility to the dictatorship. Kanellopoulos delivered a memorable funeral oration; but unfortunately one of Papandreou's
followers used the occasion to make a speech eulogizing the
'relentless struggle'.

When Karamanlis replied to Averoff on 24 November, this
occasion called for comment as well as the contacts with the
Junta. The significance of his wreath, he said, had been forgive-
ness and reconciliation; but the allusion to the 'relentless
struggle' was typical of the spirit which had destroyed Greek
democracy and led to the dictatorship. As for the idea of talks
with the dictators, he could not approve it until they were
ready 'to seek the honourable solution of a return to secure
normality'. His own policy, he added, was now to enlist the
pressure of foreign opinion against them.

His channels for enlisting foreign pressure during 1969 were
through NATO in Paris and through Archbishop Iakovos in
the United States; but they had little success. The new
American President, Richard Nixon, as Karamanlis wrote to
Xanthopoulos-Palamas on 1 February, found himself pressed
by Greeks supporting the Junta on the one side and Greeks

opposing it on the other side, so that he could only have the worst impressions of the Greeks. Palamas' reply, on 14 April, showed things to be even worse than Karamanlis feared.

On the occasion of Eisenhower's funeral on 2 April, the King and Pattakos had been in Washington simultaneously. Nixon had refused to see the King or to intervene in Greece; but he had met Pattakos and formed a favourable opinion of him. In view of the defence talks initiated by Nixon with the Colonels, there was little prospect of American pressure on them. Similar indications reached Karamanlis from friends in Athens who were in touch with US officials there.

It was suggested from Athens that the US government might be more receptive to persuasion if the democratic parties in Greece could be induced to present a united front. Karamanlis was sceptical, but the suggestion was pressed by both Kanellopoulos and Andreas Papandreou. The latter wrote to Karamanlis on 13 February from Canada, where he had settled, to say that he not only accepted but prayed for 'a Karamanlis solution'. Soon afterwards George Papandreou's lawyer conveyed to Karamanlis the late leader's political testament, which stressed the need for co-operation between Karamanlis and Andreas, not forgetting the King but excluding the Communists.

Gradually a proposal took shape to draft a joint declaration of all the political parties, perhaps leading to a merger under Karamanlis' leadership. But Karamanlis wrote twice to Averoff in the spring of 1969, on 2 April and 3 May, asking that the talks should not proceed. Kanellopoulos also expressed doubts, in a letter of 16 June, whether co-operation was possible with Andreas Papandreou so long as he went on attacking the Americans. But he also reported advice from Washington that a merger under Karamanlis would have a good effect on American opinion.

Despite Karamanlis' disapproval, the talks in Athens went on during the summer of 1969. His friends, especially Kanellopoulos, reported regularly on their progress, which was slow and difficult. Karamanlis' replies were sceptical but not wholly negative. On 1 August he wrote approving the co-option of George Mavros, the new leader of the Centre Union, and Markezinis; but he was doubtful about Andreas

Papandreou, with whom he had no common ground. 'One and one do not always make two,' he commented: 'often they make zero.'

He also hinted that he was contemplating an initiative of his own. This was more important to him than inter-party talks, which in any case broke down because the Centre Union refused to allow the 'apostates' who had supported Stephanopoulos to sign the draft declaration. Kanellopoulos told Karamanlis that only his reputation was equal to the task of leadership; but he had insisted that his name should not be used, so it was not to be.

Meanwhile the Colonels tried again to start a dialogue with him. Xanthopoulos-Palamas, now an Under-Secretary in the Ministry of Foreign Affairs, wrote on 16 August urging him to agree, but he replied on the twenty-eighth that no dialogue was possible without good faith. Papakonstantinou also wrote on 2 September about the Colonels' desire for a dialogue, but he replied tersely on the fourth urging him not to be taken in.

On 28 September he wrote again to Papakonstantinou to say that he was about to issue a public statement, and asking that the party leaders, especially Mavros, should support it at once. It was published on 1 October, the first anniversary of the Colonels' new constitution, and the politicians in Athens duly supported it. The statement constituted much the strongest attack that Karamanlis had yet made on the Junta. Their regime was a 'tyrannical and illegitimate institution'; they had never intended, as they said, to restore democracy; their political ideas were 'medieval and theocratic'. By their blunders they had caused the disintegration of the armed forces; they had undermined the economic future of the country; they had isolated Greece both politically and morally. Now they were resorting to 'terrorization of the Greek people and deception of international public opinion'. He saw their downfall as inevitable. Before it was too late, they must hand over power. They must recognize that 'the geopolitical position of Greece and the character of its people' were quite unsuited to dictatorship. Their only alternatives were to withdraw peacefully or to be overthrown. It was the duty of their fellow officers to impress this fact on them. In conclusion, he himself was ready 'if necessary, to contribute personally to the task'.

Uncompromising though this statement was, he hoped it would provide the Colonels with the opportunity to start a 'serious and honourable dialogue'. With this in view, he decided to make use of Lieutenant-General Solon Ghikas, a retired Chief of the General Staff, with whom he had a relationship of confidence and friendship. In a letter to Ghikas dated 28 September, he asked him to use his influence with the Colonels. But he added that 'if the government chooses war, you must examine with a group of your friends and colleagues what should be done next with my initiative, so that it does not fall into the void'. This could have been read as an invitation to a military counter-revolution.

Ghikas reported on 11 October that the Colonels were adamant. Papadopoulos and Makarezos attacked Karamanlis at a press conference; Makarezos and Pattakos told Ghikas that they would not discuss the matter. They blamed Karamanlis for what they called 'terrorist activities' against them, which he publicly repudiated on 23 October. The most disappointing outcome was that only one courageous newspaper, *Vradyni*, and one retired General openly supported Karamanlis' initiative. There was to be no counter-revolution.

The year 1970 was perhaps the most depressing time of Karamanlis' self-imposed exile. Apart from the failure to make any impression on the Junta, it was also the year in which his marriage finally broke down. That he did after all contemplate a return to political life was confirmed, if it had ever been in doubt, by a question he put to Tsatsos: would a divorce damage him politically? Tsatsos' reply was that it would not, but a remarriage would. Amalia divorced him and returned to Athens in 1970. She remarried, but Karamanlis did not. The episode left no aftermath of bitterness, but the year was notably barren of correspondence with Athens.

Having failed to spark any internal movement against the Junta, Karamanlis turned again to the possibilities of external pressure. There was limited satisfaction to be had from the enforced withdrawal of Greece from the Council of Europe, to forestall expulsion, on 12 December 1969. Karamanlis commented that 'the dictatorship has cut off Greece from the body of Europe'. But such weapons were two-edged: they encouraged opposition, but they humiliated all Greeks. There was a similar ambiguity about Karamanlis' approaches to the Americans. As he wrote to Tsatsos on 31 March 1970, it was deplorable to have to give the impression that 'it is for the Americans to decide how the Greeks are to be governed'.

It was deplorable but unavoidable. Nixon's defence advisers attached great importance to Greece, and his Vice-President, Spiro Agnew was half-Greek and devoted to the Colonels. Early in 1970 the faithful Archbishop Iakovos had a meeting with the President, for which Karamanlis armed him with a long memorandum when he passed through Paris. In it he wrote that he appreciated the US policy of non-intervention, but stressed that the Greek problem was also a problem for NATO, especially because of the growing threat from the Soviet Union to the Mediterranean and the crisis in the Middle East. Soviet propaganda against the USA and Turkish propaganda against Greece must compel the US government to take a position on Greece. What was it to be?

The problem, he argued, was military and national as well as political and economic. Greek morale was low, especially because of the failure of the Americans to intervene, which was leading to anti-American feeling. There was a need for urgent pressure to force a change of government. The Junta would resist it, but must be told that Greece could not endure another 'show-down'—he wrote the word in English—like that at the Council of Europe. By implication, he meant an attempt to expel Greece from NATO.

There were only three possible courses, he wrote: first, a violent overthrow of the Junta, which ought to be avoided; second, its voluntary withdrawal, which it would resist; third, elections to be held under the Junta, which could not possibly be fair or satisfactory. Of these three courses, the second was the preferable one, despite the unavoidable resistance of the Colonels. He recommended pressure by the USA to bring it about.

The memorandum was handed to President Nixon on 20 February 1970, but the results were disappointing. The Americans feared that if the Colonels fell, chaos and eventually Communism would be the result. They valued their bases in Greece, and they hoped to negotiate home-port facilities for the Sixth Fleet at Peiraeus. It was not until a year later that Averoff was able to report to Karamanlis, in a letter from Athens on 10 February 1971, the first signs of American disappointment with the Junta and the beginnings of pressure on it.

Even then the indications were ambiguous. Some of Karamanlis' correspondents—notably his brother Akhilleas, George Rallis, and Averoff—reported a state of confusion in American policy. This arose chiefly from a conflict between the White House and the Congress. On 24 April the President wrote to Papadopoulos congratulating him on the economic progress of the last four years; but on 3 August the House of Representatives voted to suspend economic aid to Greece. The latter decision was a gesture of disapproval, and not, as it would have been in Karamanlis' day, a vote of confidence.

But at least the US Ambassador in Athens, Henry Tasca, seemed willing to listen to reason. On 7 July 1971 the King telephoned Karamanlis from Rome to say that he was expecting a visit from Tasca the next day. Tasca told the King on the eighth that his government was pressing Papadopoulos to restore democracy, which he said he was willing to do but for his internal difficulties and the risk of a crisis in Cyprus. These were perennial excuses, but the King thought it worth while to advise Tasca to visit Karamanlis in Paris.

Karamanlis was extremely sceptical, for Tasca had hitherto been notoriously sympathetic to the Colonels. Besides, he was about to go on holiday. He was therefore in no hurry for a meeting. It did not take place until 30 September, and nothing new emerged from it. But it was given a false significance by the Americans' decision to publish the fact that it had taken place. The Colonels reacted with a denunciation of both Karamanlis and Tasca. But their annoyance did not prevent the conclusion of an agreement with the Americans to allow the home-port facilities required by the Sixth Fleet at Peiraeus.

Meanwhile discussions had been resumed in Athens on the possibility of a common front between the parties. All of them, including Andreas Papandreou and the Communists, had responded favourably to Karamanlis' statement on 1 October 1969. Several of Karamanlis' colleagues tried to pursue discussions with that as their basis, but the results were disappointing. Their letters to Karamanlis at regular intervals over the next two years kept him informed of the difficulties. But it was clear that many difficulties would be removed if he himself were willing to assume the leadership.

Tsatsos wrote to him on 16 June 1971 that 'if anything unforeseen happens—and the more unforeseen the better—your immediate presence will provide the way out, the only way for us to proceed in a normal fashion back to normality'. The assumption that he alone could command the necessary support was confirmed when George Mavros told the Italian newspaper, *Messaggero*, in November 1971 that the Centre Union would accept the leadership of Karamanlis.

Some members of ERE, however, while completely loyal to Karamanlis, had ideas of their own with which they thought it worth while at least to experiment. There was a revival of the possibility of a dialogue with the Colonels, who made an indirect approach to Averoff in April 1971. He had several times written to Karamanlis during the previous year expressing the conviction that the Colonels had no intention of restoring democracy, whatever they might say. But he did not immediately rebuff their approach. He wrote on 21 April—the fourth anniversary of their coup—to assure Karamanlis that he would handle Papadopoulos' approach with extreme care. It was not long before he returned to his original conviction that it was a waste of time to discuss political changes with the Colonels. From the beginning of 1973, his mind turned to another and more drastic course.

Meanwhile a group of less important members of ERE, together with colleagues in the Centre Union, decided on an initiative of their own. Tired of the fruitless discussions of a common front among their leaders, they issued a joint declaration in October 1972 that past animosity between their parties must cease. They themselves would support any initiative and any tactics which Karamanlis might prescribe. They simply wanted him to come back and take control.

Their initiative displeased both Kanellopoulos and Mavros. Papakonstantinou and Tsatsos both wrote to Karamanlis on 27 October to say that they had discouraged members of ERE from signing the declaration, and only some thirty had done so. Karamanlis published a statement on 7 November dissociating himself from the declaration. What annoyed him, as he wrote to Papakonstantinou on the ninth, was the implied suggestion that he should lead a transitional government, which he had consistently refused to do.

Tsatsos wrote again on 5 January 1973 to say that he recognized Karamanlis' unwillingness to have his name associated with transitional plans. But support from abroad, especially from the USA, was indispensable, and only Karamanlis' name carried any weight there. On 2 February Papakonstantinou also wrote again, to say that a common front could still be achieved, with the tacit implication that Karamanlis' name was essential to it. Once more Karamanlis insisted that his name must not be used in any way.

Numerous letters followed during February and March from these and other colleagues, all with a common theme: the talks were continuing, they had American support, but the Americans wanted Karamanlis involved. Still he refused. But on 23 April he issued another long statement of his own. It was boldly published by *Vradyni* in Athens, and by one newspaper in Salonika.

Once more he analysed in detail the crimes and follies of the Junta. He particularly emphasized the demoralization which they had caused in the armed forces, and their responsibility for creating 'a psychological gulf between the armed forces and the people, with incalculable damage to the nation'. He reaffirmed that 'the highest national interests require the restoration of democratic normality'. He even told the Colonels exactly how to bring it about: 'Let the government recall the King, who is the symbol of legality, and surrender its position to a strong, experienced government.'

The statement had a greater impact than its predecessor in 1969. All the party leaders and the foreign press welcomed it. Tsatsos wrote on 3 May that its publication had greatly increased Karamanlis' popularity. Similar reports came from other friends. His brother Akhilleas wrote on 25 May that the impression made on the armed forces had been favourable, except that the reference to the King as 'the symbol of legality' had caused some reservations. This last point was undoubtedly made in the light of a startling event which occurred the day

before, when the Junta announced the frustration of a conspiracy in the Navy. They claimed that Karamanlis' statement
had been issued in order to provide 'political cover' for the
conspiracy.

It was true that Karamanlis had heard in advance of the
plot, but not that he had any part in it. It was not the first
naval plot that had come to his ears. Twice in September 1969
emissaries had come to seek his advice on behalf of the King
about a conspiracy of naval officers, but he had given them
no encouragement. He had not then regarded the supposed
plans as serious, nor had he sought details of them. The memory of the King's fiasco in December 1967 was too recent.
But in 1973 the emissary was Averoff, and he was not coming
on behalf of the King.

The naval conspiracy included retired officers and others
still on active service, led by Captain Papadongonas. The
intention was that as many naval units as possible should con-
centrate at Syros and send an ultimatum to Athens demanding
the resignation of the Junta. If that was refused, the ships
would sail to Peiraeus and establish a blockade. If necessary,
they would cut the main routes into Athens by gunfire. The
blockade would continue until the Junta resigned. Naturally
the plotters placed no reliance on the Army, but they thought
they had secured the neutrality of the Air Force.

Early in 1973 Papadongonas approached Averoff to seek
'political cover' for the attempt. Averoff replied that his own
name was insufficient for their purpose, but he agreed to
approach Karamanlis. He went to Paris with this aim in early
March. When Karamanlis heard of the plot, he expressed
doubts about its feasibility. He would not immediately com-
mit himself, but asked Averoff to come back the next day. He
then dictated a note, which Averoff wrote down. Karamanlis'
recollection of it was terse: 'I told him that I cannot take
responsibility for a movement over which I can have no control.' Averoff's account from memory slightly expanded these
words: 'I respect the intention. I cannot either encourage or
discourage something of which I know nothing. If it occurs,
I will assist by declarations from here aimed at achieving a
compromise solution.'

Averoff returned to Athens with this reply, which he read

out to Papadongonas. The latter said it was satisfactory, although Averoff insisted that it was neutral. The Junta was later to claim that it did not satisfy the conspirators, and that Karamanlis therefore issued his statement of 23 April to give them more encouragement.

In fact Karamanlis had no intention of encouraging them when he drafted his statement, which was indeed neutral. He twice sent messages to Averoff through third parties, to tell him that there were widespread rumours of the conspiracy current outside Greece. Both of them concluded that it was badly organized and not to be taken seriously. Averoff therefore insisted on seeing Papadongonas again, but was unable to do so until 21 May, only three days before the plot was exposed. In fact it had already been betrayed. Only one destroyer, under Commander Pappas, avoided seizure by the security police and sailed for the western Mediterranean.

The Junta at once sought to implicate the King and Karamanlis in the plot. They issued a statement accusing both on 1 June, which Karamanlis repudiated the next day. On the fourth Averoff sent Karamanlis a brief note to say that he was under surveillance. He added that, whatever happened, 'I will insist on the truth: that I had no contact with anyone in the naval conspiracy and that I brought you no message and received none from you.' He wrote another letter to Karamanlis on 13 June, setting out the same line in greater detail. Both letters were clearly phrased on the assumption that they might be intercepted. Eventually Averoff was arrested on 3 July. At his interrogation he admitted his meeting with Karamanlis, but insisted that neither he nor Karamanlis had given the conspirators any encouragement.

Karamanlis also repeatedly denied any connection with the conspiracy. Of greater importance to him was the exploitation of it by the Colonels to overthrow even their own parody of a constitution. On 1 June they announced the abolition of the monarchy and the introduction of a republican constitution with Papadopoulos as President. There was to be a plebiscite on the new constitution and the Presidency within two months, and elections by the end of 1974. Karamanlis at once denounced the new constitution, as did Kanellopoulos and other political leaders in Athens and the King from abroad.

The King twice declared, on 9 June and 24 July, that after the dictatorship was overthrown there would be a free plebiscite on the form of the constitution. Karamanlis cited the first of these statements, in his own statement of 19 June, in order to encourage anti-monarchists to vote 'No' on the Colonels' constitution. It was on his encouragement that the King repeated his undertaking. Karamanlis issued a further attack on the Colonels on 16 July, to which they responded in their accustomed manner.

During June many of Karamanlis' friends wrote to urge him to return at once to Greece, since this alone might cause the immediate collapse of the Junta. But Karamanlis had a more realistic appreciation of the determination of the Colonels. They were still accumulating evidence against him in connection with the naval conspiracy, the tale of which was still unfolding. On 13 July they claimed to have further proof of the complicity of the King and Karamanlis.

The evidence was that on 9 July the commander of a destroyer had been approached at the French port of St. Raphael by Pappas and a civilian with a proposal that they should sail to the Italian port of Fiumicino, where they would take aboard the King and Karamanlis to go to Athens. Karamanlis' friends admitted that this encounter took place, but denied that Karamanlis knew of it. Formal charges were laid against him, however, on 21 July, and a court order was issued for his interrogation, which never took place. The Colonels were satisfied that they had achieved their object of discrediting Karamanlis and the King in preparation for the plebiscite, which took place on 29 July.

The poll amounted to three-quarters of the electorate. Of those who voted, slightly more than three-quarters supported Papadopoulos and the Republic. On the next day Tsatsos wrote despondently to Karamanlis withdrawing his advice of an early return. The political leaders in Athens, with Kanellopoulos in the van, issued a general denunciation of the plebiscite on 14 August. On the nineteenth Papadopoulos was sworn into office as President. He announced an amnesty for crimes committed against the regime since 21 April 1967, which led to the release of Averoff and Captain Papadongonas among others. But the amnesty was expressly framed to cover

only crimes committed within Greek jurisdiction. This defini-
tion excluded Karamanlis; not that he had any intention of
returning to Greece at the time.

During the next few months an inconclusive correspondence
took place between Karamanlis and his colleagues on the
question whether ERE should take part in the elections if
and when they were held. Karamanlis' advice was that the
political parties should prescribe specific conditions to the
Colonels, which would amount to complete guarantees of
free elections. Then either the Junta would accept them, im-
probable as it seemed, in which case the deadlock would be
ended; or it would refuse them, which would bring it into
public disrepute and give a psychological boost to the parties.
It mattered little, for no elections were ever to take place
under the dictatorship. The correspondence was overtaken by
events.

The last year of the Junta was not so much a Greek tragedy
as a black farce. A new twist was given to the plot when
Papadopoulos approached Markezinis, in September 1973, to
become his Prime Minister. It was rumoured that Markezinis
tried to consult Karamanlis, who maintained absolute silence.
On 1 October Markezinis accepted the derisory office, and
his government was sworn in a week later. He then announced
that elections would be held shortly; but in this he was
mistaken.

Protests against the Junta had begun among the students
early in 1973, at the Athens Law School. There were many
arrests throughout the year. The fifth anniversary of the death
of George Papandreou on 4 November gave the opportunity
for further demonstrations, and still more arrests. On 13 November the government closed the universities throughout the
country. The next day students occupied the Athens Polytechnic, supported by many of their teachers. The occupation
lasted until the seventeenth, when Papadopoulos declared
martial law and sent tanks to break down the gates. More
than twenty students were killed—perhaps as many as forty,
for the exact number could never be established. Markezinis
disgraced his reputation by appearing on television to support
the Junta's action.

After the proclamation of martial law, Kanellopoulos issued a call for 'the immediate formation of a government of national unity'. He did not name Karamanlis because he knew his wishes; and the Junta claimed that he had no authority to speak for Karamanlis. Although Kanellopoulos claimed to be speaking on behalf of the political world, several members of ERE expressed reservations in writing to Karamanlis. Support for the appeal and calls for Karamanlis' return now came from the left. Six members of the Centre Union issued a statement on 22 November that Karamanlis' return was the only way to achieve 'the reconciliation of the people and the armed forces'. From Canada Andreas Papandreou sent a telegram to Karamanlis in English, chiding him for his silence.

The King also wanted to make a statement, but only in conjunction with Karamanlis. He telephoned Karamanlis from London suggesting that they should issue parallel statements on the massacre at the Polytechnic. But Karamanlis saw no point in wasting words on events which spoke for themselves. The brutal episode had shown the dependence of the Junta on mere force, but now even its force was disintegrating. Papadopoulos had already rid himself of his chief military associates, Pattakos and Makarezos, before he set up Markezinis as his puppet. Now the Generals decided that the time had come to be rid of Papadopoulos himself. The coup which removed him was managed with practised treachery by the head of Military Security, Brigadier Ioannidis, who had once been his staunch supporter. Papadopoulos was arrested and replaced as President by Lieutenant-General Phaidon Gizikis; Markezinis was replaced by a nonentity.

Efforts were now made to dissociate the new regime from the reputation of its predecessor. Most of the arrested students were released, and the universities reopened. The curfew was lifted, and so was the censorship, at least on paper. Gizikis published a decree limiting the powers and tenure of the Presidency; he even spoke of a return to democracy. There were widespread replacements in the high command of the armed forces. An investigation was announced into corruption under Papadopoulos. The Archbishop of Athens, who admitted his collaboration with the Junta ('from disinterested motives', he said), was coerced into resignation.

But it was impossible to hide the reality that Ioannidis was the actual master of Greece, and he soon showed it. Incongruously, it was he who informed the newspaper editors of the end of censorship; but the alternative to censorship proved worse. On 1 December the courageous newspaper *Vradyni* was forcibly closed, and its office padlocked. Karamanlis' friends thought the reason was that it was widely read in the armed forces. Although the proprietor was informed that the closure would last six months, that proved to be a false forecast.

The new government naturally blamed the bloodshed at the Polytechnic on everyone but themselves, from the KKE to Kanellopoulos. The latter, together with the leaders of the Centre Union, replied on 11 December with a statement laying the blame where it belonged. Evidently the change of government had brought little relief. In the first half of 1974 the approaching climax became unmistakable. Arrests and deportations were announced every week; the island of Gioura (where Karamanlis had sheltered in 1944) was restored to use as a concentration camp; allegations of torture multiplied. The government sought desperately for a dramatic way of reversing its unpopularity. But those who were not crazy with power could see as well as the rest of the Greek people that there was only one possible candidate for the role of *deus ex machina.*

Pressure was steadily increased on Karamanlis to break his silence and make himself available. Papakonstantinou, Averoff, Rallis, and General Ghikas all wrote to him between January and June 1974 to suggest that his continued silence could be damaging. From Archbishop Iakovos he learned in April that Tasca, the American Ambassador, wanted to meet him in Paris, but Karamanlis was absent over the Easter holiday. Tasca met his brother Akhilleas instead, and repeated his desire to meet Karamanlis, but there was no response. There were good reasons for his reluctance and his silence.

Archbishop Iakovos' letters showed that although Tasca had concluded that there was 'no way out except by calling on you', his opinions had no great weight with Kissinger. A similar report came through Akhilleas on 24 April. He wrote that Makarezos, one of the original members of the Junta but now out of office, had returned from a visit to the USA with the impression that Nixon, the Pentagon, and the CIA all favoured a 'Karamanlis solution', but Kissinger was 'in no hurry to take up the Greek question'. Makarezos himself favoured the 'Karamanlis solution', but had no influence on his former colleagues. The currently ruling group was ambiguous on the subject. Sometimes Ioannidis liked to hint that he was in touch with Karamanlis, sometimes he gave the impression of regarding Karamanlis as 'undesirable'. The latter view was confirmed by the confiscation of a Patras periodical for the offence of publishing a picture of Karamanlis on 21 May, his name-day.

In these confused circumstances there was nothing to be gained by issuing general pronouncements on the political scene. Karamanlis confined himself to particular occasions, such as Ioannidis' decision to prolong the ban on *Vradyni* when the first period of six months was coming to an end. On 29 May he issued a short comment that the continued ban had a general as well as a particular significance: 'Those who exercise power in the name of the armed forces of the country not only have no intention of restoring normality but are deliberately trying to make it impossible.' His next public pronouncement was to be on a far more critical event.

The final crisis emerged in the Aegean and exploded in Cyprus. In the Aegean there were expectations of oil being found under the sea-bed, which led both the Greeks and the Turks to prepare for exploration. Rivalry between Greek and Turkish claims, which included not only the continental shelf under the sea but also territorial waters and control of the airspace, came to a head in the spring of 1974. The Greeks withdrew from a NATO exercise in protest at Turkish violations of Greek airspace. At the end of May a Turkish survey-ship sailed into the Aegean, and soon afterwards the Greek government threatened to extend Greece's territorial waters unilaterally. The US government offered to mediate, but in vain. The remnants of the Junta were set upon the course of the Gadarene swine.

Two comments written by Karamanlis' correspondents summarize the disastrous situation. On 24 April Akhilleas wrote that 'the militarists . . . do not understand the problems which are accumulating, so as to apply proper solutions, and think they are doing well.' On the nineteenth Averoff sent a memorandum to Gizikis, with a copy to Karamanlis, arguing that not only Cyprus and the Greeks of Istanbul were now at risk but also 'still worse, the fate of the root and the body of Hellenism is in jeopardy.' He foresaw war 'within the year'.

Ioannidis, however, saw a characteristic way out of the impasse. It was to achieve *enosis* in Cyprus by means of yet another coup. Success would both forestall action by the Turks and re-establish the prestige of his regime. But it would first be necessary to remove Makarios, who now preferred his status as head of state to the achievement of *enosis*. It seems probable that Ioannidis discussed his plans with agents of the CIA. Certainly rumours of them were leaked and reached Makarios. He sent a long letter to Gizikis on 2 July, alleging a conspiracy to murder him and demanding the removal of Greek officers with the Cypriot National Guard. On the next day the Greek Foreign Minister resigned; so did his Secretary-General, Angelos Vlakhos, who knew Cyprus intimately and had grave suspicions of what was afoot.

Makarios made no secret of his letter to Gizikis. It was released to the Press, after copies had first been sent to the King in London and Karamanlis in Paris, carried by Makarios' private secretary. Both immediately recognized the peril of the challenge to Ioannidis. The King advised the emissary to be guided by Karamanlis; he also discussed the letter with British ministers. Karamanlis asked the emissary whether Makarios had taken steps 'to guard his back against the probable reaction of Ioannidis'. When the emissary replied that there was nothing Makarios could do, Karamanlis commented that both Makarios and Cyprus were threatened with catastrophe.

Ioannidis' coup in Nicosia on 15 July succeeded, if only temporarily, but the attempt to assassinate Makarios failed. The Archbishop escaped from his residence, first to Paphos, then to the British base at Akrotiri, and finally to London. When he arrived in London on the seventeeth, the Turkish Prime Minister, Boulent Ecevit, was also there, demanding action in Cyprus under the 1960 Treaty of Guarantee. Meanwhile Ioannidis' agents in Nicosia had placed their nominee in the Presidency. He was Nicos Sampson, a journalist and former member of EOKA, who had once been condemned to death under British rule but reprieved and eventually released under an amnesty.

The time for Karamanlis to make a decisive pronouncement had now arrived. It was published (though naturally not in the Greek Press) on 16 July. After deploring the tragedy which had befallen Cyprus and threatened Greece, he castigated the 'ignorance and hypocrisy' of the military government which had brought it about. He recognized that he had a 'historic duty to address an appeal for patriotism and prudence'—but to whom? In Greece there was nothing but 'the unprecedented state of a concealed regime'. It was therefore only possible to appeal to the armed forces.

His message comprised five points. First, legality must be restored in Cyprus, in the person of Makarios; secondly, democracy must be restored in Greece; thirdly, the way was now open to find a safe retreat from the conditions of abnormality; fourthly, the opportunity to make this return to normality and to bring about reconciliation would not last long; and finally, the long-awaited undertaking that 'for the task of restoring normality and national reconciliation, I am at the disposal of the country'. It was not long before his words met with a response in the higher ranks of the services. But things had to get worse before they could get better.

Ecevit's meetings in London with James Callaghan, who had recently become Foreign Secretary in the Labour government formed in March, soon proved to be fruitless because the British were determined not to use force. The UN Security Council, which met repeatedly on the Cyprus problem between 16 and 20 July, was also unable to provide any remedy. The Turkish government therefore exercised its right of unilateral action under the Treaty of Guarantee, though its pretence of doing so 'with the sole aim of re-establishing the state of affairs created by the present Treaty' was transparently false. The invasion of northern Cyprus from Turkish ports barely fifty miles away began on 20 July. An emergency resolution of the Security Council called for a cease-fire on the same day. The Turkish forces then suspended operations for two days, but resumed their advance on the twenty-second. An attempt to mobilize the Greek forces for counter-action resulted in a humiliating shambles. Thus was exploded the delusion of the NATO powers that a military government could at least be relied upon for military efficiency.

The British government shared with Greece and Turkey the responsibility for the constitution and territorial integrity of Cyprus. There were British troops on the island, but their role was only to protect the sovereign bases. The RAF was quickly reinforced with Phantom jet aircraft. There were also two frigates and an aircraft-carrier in the vicinity. But the British government was reluctant to take risks. The only action taken by its forces was to evacuate hundreds of civilians and holiday-makers from the north coast.

The US government, which had no treaty obligations, did no more than send an Assistant Secretary of State to London, Athens, and Ankara in an effort to 'defuse' the explosive situation. But the Americans' feeling was that Makarios was finished, and they were barely restrained from recognizing Sampson's Presidency. Kissinger, though probably innocent of complicity in the plot against Makarios, was too heavily engaged in his 'shuttle diplomacy' between Israel and Egypt, and also in the death-throes of Nixon's Presidency, to give sufficient attention to Cyprus in time.

The one cause for satisfaction in the tragic story was the end of the dictatorship in Greece. Collapse would be too strong a word for it: the remnants simply vanished into thin air. The nominal Prime Minister was nowhere to be found. Ioannidis was engaged in trying to complete the destruction of Makarios. He made a notorious telephone call to Sampson urging him to 'get Mouskos' head' (using Makarios' family name). But his own days, indeed his hours, were numbered. On 22 July the senior Generals told Gizikis that they were no longer willing to take orders from Ioannidis, and that power must be re-stored to the politicians.

Gizikis summoned a Council of past Prime Ministers and other civilian leaders on the following day. At one point in their five-hour meeting Ioannidis was summoned and informed of the Council's intention to appoint a civilian government. Unabashed by the disasters he had caused, Ioannidis told them that they were making a mistake, but he would not resist. He then left the room in a temper. But the Council still found it difficult to agree on the composition of the new government.

Five years later Averoff, who was present at the meeting, gave an account of it on television. He said that Markezinis had proposed Xanthopoulos-Palamas as Prime Minister; but he was clearly not a strong enough figure, nor was Markezinis a man who had earned the right to be taken seriously. Averoff immediately proposed Karamanlis, but there was opposition from the Generals and from one politician, whom he did not name. As a compromise Averoff then proposed Kanellopoulos, whose name was generally acceptable. The meeting appeared to end with a decision in favour of Kanellopoulos, with George Mavros (who had been deported to Gioura by Ioannidis) as Deputy Prime Minister. But as the meeting broke up, Averoff stayed behind to speak to Gizikis. He pointed out that no solution could be expected to succeed unless Karamanlis was a party to it. Gizikis agreed, provided that contact could be made with him on the same day. Averoff went at once to telephone Paris.

For Karamanlis these events were a fulfilment of all his forecasts. It was impossible to witness them from afar without mixed feelings: satisfaction that the dictatorship was finished, bitterness that the Colonels had not seen their proper course in time, dismay at their evident intention to drag down the Greek people with them. His correspondence with Athens was now only spasmodic. Visitors to his flat in Paris were rare, but he had the company of his young nephew, Mikhali Liapis, who joined him in November 1973 after taking part in the students' protests. When Averoff telephoned on 23 July, it proved difficult at first to locate Karamanlis. Contact was eventually made through a cousin of Averoff's, who brought him to the telephone.

He would not make his decision hastily in response to Averoff's call. But next the Chiefs of Staff came on the telephone, begging him to return at once. He replied that he would come on the following day, but they insisted that the critical situation would not allow even twenty-four hours' delay. Gizikis offered to send an aircraft to fetch him at once, but in the meantime President Giscard d'Estaing, who had been closely following events in Athens, offered his own aircraft, which Karamanlis accepted. It was a symbolic gesture of recognition, quickly echoed round the world. The most sordid episode of modern Greek history was over.

PART IV

The Second Term
1974–1980

Chapter 9

A Sea of Troubles

ACCOMPANIED by Mikhali Liapis and a few close friends, Karamanlis landed in Greece at two o'clock in the morning of 24 July 1974. Thousands thronged the airport and the streets of Athens to welcome him. The jubilant sound of motor horns was heard all night long. Recalling the occasion three years later, Karamanlis said:

I had often thought of the emotion I should feel when I set foot again on the soil of my country. And I may tell you that the thought brought tears to my eyes in anticipation. And yet never was I calmer, never did I have myself more completely under control, than at the moment when I arrived at the airport. And the reason was that my sense of the responsibilities which I was about to undertake was so intense as to stifle, to banish every other thought.

He went straight to Gizikis' office, where the civilian and military leaders awaited him. They begged him to assume office at once. He said he would reply next day, after examining the situation; but they again pressed him, saying that the whole nation was waiting in agony beside the radio for his decision. He then laid down two conditions: that Gizikis should ensure the withdrawal of the Army to its barracks, and that the politicians should whole-heartedly support his efforts. Both conditions were immediately accepted. Thereupon he consented, and took the oath of office before the Archbishop of Athens at four o'clock in the morning.

The decree appointing him, under the one-year-old constitution, was signed by Gizikis. Inevitably both Gizikis and the constitution had to be replaced but Karamanlis announced that Gizikis would remain as a figure-head until a plebiscite could be held on the form of the state, which proved to mean another five months. Meanwhile a Constitutional Act, promulgated on 1 August, restored the constitution of 1952 with certain modifications, including one of crucial importance:

the President was substituted for the King until such time as the will of the people could be ascertained by a plebiscite.

King Constantine, who had been frequently in touch with Karamanlis and had expected to return to Greece soon after him, was shocked by the amendment. But Karamanlis argued that since the King had accepted the principle of a plebiscite by his statements in June and July 1973, it was impossible for him to return in anticipation of the people's decision without causing confusion and disturbances. A further Constitutional Act was to be promulgated in October, laying down the procedure for establishing the new constitution.

Meanwhile Karamanlis had already formed his first Council of Ministers, which was a coalition of all the talents. From his own party it included Tsatsos, George Rallis, Averoff, and Papakonstantinou. From the centre and further left it was joined by Mavros, Pesmazoglou, and George Mangakis—all former victims of the Colonels. From the professions there were General Ghikas, formerly Chief of the General Staff; Professor Zolotas, who had been and was to be again Governor of the Bank of Greece; Professor Nikolaos Louros, an eminent doctor; and the diplomat Angelos Vlakhos as an under-secretary. One regrettable exception, who no longer wished to hold office, was Kanellopoulos. Others were Andreas Papandreou and the leaders of the extreme left, who were not invited. The Communists were still technically outlaws, though the ban was soon to be lifted for the first time since 1947, and they were already active.

Every minister faced enormous problems. The gravest of all, apart from those of Karamanlis himself, were those facing Averoff, the Minister of Defence, and Mavros, the Foreign Minister. Because there was still a risk of war against Turkey, their problems were interlocked. But of the two, Averoff's position was the more critical because he could not even be sure of the loyalty of all his subordinates.

When Averoff took over his office in the Ministry of Defence (commonly known as the 'Pentagon') on 24 July, he described the government as 'the prisoner of the Army'. It was a lamentable truth. Under the dictatorship, the Chief of the Defence Staff was all-powerful. The Generals treated ministers as underlings. The incumbent CDS, General Grigorios Bonanos, still occupied the office which had formerly belonged to the Minister of Defence, and intended to remain there. For Averoff a more modest room was prepared, until he asserted himself in peremptory terms. There were even more serious problems still to come.

The most alarming of them was the disproportionate concentration of troops in Attica. A number of their officers were not resigned to the disappearance of the Junta. Ioannidis was still at liberty: he even had the impudence to push his way into the Minister's office one morning, and it required a further show of determination on Averoff's part to evict him. What was worse was that the notorious Military Security Police (ESA) still regarded Ioannidis as its commander. Other officers in key positions had signally failed to learn the lessons of the past seven years. Not only had the Army proved incapable of mobilizing against the external threat: it was seemingly incapable of anything except another *coup d'état*. The restoration of its morale and discipline needed strong measures and great tact.

Averoff began by ordering the ESA to stand down on 26 July. The next day Karamanlis visited the Pentagon, accompanied by General Ghikas, his Minister of Public Order. The appearance of the Prime Minister with a former Chief of the General Staff left the dissident officers in no doubt that they meant business. On 2 August Averoff sent Ioannidis on six months' leave—a mild disciplinary measure, but far from the last. A week later he presented decrees to the President reducing the powers of the Chief of the Defence Staff and restoring to active service the naval officers who had been dismissed for their attempt against the Junta in May 1973. General Bonanos tried to resist both measures, but his days in office were already numbered. For many reasons—incompetence, obstinacy, and disloyalty—he had to be removed.

Karamanlis was already taking the crisis in the armed forces under his personal control. The Navy and Air Force presented few problems, but elements of the Army were still in a contumacious mood. On 11 August Karamanlis presided at a conference in the Pentagon, at which he demanded the dispersal of the military units concentrated in Attica, partly because they were a threat to civil government and partly because they were needed on Greece's frontiers. When the Generals raised difficulties, they met the full force of Karamanlis' rage. Some said that this was the occasion when he coined the celebrated phrase: 'Either me or the tanks!' But he himself attributed it to the musician Mikis Theodorakis.

What he in fact said was that if his orders were not carried out within twenty-four hours, he would go to Constitution Square, call a mass meeting of the people, and use the force of public opinion to compel the Generals to obey. He then called in Ghikas, of whom they stood in great awe. Ghikas calmly persuaded Bonanos and the Chief of the Army Staff, Galatsanos, that the Prime Minister's orders were perfectly feasible. They were duly carried out.

But the internal crisis was soon brought to a head again by the external crisis over Cyprus. Legitimacy had been restored in Nicosia by the resignation of Sampson and his replacement by Glavkos Cleridis, the President of the Assembly, as Acting President of the Republic in accordance with the constitution. A precarious cease-fire had followed upon the emergency resolution of the UN Security Council on 20 July, though it was interrupted by the Turks' further advance on the twenty-second. Callaghan invited Mavros and Ecevit to meet him in Geneva on 25 July under the terms of the 1960 Treaty of Guarantee. There the cease-fire was confirmed, at least on paper. But despite five days of argument, the meeting was otherwise abortive, since the Turks were determined not to withdraw their forces.

After the Geneva conference adjourned on 30 July, Karamanlis addressed a formal request to Dr Luns, the Secretary-General of NATO, asking him to convene a meeting of the NATO Council at the level of Foreign Ministers. Luns's reply was unhelpful. He said that neither he nor most of the Foreign Ministers would be able to attend, either because they were too busy or because they were going on holiday. In any case, before Karamanlis' request could be pressed any further, the Geneva conference was due to meet again on 8 August.

A curious episode followed the adjournment of the conference. A Soviet official had arrived in Geneva from Moscow, but remained incommunicado until 31 July, when he asked to see Mavros. He claimed to have authority to ask for representation at the resumed conference on behalf of both the Soviet and the US governments, which Mavros refused to consider. In the interval before the resumption on 8 August, the Soviet Ambassador in Athens visited Mavros with a series of proposals and an assurance that his government was not hostile to the Greeks over Cyprus. Mavros did not take this approach seriously. Much more serious was a NATO report of the same period which indicated movements of Soviet military aircraft and so-called 'tourists' into the Balkan countries, coupled with an alleged guarantee by the Soviet government of Turkey's eastern frontier in the event of a Greco-Turkish war.

When the conference in Geneva met again on 8 August, it was joined two days later by the Greek and Turkish Cypriot representatives, Cleridis and Denktash. The latter simply echoed the line of the Turkish Foreign Minister, which was aggressively negative. The Turks scarcely concealed their determination to make no concessions, and harped repeatedly on the single theme of the need to relieve the pockets of Turkish population in areas held by the Greek Cypriots. They had already enlarged their own area of occupation in the week between the two sessions of the conference. After provoking a final breakdown on 13 August, for which Callaghan bitterly blamed the Turkish Foreign Minister, they renewed their advance in Cyprus at 5 a.m. on the following day.[1]

As soon as Karamanlis heard of the new attack, he convened a meeting at the Pentagon at 6 a.m. on 14 August. It was attended by Averoff, Rallis, and the Chiefs of Staff. Karamanlis asked the Chiefs of Staff whether any military action was possible. In particular, he proposed to dispatch three submarines to Cyprus to attack Turkish ships, and jet aircraft from Crete to attack targets on land. After a staff conference which lasted half an hour, the Chiefs of Staff replied that these operations were impossible. Karamanlis accepted their advice, but ordered the concentration of a division in Crete, with armoured fighting vehicles, for convoy to Cyprus.

As soon as the meeting ended, he summoned the full

---

[1] Detailed accounts of the conference have been published by Stanley Mayes, *Makarios* (London, 1981) and Stavros P. Psykharis, *Oi 70 krisimes imeres* (Athens, 1976). The latter includes the Greek record of the final meetings (pp. 187-226) and the Turkish proposals (pp. 227-31).

Council of Ministers, together with Kanellopoulos and other former Prime Ministers. With their agreement, he instructed the Ministry of Foreign Affairs to inform the NATO Ambassadors that Greek forces were withdrawn from NATO command, though Greece would remain a member of the alliance. The remarkable speed of his reactions can be judged from the fact that this decision was made public at 9 a.m. on the fourteenth, four hours after the Turkish attack began. Meanwhile the Turkish advance in Cyprus continued towards its final target, known as the Attila Line, which would comprise forty per cent of the island.

On the fifteenth Karamanlis gave his British allies a last chance of making amends by asking their Ambassador, through Mavros, to protect the passage of the Greek division from Crete to Cyprus. He let it be known that he and Averoff intended to accompany the convoy. Two days later came a letter from the British Prime Minister, Harold Wilson, refusing his request. It was in any case already too late.

All attempts by NATO leaders to persuade him to reverse his decision were rebuffed. First Luns, at last taking the matter seriously, proposed on 14 August to visit Ankara and Athens, in that order; but as the Turks peremptorily refused to receive him, Karamanlis also rejected his proposal on the fifteenth. Early the next morning Kissinger telephoned Karamanlis, expressing (in the words of the Greek record):

the opinion that the Turkish forces ought to stop where they were and negotiations should follow. Prime Minister replied that there was no possibility of negotiations in the face of *faits accomplis*. Then Mr Kissinger proposed that Mr Karamanlis should meet personally with President Ford in Washington, receiving the reply that under present circumstances it was impossible for the Prime Minister to leave Greece.

At this point the American Secretary of State asked what the USA could do. Mr Karamanlis replied that the negotiations could be resumed if the Turks were persuaded to evacuate Famagusta immediately (their forces had not yet advanced to Larnaka) and to withdraw subsequently to the line of stabilization.

There followed a letter from Kissinger purporting to contain reassurances, but they amounted to no more than a promise that the Turks would cease hostilities within a few hours. That they duly did on the sixteenth, having reached all their objectives.

In an address to the people on television, Karamanlis at once explained why he had no alternative to the decision which he had taken. Later he justified it on further grounds. He had to give some satisfaction to public opinion and to the armed forces; his decision gave enhanced prominence to the fate of Cyprus in the eyes of the world; it also created a reasonable expectation that the allies would take some initiative over Cyprus as the price of Greece's full return to NATO. Finally, under the threat of war, he had to have full control over the country's armed forces.

During the next six years there were countless conferences and resolutions of the Security Council and the General Assembly of the United Nations over Cyprus, but practically no significant change. The Turks remained undisturbed on the Attila line. Karamanlis could hold out no hope of a return to the status quo ante. In any case, since Cyprus was an independent state, Greece was no longer the protagonist. He could not make policy for the Greek Cypriots, only give them diplomatic, moral, and economic support. Besides, he had problems enough at home.

First and foremost, he had to complete the regeneration of the high command, which had failed the country so abysmally. On 19 August he convened, in great secrecy, a meeting of the Supreme Council of National Defence at the Ministry of Foreign Affairs. Only a few of those present knew that the purpose was to review the positions of the Chiefs of the Defence Staff and the Army Staff, Generals Bonanos and Galatsanos. Both were tainted with at least nominal complicity in the plot against Makarios; both had resisted the proposal to disperse the military concentrations in Attica; both had shown a lack of determination in the discussion of armed intervention in Cyprus. Without hesitation it was agreed that both must be retired and replaced. The order was carried out by Averoff within twenty-four hours. Fortunately no such action was needed against the Chiefs of Staff of the Navy and Air Force, whose conduct had been impeccable. The crisis in the armed forces was not yet over, but the first essential steps had been taken.

Neither Karamanlis nor Averoff could yet sleep wholly secure. Karamanlis himself, in fact, seldom slept in the suite he occupied at the Grande Bretagne Hotel. He preferred a small motor yacht, anchored off Glyphada, within easy reach of a destroyer in case of any attempt against him. Such an attempt was still possible for many weeks to come, so long as the Army had not been purged of Ioannidis' sympathizers. A few disloyal officers, mostly of junior rank, looked to Gizikis for support against Karamanlis. Gizikis, however, only wanted to retire as soon as possible, and kept Karamanlis informed of every breath of conspiracy that reached him. Nevertheless Greece's crisis was far from over. Two years later, it was revealed by Karamanlis' Minister of Press and Information that there had been four attempts to eliminate him during the first six months after his return.

Like Hamlet, Karamanlis faced a sea of troubles. For him the phrase could be taken in a dual sense: literally, in the Aegean; and metaphorically, in the disastrous legacy of the Colonels. For the latter, the Greek language has an apt idiom: 'They made a sea of it'. But for Karamanlis, unlike Hamlet, patience and despair were equally alien alternatives. He did not pause to ask whether to be or not to be.

The task was immediate. While the dangers of war abroad and counter-revolution at home were being contained, he had also to restore the foundations of constitutional government. There were three phases to the task: first, to re-establish an elected government; second, to determine whether Greece was to be a republic or a monarchy; third, to draft and legislate the articles of the constitution. On 2 October the first step was announced: there was to be a general election on 17 November. Two days later a second Constitutional Act laid down the subsequent procedure.

It provided that within fifteen days after the election, the incoming government was required to proclaim a plebiscite on the form of the constitution, which would be held within thirty days. According to the outcome, either the King would immediately return to the throne or Parliament would elect a temporary President. The government was then required to submit a new constitution in draft to Parliament. Parliament would have the right to amend and supplement the draft, but must complete its work within three months. Failing that, the government must submit its own draft, as so far completed and amended, to a national plebiscite. This procedure was devised by Karamanlis to avert the interminable delays to which previous constitutional changes had been subjected by Parliament. The previous constitution, for example, had been under debate from 1946 to 1952.

So Karamanlis began his huge and complex task. His burden was far heavier than when he first took office in 1955. When he succeeded Papagos, recovery had already begun from the years of war and civil war. Now both war and civil war threatened Greece again. At home he had to make democracy work again, to eradicate all traces of the Junta, to purge the public services, to re-equip the armed forces, to restore their morale and discipline, to revive the crippled economy, to modernize the country's institutions and education, to restore the people's self-respect. Abroad he had to re-establish Greece's alliances, to resist the encroachments of the Turks, to build new relationships with Greece's neighbours, and above all to join the European Economic Community. Not only were all these tasks interdependent, but all had to begin at once.

Although he had every reason for confidence in his exceptionally able Council of Ministers—probably the most popular government Greece had ever known—it was clear that only Karamanlis himself could be the architect of reconstruction. In exile he had mellowed and formed a wider vision of Greece's place in the world. He acknowledged that he had become more tolerant, but chiefly because circumstances had changed. He had to overcome bitterness by his own example because of the extreme danger to the country: 'I should be a poor general if I opened up a front at home when I have so many fronts open abroad', he said; and he believed that he had actually sacrificed popularity by his excessive tolerance of criticism and opposition.

But his tolerance could not be unlimited, for he had also witnessed from afar events which shook even his limited confidence in Greek habits and institutions. The single word in which he most frequently summed up the weaknesses of Greek politics was 'demagogy'. This was what he had in mind when he admitted to questioners that 'to some extent' he felt inhibited by the parliamentary system. In his last year as Prime Minister, he elaborated his answer:

Of course that does not mean that I am against the parliamentary system. Precisely the opposite: I am in favour of it, because it is the only way of securing the people's liberties. But I am personally repelled by some of its aspects: the verbalism, the often intolerable rhetorical exhibitionism which not only does not contribute to the solution of problems but complicates and perpetuates them; the theatricality which is more or less inseparable from parliamentary activity; the compromises and demagogy which are also to some extent inherent in the nature of the parliamentary game.

When he looked back on his final years as Prime Minister, he was able to claim some success in the aims he had set before himself, but he also had to recognize the limits of that success. His aims were three: to bring Greece into the 'European family', as he called it; to restore a properly functioning democracy; and to prove to the Greek people that it was capable of standing on its own feet. There were also, in his own judgement, three insuperable handicaps: the unhealthy political atmosphere; the poor quality of the Opposition; and the running sore of Cyprus. He defined them only in retrospect, but he foresaw them from the start.

In a speech which may conveniently be quoted in anticipation, he warned the Greeks of their failings in pungent and epigrammatic terms. 'History shows', he told Parliament on 16 October 1975, 'that what the Greeks win in war, they proceed to lose in the peace.' He cited 1920 and 1940 as examples. 'We lose because we have the bad habit of putting political antagonism first and our national interest second.' Foreign enemies could take advantage of these weaknesses, because 'we are incapable of accurately assessing international circumstances.' The Greeks imagined that Greece was the centre of the world's political interest—'the navel of the earth'—which led to the delusion that 'we can dictate our own policy to others, both friends and enemies, great and small.' He described how once when the archaeologists at Delphi told him they had found the original stone known as the 'navel of the earth', he begged them to throw it into the sea.

No one else could have talked to a Greek audience like that, and left them in reflective silence. Nor could even Karamanlis have done it twenty years earlier, as he did now, with a combination of unquestioned authority and genial irony. He could do it partly because he had returned with an uncompromised reputation and partly because he had spent a decade meditating on and maturing his conception of Greece. Those years had been spent mainly in France; and his speech in October 1975, no less significantly, was made a few days after returning from a visit to England. Like no Greek since Venizelos, he had a clear vision of what he wanted his country to become, and where he wanted it to stand. He could have said, adapting the memorable words of de Gaulle, 'I have always had a certain idea of Greece'. The time had now come to give it form. But it was not enough to restore only the form, without the content, of democracy.

Political activity began again in the late summer of 1974. Karamanlis made his first major political speech in public at Salonika on 31 August. It was his first appearance in over thirteen years in the capital of his native province. The occasion attracted a crowd of some half a million, who sang and danced in the square before his hotel until late in the night. He went on to open the Trade Fair with a speech of three words: 'Greece is free!' But even on this memorable and exuberant occasion there was a threat to his life from supporters of the Junta, which was successfully foiled.

During September decrees were promulgated to rescind the Junta's ban on political parties, and specifically to legalise the KKE. Towards the end of the month Karamanlis formed his own new party, in place of ERE, under the name of 'New Democracy'. His intention was that the new party should be 'freed from all the commitments and passions of the past'. He wanted to make it easy for 'all healthy elements of our political life, irrespective of their affiliations', to join it. On 30 September he expanded these ideas in a speech inaugurating the new party.

'The great theme of our age is democracy', he began. Only nineteen out of 140 countries had a true democracy. In Greece democracy had failed because of the lack of a 'calm political atmosphere and calm political habits and customs'. It had succumbed to 'recurrent plots, revolutions, dictatorships, constitutional upheavals, civil wars'. It had functioned 'imperfectly and subject to long and frequent lapses'. The last few weeks had witnessed a political miracle, which he now sought to consolidate: 'to make a reality of the name of the party—to give the country a New Democracy'.

His emphasis was on co-operation with the people, especially the young. He listed the specific aims: to rise above 'the misleading labels of right, centre, and left'; to treat all Greeks as equals before the law; to promote rapid development in all sectors; to support free enterprise, while leaving a distinct role to the state sector; to ensure the constant renewal of the party's membership; to invest generously in education, 'not only from our surplus but from our deficit'; to make a reality of 'popular sovereignty'; to contribute to the 'realization of the idea of united Europe'. While much of the language was familiar, the combination of aims went far beyond any previous party's programme.

During October all parties were actively preparing for the general election in the following month. The voting system, unanimously agreed in the coalition government, was to be reinforced proportional representation. Some indignation was expressed at the speed of the election, especially by Andreas Papandreou, who had returned only in mid-August. But all the party leaders managed to establish their organizations in time.

Most of the former Deputies of ERE joined New Democracy (ND). Papandreou established the Panhellenic Socialist Party (PASOK). Mavros and Pesmazoglou joined in establishing the Centre Union–New Forces. Two distinct Communist Parties emerged, known as the KKE (Exterior), which followed the Moscow line, and the KKE (Interior), which did not; but they combined for the general election, together with the surviving Union of the Democratic Left (EDA), led by Iliou. There were thus four parties or alliances in serious confrontation. Smaller groups also campaigned, but won no seats.

On 8 October Karamanlis accepted the resignations of all his ministers except Mavros and Averoff, who were still needed to handle the external crisis (though Mavros also resigned a week later). In their places he appointed non-political ministers to conduct the election, with no other function except the privilege of lifting military law. Meanwhile he was carefully nurturing the mood of the country for the restoration of democracy. There was naturally boundless enthusiasm for the idea, but he feared that enthusiasm would blind people to the reality and responsibilities. Between August and November he addressed frank and solemn admonitions to representatives of every sector of public life, especially those which had been most disrupted by the dictatorship: the senior officers, the lawyers, the trade unions, the agricultural co-operatives, the civil servants, the election officials. In holding elections only four months after his return, he knew that he was taking a calculated risk.

His own electoral tour was shorter than in the past, largely because he still had to keep watch on the remnants of the Junta. He learned of a conspiracy to kidnap him on the very day when he was taking the election decree to the President. Other plots also became known to him at the time: one, for instance, was to create an incident at the Turkish frontier on the River Evros, in order to force a cancellation of the whole election. But although he was obliged for these reasons to remain mostly in Athens, he could now address his people by television, which he did three times.

Outside Athens, he spoke first in Salonika, where his first audience was not the civil population but the officer corps. He addressed them bluntly on their duty and the disgrace of the dictatorship. Next he spoke to the people on the problems of the future. Elsewhere, only Larisa, Crete, Patras, and Athens were to hear him further in person. His themes were constant. First came foreign policy, which he described as a triptych of 'national independence, national security, national dignity'. He spoke of the need for loyalty among the armed forces, of the threat to Cyprus, and of Greece's unwavering commitment to the Western world. He traced out all the formidable problems of domestic policy, including the eradication of all remnants of the Junta. Finally he announced his intention to propose a revision of the constitution and to hold a plebiscite on the monarchy. Past, present, and future were interwoven, and there was a precarious balance in all the aims which he was defining.

The Army must be strong enough to withstand Turkish threats, but its strength must not threaten the civil power.

Greece must be loyal to the West, but it could not be forgotten that the West had betrayed Greece's loyalty. It was easy for opponents to attack Karamanlis on mutually contradictory grounds during the campaign. Hostile newspapers accused him of being party to a conspiracy against Cyprus, and of conceding a tacit amnesty to the Junta. The proposal of a plebiscite was attacked both by the monarchists, who wished that Karamanlis had brought back King Constantine with him, and by extreme republicans, who regarded the monarchy as a chapter to be closed without appeal. But Karamanlis' moderation and common sense struck the national chord, as became clear on 17 November.

New Democracy won over fifty-four per cent of the votes and 220 seats out of 300. The Centre Union came a poor second with sixty seats; PASOK won twelve, the left-wing front eight, the rest none. It was a uniquely complete victory: no Greek leader had won a properly contested election so decisively before. Karamanlis was now able to form a strong single-party government: indeed, with such a majority he was obliged to do so, even if his instinct might have preferred to include some of his ex-colleagues from outside ND. His statement on the results was notably restrained and even sombre. 'The problems which the nation faces are many and critical,' he said: 'so we must all alike, victors and vanquished, respect the verdict of the people and the rules of democracy; we must work together in a calm, orderly development of our national life.'

To settle the constitutional problem took more time than to restore democratic forms. There were two separate questions: the form of the constitution and the designation of the head of state. Like Elevtherios Venizelos before him, Karamanlis had no prejudice against monarchy as an institution, though he had suffered much from individual members of the Royal Family. He intended that the plebiscite should be a genuine test of public opinion. In order to avoid Venizelos' mistake of identifying his party with a particular system, he not only took a strictly neutral attitude himself but forbade his ministers to express their preferences publicly, while at the same time allowing them a free vote. (George Rallis, who was Minister in the Prime Minister's office and eventually

Karamanlis' successor, let it be known some time afterwards that he had voted for the King; and the party which Karamanlis led was itself traditionally monarchist in sympathy.) The monarchists were also allowed four television broadcasts, including two by the King himself, in which he stressed the depth of his family's devotion to their country.

Polling day was 8 December. There was a heavy poll, which went in favour of a republic by a margin of two to one. Karamanlis immediately offered to support Kanellopoulos as a candidate for the Presidency during the interim period before a new constitution was drafted, but the offer was declined. Kanellopoulos did not hide his dissatisfaction with the temporary character of the office, as well as the constitutional proposals which Karamanlis outlined to him. Ten days passed before a suitable candidate—Professor Michael Stasinopoulos—could be found to replace Gizikis. Even he was not an uncontroversial choice, for he was elected on the votes of New Democracy alone, with almost the whole Opposition voting against him.

Meanwhile the first Parliament for over seven years had assembled on 9 December. Karamanlis' speech setting out his programme was delivered two days later. It was much longer than his first inaugural speech nineteen years earlier, for the problems were much more complex. He began with something like a formal lecture on the duties of parliamentarians. Their aim, he told them, must be 'healthy politics and social democracy; the strength and well-being of the nation; the cultural development and international prestige of Hellenism'. Neither social democracy nor cultural development were to be found in his speeches before the years of exile.

He spoke of the need to revise the constitution, to modernize the machinery of state, to decentralize government. Then he turned to foreign policy, repeating the arguments which he had used in election speeches. But there were also innovations. He announced for the first time his intention to secure full membership of the European Economic Community. Also for the first time, he foreshadowed closer co-operation in the Balkans and with the Arab countries of the Middle East. He promised moral support for the Cypriots, but emphasized that

'Greece prefers negotiation to confrontation'. He reasserted Greece's loyalty to the Western alliance, but added that it was impossible to overlook the failure of the alliance to avert Turkish aggression.

All in all, it was a manifesto of a much wider role in the world than Greece had played before. To achieve it, he argued that Greece would need many guarantees: strong but democratically controlled forces; an independent judiciary; an effective economic and social programme. There followed a long and devastating analysis of the legacy of the dictatorship; then an even more detailed exposition of the economic targets for 1975 and a long-term scheme of reconstruction. Next he spoke of education in words which reflected the experience of his years abroad. Greek education, he said, must be so modernized and improved at all levels that young Greeks would no longer flock to foreign schools and universities, to find what they could not find at home. In a brief peroration he called on his people to rise to the level of their historic circumstances, and to give him their confidence. Parliament duly did so by 217 votes to seventy-eight.

The whole country, too, was with him so far. Even the Opposition offered only token criticisms. The real struggle began only on 23 December, when Karamanlis published his plans for constitutional reform. They were aimed, characteristically, at strengthening the executive and eliminating parliamentary delays. But they did not, as had been forecast, embody a Gaullist model borrowed from France. On the contrary, Karamanlis had devised a new model adapted to Greek conditions, and one which by no means favoured himself when he stood for the Presidency in 1980.

The President was to be elected by Parliament, not directly by the people. The aim was to avoid the division of the people into two factions, one for and one against the President, who would then become the prisoner of the former. His election would be determined in up to three ballots at intervals of one week. In the first two ballots a majority of two thirds was required, in order to ensure that the President was not elected on the votes of one party alone, since very rarely would one party hold sixty-seven per cent of the seats. At the third ballot, if it became necessary, a majority of three-fifths would suffice.

But if even that was unobtainable, Parliament would be dissolved and the new Parliament would elect the President by a simple majority. Deputies were thus put under pressure to decide the election by cross-party voting, at the risk of losing their seats.

The powers of the President were carefully and ingeniously defined. He could not initiate legislation, but he could refer back laws passed by Parliament; whereupon they had to be passed not by a majority of those present and voting but by a majority of the total membership of Parliament. He also had the exclusive right to order a national referendum on matters of major national interest. His powers of dissolution were limited—less, indeed, than the King held before him. But since it was assumed that he would himself succeed to the Presidency (though he disclaimed any such ambition at the time), his proposals were scrutinized with that prospect in mind.

Debates on the constitution occupied the next six months, and were often acrimonious. The most contentious points concerned civil rights. There were, for example, articles restricting the right of public servants to form trade unions or to go on strike. There was to be a right to ban public meetings in the open if there were a serious risk of disorder. Parliament was to have power to prescribe the conditions and qualifications for journalism. Freedom of religion was not to carry exemption from obligations to the state. These were not onerous or unusual provisions. Nor was the right of the President to suspend certain non-fundamental articles of the constitution in the event of war, mobilization, or a serious breakdown of public order.

Karamanlis conceded a number of amendments, which he later called the only weaknesses of the constitution. One point which he would not concede, however, was the provision that if a presidential term were cut short for any reason, the new President should have a full term of five years and not simply serve out the remainder of his predecessor's term. This point too was scrutinized with his own succession in mind. In any case, no concessions would appease the Opposition.

During May 1975 the PASOK Deputies walked out of the debates, and the whole Opposition abstained from the final vote. On that occasion Karamanlis made a major speech in defence of the draft constitution, describing it as the only one in Greek history that had ever been enacted 'in a constitutionally orthodox manner and in a short space of time'. To introduce it, he said, had been 'one of the basic aims of my political life', which he had pursued since 1961.

He called it 'truly Greek' in character, not copied from any other country, though he had studied many models. 'From the point of view of the separation of powers,' he went on, 'it lies between the French and the German constitutions.' But he claimed for it stronger provisions than either to guarantee 'popular sovereignty'. He deplored the absence of the Opposition from the debate, despite the amendments which they had secured in the draft, but he intended to answer their known objections.

They complained, firstly, about limitations on civil rights. But there were none which were not common form in Europe, and they accorded with the Treaty of Rome. Without such limitations democracy would collapse, 'for Anarchy was the daughter of Freedom who swallowed up her mother, as Aeschylus would put it.'

Secondly, they complained about the excessive powers of the President; but these were less than those of the Presidents of the USA, France, and other democracies. The error of the Opposition, he contended, was 'to link the constitution with my person'. Of course he could have taken the Presidency if he had wanted, but he did not. If they had any sense, he added sarcastically, 'the possibility of my becoming President would be their dream instead of their nightmare.'

In any case, he pointed out, a constitution was only the framework of democracy. How it worked would depend on 'a calm atmosphere, calm political habits, and above all a responsible Press and leadership'. The Greek people must supply these, or the result would be failure. Urging them to avoid the mistakes of the past, he quoted the French Admiral De Rigny (one of the victors of the battle of Navarino): 'These Greeks take to mutual destruction just when Fate smiles on them.' It must not happen again.

Parliament agreed with him by 208 votes to none. But Papandreou called the constitution 'totalitarian' and Mavros called it 'reactionary'. When Karamanlis nominated Tsatsos for the Presidency, Mavros forced a vote by nominating Kanellopoulos. This untoward contest between two of Greece's most eminent intellectuals resulted in an easy victory for Tsatsos by 210 votes to sixty-five. But the Opposition was already heartened by the turn of events in recent months.

Candidates of PASOK had striking successes in the student elections in November 1974, and also in the first local elections and parliamentary by-elections in the New Year. Papandreou and his Deputies exploited their successes by encouraging demonstrations and protest meetings, by condoning the violence which accompanied strikes, by criticizing the police and the judiciary, and above all by accusing the government of undue tolerance towards the supporters of the dictatorship. The 'calm political atmosphere' was not to be.

The process of what was called 'de-juntification' was unavoidable a slow one, for Karamanlis insisted that legal procedures should be respected. The armed forces and police must not be demoralized, nor the civil service and judiciary reduced to impotence. Despite these constraints, the purge was very far-reaching. It went much deeper, for instance, than in Spain and Portugal, where the dictatorships lasted much longer. The total number of dismissals and replacements was about 100,000. They included all local councillors and mayors; all the members of agricultural committees; all the directors of state legal organizations. Public prosecutors were subjected to investigation by a special decree. The purge of Army officers extended to all those who had played an active role in overthrowing the democracy or supporting the dictatorship. They included nine Generals and more than fifty other senior officers within the first few weeks. In later years Karamanlis spent much time in Officers' Clubs and military gatherings elsewhere, to form his own impressions of the mood of the Army and to assure himself of its reliability.

The Public Prosecutor began proceedings against the major criminals on 21 October 1974. Papadopoulos, Ioannidis, and their colleagues were arrested and removed to the island of Kea to await trial. The trial required careful preparation, including a resolution in Parliament to the effect that the action on 21 April had not been a revolution (which would have been deemed to generate its own legality) but a *coup d'état*. Consequently their cases came to court only in May 1975. Other trials followed throughout that year, and the next, and even into 1977.

There were many separate indictments, almost all of which involved Ioannidis: for crimes under the dictatorship, for the assault on the Polytechnic, for torture, for bribery and corruption, for destroying criminal records. Concurrently there was the purge of officers not liable to criminal prosecution, which Averoff was only able to declare completed in 1976. Even so, the Opposition found scope for criticism. In Karamanlis' judgement, the demands of Papandreou and others would have been tantamount to the disintegration of the state. They complained that all the civilian Ministers who had served under the dictatorship were acquitted; that the convictions of seven officers involved in the Polytechnic massacre were set aside on appeal; and that officers, civil servants, and lawyers who had served under the Junta were retained and eventually promoted. But it could not be otherwise if the fabric of the state was to be preserved.

The most serious blow to the whole process was the discovery of a new military plot in February 1975. Karamanlis had a rough passage in Parliament on the last day of that month, when he made a statement on the new conspiracy. But he insisted that he had no call to apologize: the government had the situation under control, the conspirators had found no support in the armed services and had been under surveillance from the first, and 'most important of all, the government had acted with lightning speed to destroy the conspiracy before it came out into the open'. He even taunted the Opposition with its passion for criticizing instead of congratulating the government. 'Their behaviour reminds me', he said, 'of Iago's words in Shakespeare: 'For I am nothing if not critical.'

The conspiracy had indeed been frustrated. But within a week over sixty more senior officers had to be removed from their posts, and in the summer twenty-three officers were indicted for the new conspiracy, inevitably including Ioannidis. Two further criticisms arose from the process of 'de-juntification'. One concerned the sentences on the three leading Colonels; the other, the failure to prosecute Ioannidis for the coup against Makarios. Ioannidis already had half a dozen sentences of life imprisonment awaiting him, but his crime against Cyprus was not the least black of them all.

In the case of the three Colonels it was foreseeable that sentences of death would be passed on them. As soon as the sentences were announced, on 23 August 1975, Karamanlis summoned the Council of Ministers. With their approval, he recommended to the President that the sentences should be commuted to life imprisonment, which was done on the twenty-fifth. There were protests, especially from Papandreou. It was alleged, but denied by Averoff, that there had been pressure from the armed forces. Karamanlis chose to reply to the criticisms in a speech at Drama on 29 August, addressed to officers who had been taking part in a major exercise.

He accepted full responsibility for the decision, pointing out that it was for the courts to pass sentence but for the executive—namely, the President on the advice of the Prime Minister—to exercise the prerogative of mercy. He added that in the case of the Colonels, life imprisonment would really mean imprisonment for life. He had no need to add that there was nothing soft-hearted about the decision. It was also politically wise, for Greek democracy would have been in much greater danger from the memory of three executed martyrs than from three foolish old men squabbling in gaol.

The decision not to prosecute Ioannidis for the coup in Cyprus was more difficult. Before issuing a decree suspending the prosecution on 7 March 1975, Karamanlis had consulted Mavros, Papandreou, and others. At the time they accepted his view that the prosecution would be contrary to the interests of Greece's external relations. It would, he argued, have provided a justification for the Turkish invasion. It would have led to recriminations with the United States, since Ioannidis would have produced evidence in court of his contacts with the CIA. And it would have led to the further prosecution of hundreds of officers who had been unable to escape nominal implication in the coup, at a time when the country faced the risk of war. Embarrassing consequences were nevertheless inevitable. The Press continued to speculate on the supposed implication of the United States. Mavros and Papandreou later criticized the decision, although they had accepted it at the time. They demanded that 'the file on Cyprus' should be opened. The criticisms naturally were intensified after Sampson was prosecuted in Nicosia and sentenced to twenty years' imprisonment at the end of August 1976, for his part in the same conspiracy of which Ioannidis was accused.

Once the trials and purges were over, Karamanlis hoped that the past would be forgotten. He insisted that he had never used the slogan attributed to him, or at least to his supporters, 'Either Karamanlis or the tanks'. But memories of the dictatorship died hard. The anniversary of the Polytechnic massacre was celebrated every year with marches and demonstrations, invariably orchestrated by the extreme left and often leading to violence. In December 1976 one of the policemen convicted of torture was murdered, in an act of private vengeance. At his funeral an inflammatory speech was made by a former propagandist of the Junta (who was also a former Communist, condemned to death *in absentia* during the civil war). Another policeman, convicted of the conspiracy of February 1975, was allowed to escape from a prison hospital in 1977; and seven of his colleagues were dismissed for complicity in his escape. Accusations and violence followed from both sides, and continued intermittently for more than two years. In December 1978 more than thirty bombs were exploded in Athens by sympathizers with the Junta; in the following month another convicted torturer was murdered; and neo-Fascists were still being sentenced for terrorist offences as late as the middle of 1979. Such was the legacy of the Junta, of which Karamanlis was unavoidably the principal legatee.

Frequent reassurances did not dispel public anxiety, and some public statements incidentally fed it. Averoff's answers to questions in Parliament and the Press were sometimes disturbing. He announced the end of the purge of the armed forces in April 1975, and repeated it in February 1976; but in January 1977 he admitted that about 200 officers who had supported the Junta were still on active service, and six months later he issued a stern warning to the 'driblets' (*stagonidia*) of the Junta which still survived. More serious still, at the end of August 1977 he announced that a new 'officers' movement' had been neutralized. In every case he added reassuring comments: the residue of the Junta presented no danger, the leader of the 'officers' movement' was only a colonel undergoing psychiatric treatment; but Papandreou and his party refused to be reassured.

Karamanlis was not dissatisfied with the process of 'de-juntification', which had been both strict and fair. It had not demoralized the public services, and it had forestalled fresh eruptions, if only by a narrow margin. But it left Karamanlis a target for endless criticisms, which were endlessly exploited. Papandreou in particular seemed to be imitating his father's example of opposition for opposition's sake. Some of his left-wing followers were even more violent in their language.

There were, however, a few remarkable exceptions on the left who regularly praised the new Karamanlis. One of his least probable supporters was the celebrated musician, Mikis Theodorakis, once a pillar of the extreme left. Another who spoke approvingly of him was Iliou, the leader of EDA. Even the two Communist Parties occasionally had a good word for him, while they had none for each other. On the other hand, some of his former supporters turned away from him. His former Foreign Minister, Spyros Theotokis, repeatedly accused him of reviving policies of the Junta. Others accused him of having become practically a socialist. Both kinds of criticism were naturally pressed by the Opposition.

The two principal parties of the Opposition were both pursuing aggressive tactics: the Centre Union, which had re-named itself the Union of the Democratic Centre (EDIK), because it was suffering from internal dissension; and PASOK because it was growing in strength and confidence. Of the sixty Deputies representing EDIK in Parliament, one was expelled in July 1976 and three more resigned two months later. At least two others were widely regarded as undeclared supporters of Karamanlis, and later joined ND. PASOK also had its troubles, largely due to Papandreou's autocratic leadership. He expelled several of his members during 1975, but readmitted them in time for the next election. More important, however, was the fact that he was clearly gaining ground over EDIK, especially in establishing PASOK'S provincial organization.

Karamanlis regretted the course taken by the Opposition: not so much its aggression as its disarray and reversion to 'demagogy'. He was still determined to establish Greece as a democracy on the Western model; and for that it was necessary that the Opposition as well as the government should play its role. This was not yet happening. But Karamanlis' grip, both on the country and on his own party, remained as strong as ever.

Chapter 10
Democracy on Trial

AN important aspect of Karamanlis' determination to Europeanize his people—if necessary, against their will, as he put it himself—was his plan to establish New Democracy as a political party in the Western sense. Traditionally almost every party in Greece, with the interesting exception of the KKE, had been simply the personal entourage of its leader. Invariably they dissolved when he was taken from them, or often even earlier. A political party, to survive, must have principles, discipline, and continuity. Karamanlis' discipline was firm and occasionally severe: he regularly lectured his Deputies, and unhesitatingly expelled one who was implicated in an arms scandal. But there were more important issues than that.

In announcing the establishment of ND on 30 September 1974, he had defined its principles more explicitly than he had done in the case of ERE. Later he went further still. In July 1975 he published a formal statement of 'ideological principles'. His next innovation was the first national congress of the party—indeed, the first of any party—which was held on the Macedonian peninsula of Khalkidiki in May 1979. More significantly still, it was succeeded by half a dozen regional conferences in the following year, from all of which Karamanlis conspicuously absented himself, in order to emphasize his often-repeated desire to 'dissipate the impression that I am irreplaceable'. Even political opponents acknowledged that these innovations were highly successful.

Conservative politicians usually abhor ideology as an embarrassment, but Karamanlis repudiated the idea that he was a conservative. The Communists and EDA tacitly recognized his difference from the common run when in November 1974 they published a joint statement after the election, that 'the vote for Karamanlis was not a vote for the right.'

In formulating the principles of ND, he subtly stole the phrase 'popular sovereignty' from the extreme left, 'social democracy' from the moderate left, and 'new forces' from the Centre Union. Words like 'radical' and 'progressive' had already taken root in his vocabulary. But they were accompanied by abstractions dearer to the hearts of true conservatives, about patriotism, freedom, independence, order under the law, and social stability. At other points he gave commitments which seemed ambiguous to both the right and the left, such as the combination of private enterprise and a market economy with state intervention. In other areas, such as the modernization of the armed forces and the administrative machine, his commitments were stimulating but also disquieting. Such was the tone of the new Karamanlis: exciting to almost everybody, but still a puzzle to some.

To modernize Greece was easier said than done. It was least controversial in technical and professional fields, such as the armed forces. In that case even Papandreou had to support Karamanlis, after demanding a more belligerent policy towards Turkey. Almost a quarter of the new government's first budget was devoted to the armed forces, without challenge in Parliament. Karamanlis personally presided at meetings in the Ministry of Defence which decided to order new equipment from France and West Germany. At the same time it was decided to establish arms factories in Greece, capable of assembling and servicing weapons and aircraft and small ships.

The structure of the forces was also overhauled under Karamanlis' close supervision. The most senior appointments required personal approval from him as well as Averoff. New legislation was passed to separate the control of the three armed services, which had been amalgamated under the Colonels because the Army was the only one they could trust. These were necessary safeguards to ensure that there could be no further threat from within. The nature of the threat from without was clearly indicated by two further measures: first, the creation of a fourth Army Corps with its headquarters at Xanthi in western Thrace; and secondly, the fortification of the easternmost islands of the Aegean.

At home Karamanlis could safely leave the management

of the economy in expert hands. But he regularly presided at ministerial committees in the Ministry of Co-ordination on important decisions. Whenever he had a major speech to make, especially at the annual opening of the Salonika Trade Fair, he included detailed analyses of economic developments. Such close attention to economic issues was a necessary consequence of the importance he attached to negotiating Greece's entry into the EEC.

His interventions were, as always, based on pragmatic grounds rather than dogma. He had made it clear from the first that his commitment to free enterprise did not exclude a measure of *étatisme*. He confirmed it in practice by three major acts of nationalization. The government took control of Olympic Airways from Onassis and the oil refinery at Aspropyrgos from Niarkhos; and it also took over the administration, but not the ownership, of the Andreadis group of banks, which had been grossly mismanaged. Thus a government which its critics accused of being the tool of capitalism came into conflict with three of the most powerful capitalists in Greece. In the case of the banks, which he pressed to form new consortia for industrial investment, he hinted at further interventions by the state if they failed to respond.

Every ministerial committee knew that it would find the Prime Minister in the chair whenever a project needed a specific impetus. In fact, his presence was the clearest indicator of priorities. Among the highest priorities by this criterion were the exploitation of the country's mineral wealth, the transport and environmental problems of Athens, the planning of a new international airport, the development of nuclear power, the reafforestation of Attica. He also presided at meetings on the economic and financial framework of development: to draft a new five-year plan, to introduce rules of competition in conformity with the EEC, to break the link between the drachma and the dollar.

Although Karamanlis was the principal fount of decision, others had to be urged and cajoled to make their collective contribution. The forum was provided by public occasions like the Salonika Trade Fair, or professional conferences of business men, trade-unionists, civil servants, agricultural workers and co-operatives, which he regularly addressed. At

Salonika in particular he liked to be able to forecast major new developments. But for a time, unfortunately, there was a scarcity of opportunities for inaugurating newly completed projects, which had been so impressive a feature of his first premiership. This was a legacy of the industrial stagnation under the dictatorship. The Colonels had been able to exploit the economic growth of Karamanlis' first term, but had contributed little themselves. It was a heavy task to repair their own unhappy legacy, which included a high rate of inflation, a low rate of growth, large deficits in both the budget and the balance of payments. Modernization had to begin by overcoming all these handicaps. By the end of 1975 most of the indicators had moved in a favourable direction, but Karamanlis still had to warn employers and workers of fresh dangers: the rising price of oil, the burden of defence, the impact of unreasonable wage demands under threat of strikes.

He refused, however, to be deflected from his policy of public investment. The budget announced in November 1976 included a capital programme of £750,000,000. Roads and agriculture were to be major beneficiaries, and there was special provision for projects in northern Greece. There was also the major innovation of a plan to establish an indigenous arms industry, for which legislation was introduced during the year. In February Karamanlis laid the foundation-stone of an aircraft factory at Tanagra, and forecast plans for a naval construction-yard at Skaramanga. In October Averoff opened a small-arms factory, partly financed by German funds. Later in the same month it was announced that the aircraft factory would be in operation by the summer of 1978. Greece was gradually ceasing to be wholly dependent on foreign aid for her defence.

Foreign aid was already diminishing, since the progress of the Greek economy had become 'better than satisfactory', in the words of the US Department of Trade at the beginning of 1978. But loans for capital investment were correspondingly easier to negotiate, both from international institutions such as the World Bank and the European Investment Bank, and also from private banking consortia in Paris and London. With their help Karamanlis was able to plan a new international airport at Spata, near Athens, and an extension of the underground railway in Athens. Although neither came to fruition while he was Prime Minister, the expression of foreign confidence in his management was clear.

Because he wanted to establish the same degree of confidence at home, he was keenly concerned that his pledges to education and social policy should be fulfilled. The budget for 1977 provided an increase of twenty per cent for education and almost seventeen per cent for welfare. Both figures were well above the current rate of inflation, which had been reduced from fifteen per cent in 1974 to below eleven per cent by the end of 1976. But it was not enough to vote the money. Karamanlis was constantly urging his ministers to show greater drive, to overcome the frustrations of bureaucracy, to set an example of austerity and imagination in their departments. They could never afford to forget that he was watching their performance with a severely critical eye.

On 10 January 1977 he took the chair at a ministerial meeting in the Ministry of Health, to insist on improvements in social insurance and public health, particularly in the rural areas. His ideas took more explicit form in a statement issued two months later, which listed twelve specific projects: five new hospitals providing 3,500 beds; a full-time hospital medical service; 200 health centres; a service of rural doctors; a system of drug supply in agricultural communities; training for nurses at university medical schools; a twenty-four-hour service in all Athens hospitals; a reduction of hospital wards to six beds or less; inspection of both public and private hospitals by the Ministry of Social Services; establishment of a National Health Council; preparation of a national register of prescriptions; re-establishment of the Athens School of Public Health, which had been closed under the dictatorship. Ministers needed no reminding that Karamanlis had once performed their functions himself. Six months later he held another meeting at the Ministry to review progress.

His formidable programme of innovations was one of the reasons for the fear among reactionary politicians and the wealthy bourgeoisie that Karamanlis had virtually become a socialist. The truth was quite different. Unlike many of his countrymen, he had learned from experience. He had known the hardships of rural life as a boy in Macedonia; he had served

his political apprenticeship in the most underestimated departments; and he had lived for a decade in Western Europe, where
he saw that the Welfare State had become part of the accepted
order. If Greece was to be integrated into Western Europe,
which was his supreme ambition, then the Greeks must
modernize their way of life; and this was how it had to be done.

The same principle applied to education. At the beginning
of 1976, in a weighty address to officials of the Ministry of
Education, Karamanlis defined four problems; first, the relative scale of the educational budget; second, the provision of
competent teachers; third, the content of the educational
programme; fourth, the language of instruction. He did not
claim to have ready-made solutions, but he called for an im-
partial study: education, he said, was to be 'above party'. He
appointed an inter-party committee to consider the problem
of the language, which had been bedevilled for more than a
century by the conflict between the official *katharevousa* and
the demotic which everybody spoke. The tenor of his own
thinking was shown by decisions taken in the next two years.

First priority was to be given to vocational education, as it
was in Karamanlis' first term of office. Early in 1977 it was
announced that new medical faculties would be established
in the Universities of Patras and Ioannina. New legislation
was introduced to expand technical education, including a
Polytechnic in Crete at Khania, in addition to a new university
at Iraklion. A training-school for civil servants was also
planned, not without opposition. The question of the language
of instruction was settled, again not without opposition, by
the decision that demotic should be introduced in all schools,
and eventually in higher education as well. In August 1977 an
Education Bill including this provision was introduced by the
responsible Minister, George Rallis, who also held the powerful position of Minister in the Prime Minister's office.

The opposition to these and other measures was not wholly
drawn on party lines. The universities resisted the introduction
of demotic; the students marched in protest at the training-
school for civil servants; the schoolmasters several times went
on strike; and the Senate of the University of Athens came
into conflict with the Minister of Public Order over the conduct of students. A more purely ideological conflict arose in

1977 over legislation to supervise private schools, of which there were a great many in and round Athens, because the left-wing opposition wanted to abolish them entirely.

Whatever the matter at issue, it was to be expected that left-wing students would take the lead in protesting. Early in 1978 university students were boycotting their classes, and their teachers went on strike for more than two months, in protest at legislation on higher education. A year later, in August 1979, the campus of the University of Athens was in uproar against the government's measures to conserve fuel. Early in 1980 the students were protesting at legislation, which had been approved by the University Rectors, limiting their right to resit examinations in which they had failed. Karamanlis patiently requested the University Rectors to reconsider it. His critics thought he was too indulgent towards the young, but it was part of his political philosophy to be so; even to the point of reducing the length of military service.

In trying to widen the horizons of Greek society, Karamanlis inevitably met obstacles. One of the most conservative of national institutions was the Church. Karamanlis was criticized for calling on the Pope in September 1975; a bishop accused George Rallis of being a Freemason; another bishop denounced tourism as a cause of ungodly corruption. The Archbishop of Athens refused to sanction a concordat with the Vatican, and opposed the establishment of diplomatic relations, though unsuccessfully. Forty other bishops joined the Archbishop in declaring their lack of confidence in the man chosen by Karamanlis as Under-Secretary for Education. The Holy Synod vigorously condemned the government's draft law on divorce by consent, but it was nevertheless enacted on a trial basis in 1979. It was only to be expected that the Church should also resent Karamanlis' decision to transfer four-fifths of its property to the State, which was also carried into law.

The Church, like the rest of Greek society, had in the end no alternative but to move with the times. The Patriarch of Constantinople followed Karamanlis' example shortly before Christmas 1975, when he met the Pope in the Sistine Chapel, and the mutual anathemas of the Orthodox and Catholic Churches were rescinded. Their successors met again four years later in Istanbul to discuss the possibility of reunion.

In the meantime, during 1976, the archbishop of Athens visited the godless capitals of Bulgaria and the Soviet Union. On the whole, however, the Church was little touched by Karamanlis' policy of modernization.

He was not discouraged by political, academic, or ecclesiastical opposition. He had a clear conviction that he was setting in motion a trend which could not be stopped or reversed. Sometimes he called it 'making the Greeks Europeans'; sometimes he spoke of 'raising the cultural level of the people'. In practice it took the form of an endless stream of social and cultural initiatives: lowering the voting age to twenty; setting up a new Ministry of Land Use, Housing, and the Environment; proposing financial provision for the political parties (though this was frustrated by the extreme left, which did not wish to disclose its other sources of income); broadcasting the Voice of Greece; introducing colour television; supporting the International Year of the Woman; abolishing the dowry system; imposing compulsory service on women in time of war or emergency; establishing a National Cultural Centre; inaugurating an Olympic stadium near Athens and proposing a permanent site for the Olympic Games in the Peloponnese; setting up a Social and Economic Policy Council; co-operating in the construction of a North–South motorway through Greece to the Middle East; and much else. No previous Prime Minister would have dreamed of most of these innovations; or if any had, they would have remained dreams.

It was part of the same policy of modernization to exploit Greece's ancient heritage. 'Those peoples have prevailed', he once said, 'who have created a culture and written history with their culture.' No country, he pointed out, had either possessed greater wealth of culture than Greece or been more backward in exploiting it. He astutely used the magnificent treasures found at Vergina to enhance both Greek and Macedonian pride; but he sadly observed that in a scholarly publication on the subject, only two articles out of ten were written by Greeks. When he tried to send the treasures of Cnossos for exhibition abroad, he was frustrated by short-sighted obstruction. Even his efforts to save the Acropolis and the seas round Greece from pollution came almost too late.

Every original endeavour found opponents more vocal

than supporters. Measures against pollution antagonized industrialists and taxi-drivers; developing new industrial sites antagonized archaeologists and conservationists; almost everything antagonized students. Although the trend of economic growth continued, international conditions were becoming difficult and inflation was again a threat. Ministers were demanding supplementary estimates, and some desirable objectives had to be postponed. Leaders of the Opposition began to prepare themselves for a general election, though it was not due until the end of 1978. The expectation grew when a new electoral law was introduced in June 1977, which lowered the age of voting and made concessions for the benefit of the smaller parties.

Karamanlis still told his parliamentary supporters that 'we are far away from elections.' When he changed his mind in September, the decision had nothing to do with the state of the economy. There were three related crises coming to a head, he told his Council of Ministers on 18 September: over Cyprus, over relations with Turkey, and over negotiations with the EEC. A government with 'increased prestige and renewed confidence' was needed to confront them. He therefore proposed to ask the President for an early dissolution.

The request was conveyed to the President by George Rallis, because Karamanlis was confined to his home with lumbago. Polling day was fixed for 20 November. In accordance with convention, Karamanlis replaced the Ministers of War, Justice, Northern Greece, and the Prime Minister's office, but remained head of the government himself. Despite his indisposition, he carried out nearly the same electoral tour as in 1974, apart from the omission of Crete. As usual, his first public meeting was at Salonika, where he emphasized again the three concurrent crises in external relations, but added a resolute justification of his economic and social policies.

In his later speeches at Larisa and Patras, in Athens, and on television he laid greater stress on domestic politics. 'Greece is not a Paradise,' he told his audiences, 'but neither is it an Inferno.' It had recovered in three years from the agony of the dictatorship. Its future task was to consolidate what had been won, to intensify the growth of the economy, and to achieve a fairer distribution of the nation's wealth. The only alternative was a left-wing government aiming, 'by the isolation and impoverishment of our country, to deliver it into the arms of Communism'. Everything that Karamanlis claimed about the past was justified, but for once his outlook on the future seemed defensive and cautious in comparison with the heady rhetoric of Papandreou.

The outcome of the election was a disappointment for Karamanlis. New Democracy's share of the poll dropped from fifty-four per cent in 1974 to forty-one per cent. The party took 173 seats, a loss of more than forty. PASOK increased its share of the poll to twenty-five per cent and took ninety-two seats, a very considerable advance. Mavros's party, EDIK, took only fifteen seats, a disastrous drop in popularity. Of the remaining seats, the Communists won eleven, the right-wing Nationalists five, and two small parties two each. Papandreou correctly claimed to have made extensive gains at the expense of New Democracy as well as EDIK. Mavros acknowledged his personal failure by resigning the leadership of EDIK, which began to disintegrate, some breaking away to the left and some to the right. Ioannis Zigdis, who became the parliamentary leader of the rump of EDIK, weakened it still further by quarrels with his colleagues.

Papandreou was now the official leader of the Opposition. Karamanlis acknowledged that he had every reason to be triumphant. It was the worst result for the leader of ND since the elder Papandreou had defeated ERE in 1963. But the set-back of 1977 was less damaging than the defeat of 1963, for he still had an overall majority of nearly fifty, which was to be reinforced in 1978 by two major defections from the Opposition, Mitsotakis and Athanasios Kanellopoulos. And Karamanlis was still Prime Minster.

Publicly, he attributed the set-back to 'dirty tricks' (*doliophthora*) by the Opposition and to mistakes by New Democracy. Perhaps it had been a mistake to give so much emphasis to the three issues of foreign policy: Cyprus, Turkey, and the EEC. On the first two there was hardly room for disagreement, since any Greek government could be counted on to give whole-hearted support to the Greek Cypriots and to resist Turkish claims. On the EEC Karamanlis could still claim a substantial majority of votes for parties favouring Greece's entry, since only PASOK and the extreme left were against it. Perhaps also Karamanlis behaved too honourably for his own advantage in refraining from tempting promises. It was not until after the election that he revealed a number of attractive aspects of the budget for 1978: reductions in tax levels and increased priority for investment in agriculture and education. These might have reinforced his vote, for it was undoubtedly among agricultural workers and the newly en-franchised students that PASOK made its biggest gains.

On later reflection, Karamanlis noted two other factors in the reduction of his vote. One was the emergence of the extreme right, which subtracted some seven per cent from his vote with criticisms of his supposedly socialist policies. The other was the anti-Western feeling, which was growing as a result of the failure of the Western allies to help Greece over her national problems, such as Cyprus and the Aegean. Karamanlis was thus penalized for pursuing a pro-Western policy. But over neither of these two adverse factors had he the slightest regret.

Although he was naturally disappointed by the result, his regrets were not on his own account. Such set-backs only reinforced his determination. As he had once told his French biographer, Maurice Genevoix, he had 'dried up his soul' in order to succeed. But he was sensitive to the misfortunes of his friends. Many of them had lost their seats: even George Rallis came near to defeat. As the depressing count proceeded, Rallis saw tears in Karamanlis' eyes, and chided him for trying to conceal them. Karamanlis saw the deep disappointment reflected in Rallis' face, and promised him a place in the government even if he failed to retain his seat.

It did not take long for the party to recover from its set-back. Karamanlis reconstructed his government to face the critical situation which he had foreseen, with Averoff at the Ministry of Defence as before, Papaligouras at the Ministry of Foreign Affairs, and Rallis (who had in the end retained his seat by a narrow majority) at the Ministry of Co-ordination. These were the three crucial departments in the next phase, and the three men who held them were generally regarded as the natural candidates for the succession to Karamanlis if the new Parliament should be his last. Within six months Papaligouras had resigned on grounds of ill health, and Rallis had moved to the Ministry of Foreign Affairs in his place. Since Karamanlis had emphasized the overriding importance of foreign policy in the immediate future, Rallis was then strongly placed to gain the succession. But Karamanlis never gave any indication of personal favour in the matter. It was for the party to choose its own leader, when the time came.

The three crises which had led Karamanlis to risk a premature election came to a head at different speeds. Two of them—those over Cyprus and the Aegean—were long-drawn-out and in the event practically insoluble. The third, over the EEC, was intractable but came in the end to a satisfactory conclusion. However, these were only three of the many strands which had to be woven together in the fabric of Greek foreign policy; and whoever was at the Ministry of Foreign Affairs, only Karamanlis had all of these strands in his hands.

Cyprus and the Aegean were naturally connected problems, since both involved relations with Turkey. But they were also distinct, as Karamanlis repeatedly pointed out, because Cyprus was an independent state. The policies of the Cypriot government were made in Nicosia, not in Athens. Karamanlis had no intention of interfering in its internal affairs: he would contribute moral support, but never guidance. The story of Cyprus in the years 1974-80—the interminable exchanges at the United Nations and in Nicosia, Athens, Ankara, Geneva, Vienna, Brussels, London, Washington, and Moscow—is important in the history of international relations but only marginal to the biography of Karamanlis. It took up a vast amount of his time, but the crisis which he foresaw in 1977 passed without any significant change in the status of the island.

Karamanlis never denied—in fact, he constantly emphasized —that the catastrophe of July 1974 was caused by Greek actions under the dictatorship. But it was also undeniable that the Turkish reaction was unjustified under the 1960 Treaty of Guarantee. Not only was it clearly not intended simply to restore the status quo ante, as Article IV of the treaty required. It had also been expressly stated by the legal advisers of the

UN in 1960 that armed force was not permissible under that article in any case. Still less could justification be found for the Turkish refusal, after the invasion, to carry out the resolutions of the General Assembly calling for the withdrawal of foreign troops.

But since Karamanlis could not and would not retaliate by force, there was nothing he could do except mobilize moral support from the rest of the world and give his own moral support to the Greek Cypriots. He had many meetings with Makarios, usually in Athens; and he regularly received the successive Cypriot negotiators, Glavkos Cleridis and Tassos Papadopoulos. After every meeting, 'complete accord' was reported, but there was never the least progress in dealing with the Turks.

More reluctantly, Karamanlis met each of the alternating Prime Ministers of Turkey on several occasions, usually at international gatherings. He exchanged correspondence with them, and frequent public statements. The Turkish statements were conciliatory or aggressive by turns, as might suit the domestic situation of Demirel or Ecevit at any particular time. Karamanlis' statements were cool, short, and firm. But it was never possible to foresee how long any particular government would last in Turkey, so Karamanlis was cautious about accepting proposals for meetings without serious preparation at the official level, which was never satisfactorily achieved.

Meanwhile there was nothing to weaken the Turks' domination of northern Cyprus and much to strengthen it. Already before the end of 1974 they were introducing peasant farmers from the mainland and demobilizing soldiers in the island, to take over Greek properties. Their strength was increased when Callaghan visited Cyprus at the end of the year and permitted the transfer of Turkish Cypriot refugeees from the British bases in the south of the island back to the north. In February 1975 Denktash, the Turkish Cypriot leader, proclaimed an autonomous government; in June 1976 he was elected President of a so-called 'Turkish Federated State of Cyprus', which was recognized only in Ankara. Intercommunal talks nevertheless went on between Denktash and Cleridis in Vienna under UN auspices. After several false alarms, Cleridis resigned as chief negotiator and was succeeded by Tassos

Papadopoulos in April 1976. But nothing could budge the Turks.

Early in 1977 there were faint hopes of an improvement when Makarios twice met Denktash, whom he had not otherwise seen since the *débâcle* of 1974. They met at the invitation of Kurt Waldheim, the Secretary-General of the United Nations; and soon afterwards a special envoy from the American President, Clark Clifford, took a hand in the negotiations. But any prospect that these initiatives might have opened was abruptly closed by the death of Makarios on 3 August. When Spyros Kyprianou was elected as his successor, the Turkish government recognized him not as President but only as leader of the Greek Cypriots.

At the same time the Turks were proposing that Famagusta, a major Greek town and seaside resort which lay derelict under their control, should be opened to Turkish settlement. The Cypriot government demanded an emergency meeting of the Security Council, which passed a resolution on 15 September calling on all parties in Cyprus to refrain from unilateral action. So began one of the three crises which Karamanlis cited as the occasion for the dissolution of Parliament a few days later.

Whereas in Cyprus Greco-Turkish relations remained bad but static, in the Aegean they went from bad to worse. The reason was simple: in Cyprus the Turks were in possession of what they wanted, and Karamanlis was not prepared to be belligerent; in the Aegean the Greeks were in possession, and the Turks had no such qualms. There were three areas of friction: the continental shelf, territorial waters, and control of the airspace. All three had their origins in the last days of the military dictatorship, for it was the puppet government of early 1974 which had first announced the discovery of oil in 'commercial quantities' under the sea-bed and had talked of extending Greece's territorial waters to twelve miles. The conflict over the airspace then became more acute after Karamanlis withdrew the Greek forces from NATO, whereupon the Turks claimed the right of control for both civil and military purposes, which could not in practice be separated.

The issues of territorial waters and airspace proved in time to be relatively secondary. They led to a series of incidents and protests on both sides, but nothing worse occurred. The Turks complained that the Greeks were exploiting the pro-liferation of Greek islands across the archipelago to claim the entire Aegean as a 'Greek lake', but Karamanlis always denied any such claim. There was no renewal under his government of the threat to extend territorial waters. On the contrary, in February 1980 Rallis told Parliament that Greece had a right to extend her territorial waters unilaterally, as other countries had done, but made it clear by his silence that there was no intention of doing so. Similarly the issue of air-traffic control petered out, without any concession on the Greek side to Turkish claims. At the end of August 1976 civilian flights were resumed between Athens, Izmir, and Istanbul. Control of military traffic was left to be settled after Greece rejoined the military wing of NATO. From 1978 until Karamanlis relinquished the premiership, there were no further incidents.

The continental shelf was a more intractable problem, however, because of the prospect of oil being found. In the Greek view every island, as well as the mainland, generated its own continental shelf. That accorded with the current law of the sea, but it seemed inequitable to the Turks because it would virtually exclude them from any share in the prospec-tive wealth of the Aegean sea-bed. In principle Karamanlis acknowledged the force of their argument, so he proposed early in 1975 that the issue should be referred to the Interna-tional Court at the Hague. In May, at a NATO Council in Brussels, he met Demirel, who had recently become Prime Minister of Turkey. He pointed out that there were only three possibilities: bilateral talks, arbitration, or war. The first had already reached deadlock, so the only alternative to war was arbitration. Demirel at first agreed, but on returning to Ankara he was violently attacked by his predecessor, Ecevit. He therefore withdrew his agreement, and when the Greek government asked the Turkish government to sign an arbitra-tion bond in October, Demirel suggested instead that bilateral talks should be renewed on all matters relating to the Aegean. After a long interval, talks began at last between Greek and Turkish officials and experts in June 1976.

They began, unfortunately, in an atmosphere which was

already sour. Apart from the perennial bitterness over Cyprus, there were other unrelated incidents every few months which added to the tension. The Turks protested at the fortification of some Aegean islands, which Karamanlis described as purely defensive. Naval exercises and army manœuvres took place every year in circumstances which each side interpreted as threatening on the part of the other. In this case the Turks had the advantage that their manœuvres took place within the framework of NATO, but in November 1975 the Greeks had the satisfaction of a joint naval exercise with the French, the one major ally which had also withdrawn its forces from the NATO command.

Psychologically the atmosphere was further poisoned by other causes of suspicion, such as the treatment of minorities. The issue was raised from the Turkish side, although the Greeks had had far more serious grounds for complaint in the half-century since the Treaty of Lausanne. The Turks now alleged that the Muslim minority in western Thrace was oppressed by the Greeks. The Greeks complained that the Patriarchate of Constantinople was harassed by Turkish students. Constant changes of government in Ankara hampered negotiations. The precarious state of democracy in Turkey, in contrast with Karamanlis' unchallenged ascendancy, was a paradoxical asset to the Turkish government, which could hint at the danger of anarchy, military dictatorship, or even Communism, if it were not allowed to have its own way.

A real possibility of war was also still in everybody's mind. In October 1975 Karamanlis told Parliament that 'in the event of a local war, our forces are absolutely ready for decisive action in defence of the honour and security of the nation.' At the same time he emphasized that no war would be started by Greece. During the following summer the Turks carried out prolonged naval exercises in the Aegean and army manœuvres in eastern Thrace, very near the Greek frontier. Averoff responded with a tour of the Aegean islands and an inspection of Greek units in western Thrace. But he declared that 'war is excluded'; and in confirmation of it, Karamanlis wrote to Demirel proposing a non-aggression pact. At first Demirel agreed, but a month later he withdrew again under domestic pressure. He then gave an interview to *Le Monde* (20 May

1976) listing no less than six unresolved disputes with Greece.

The summer of 1976 was a time of acute crisis. In July a fleet of Turkish ships sailed into the Aegean, including a survey-ship called the *Hora* (later renamed the *Sismik*), designed to explore the sea-bed. Greek ships sailed to shadow it, and Averoff declared that the Greek forces were ready. Karamanlis called for calm. The *Hora* withdrew, but Demirel announced that it would shortly sail again. The Turkish Press published a map of the Aegean showing the extent of Turkey's claims over the continental shelf, adjoining many Greek islands. Karamanlis took the chair at a meeting of the Chiefs of Staff on 22 July, and subsequently briefed Mavros and Papandreou. On the twenty-ninth the *Sismik* (as the *Hora* had now become) was reported off the Dardanelles. A Greek survey-ship was also sent into the Aegean in early August.

After a series of ministerial meetings, on 9 August Karamanlis announced that he had addressed a protest to the Turkish government, a request for an emergency meeting of the Security Council, and an appeal to the International Court at the Hague. Papandreou was more belligerent: he said that the navy should have sunk the *Sismik*. The Security Council passed a predictable resolution urging restraint on both parties and a renewal of direct negotiations. Karamanlis welcomed it; the Turks less so; Papandreou even less.

The Hague Court also heard the Greeks' case, but the Turks repudiated its jurisdiction. Early in September the Court rejected the Greek application for an interim injunction against the Turks. Although this did not close the case, which had not yet been heard in substance, it was seen as a set-back for Greece. But it soon became clear that the Turks had no intention of making more than a demonstration. The *Sismik* returned to port once more, and the crisis died down before the end of the year.

It was only dormant, however, and it was soon to flare up again. The Hague Court had still to deliver its substantive judgement, which took so long that both parties lost interest in the prospect of a juridical settlement. In July 1977 the Greek government presented its case in writing, but the Turks again repudiated the Court's jurisdiction. For more than another year the case lay before the Court unsettled. At last, in December 1978, the Court declared itself incompetent to determine the case, in effect conceding victory to the Turks. By then other methods were being adopted.

Once more, in the spring of 1977, Turkish naval and air forces began exercises in the Aegean. To the Greeks they appeared to be directed at the Greek islands, and to be deliberately provocative. Karamanlis publicly criticized them in strong terms during March. Averoff presented a note of protest to the Turkish Ambassador, which was rejected. The Greeks then began exercises of their own. In July there was a change of government in Ankara, Demirel replacing a short-lived government under Ecevit. At first, as often happened after such changes, the new government seemed more conciliatory. Demirel announced that he had no intention of sending out the *Sismik* again. But his government lasted only six months before being replaced again by Ecevit in January 1978.

Ecevit at once began making urgent approaches to Karamanlis, who naturally viewed them with great caution. He eventually agreed to meet Ecevit at Montreux in March, and the two agreed to hold a series of meetings between the permanent officials of their Foreign Ministries. But these meetings, like those between Kyprianou and Denktash in the same period, showed only that there was no more flexibility on the Turkish side than before. The crises in Cyprus and the Aegean, which had prompted the general election of 1977, remained to haunt Karamanlis after it was over.

To the Greeks it was a disturbing feature of these disputes that the US government appeared to be favouring the Turks. An early and startling example was a remark by Vice-President Nelson Rockefeller in April 1975, that Greece ought to be grateful to Turkey for overthrowing the Junta. At the time this was an uncharacteristic view, but it became commoner later. The first reactions of the new American regime, under President Gerald Ford, to the crisis in the eastern Mediterranean were moderately encouraging to the Greeks. The US Congress voted in August 1974 to renew aid to Greece, and in September to cut off military supplies to Turkey. The Turks retaliated by depriving the US forces of their bases in Turkey. This had a dual consequence: it made the US facilities in Greece more valuable, and thus strengthened Karamanlis' hand in negotiating new arrangements with the Americans; but it also convinced the US military authorities that the embargo on arms for Turkey must be lifted in order to recover use of their bases; and this view eventually made its way through to the US political leadership.

For a time Karamanlis was able to benefit from the restored and enhanced reputation of Greece in the West. In May 1975 he was invited to personally inaugurate the NATO summit meeting in Brussels. His negotiations with the United States on defence facilities began in a friendly atmosphere. He assured the American people, through the Greek-American organization AHEPA, that the Greek people had great affection for them. The truculent behaviour of the Turks, on the other hand, was an asset in his negotiations with the US government. It was even suggested, though quickly denied, that the US bases closed in Turkey might be transferred to Crete.

Before the end of 1975, however, the Greek position had begun to weaken. It was necessary to negotiate a new relationship not only with the United States individually but also with NATO. As a powerful member of NATO, Turkey had a virtual veto over the negotiations in the latter case, and the tide was flowing in her direction. Dr Luns, the Secretary-General of NATO, openly advocated a renewal of arms supply to Turkey. In September 1975 NATO manœuvres took place in the Aegean under a Turkish Admiral. The absence of Greek forces strengthened the Turks' standing, especially in American eyes. Karamanlis insisted that Greece did not want to leave NATO, only to negotiate a new relationship But it was increasingly difficult to define what that relationship might be. Karamanlis said it would be like the status of France or Norway; but he was not helped by Papandreou's declared policy of breaking with NATO altogether.

Papandreou took the same position on the US defence facilities in Greece. In this case too Karamanlis wanted to maintain the connection, but on a new basis under 'purely national control'. Negotiations with the Americans were protracted, and were the subject of an acrimonious debate in Parliament early in 1976. By March the parallel negotiations between the United States and Turkey had reached a stage which put pressure on the Greeks. The US bases in Turkey were to be reactivated, under Turkish control, in return for a grant of one billion dollars, which would include military aid. This breakthrough so incensed the Greeks that Karamanlis temporarily recalled his Ambassador from Washington.

The outcome was a marked acceleration of the Greek negotiations with the US government. In April 1976 an agreement was reached by which Greece was to receive 700 million dollars in return for the restoration of US facilities. In a parliamentary debate on the agreement a few days later, Karamanlis again declared his willingness to end the arms race with Turkey and to sign a non-aggression pact. But the agreement was almost unanimously attacked by the Opposition. A month later violent demonstrations took place in Rhodes against a visit by the US Sixth Fleet, for which the government blamed Papandreou and the KKE. In a further debate on 12 June, Karamanlis criticized Papandreou to his face for supporting 'positions which are dangerous for the country in this matter'.

The ambiguity of Greece's relations with the USA at this time was illustrated on the occasion of the bicentennial celebrations on 4 July. Karamanlis sent a warm message to President Ford, but he also published a statement which contained not only congratulations but veiled lessons for the future, drawing attention to outstanding problems. It was also noticed that Greece was not represented at the celebrations on a ministerial level. Karamanlis himself was in Paris, talking to the French government about arms supply and obtaining an assurance that the French view of Aegean issues was 'practically identical' with Greece's. He took the opportunity of inviting the French Prime Minister, Jacques Chirac, to Athens, but the visit was never made, because Chirac resigned a few weeks later.

Greece needed all the European support that could be mobilized during the summer of 1976. While the question of US facilities in Greece was difficult enough, the future relationship with NATO was even more so. In a parliamentary debate on 20 October Karamanlis spoke of a 'special type of co-operation' which would enable Greece 'to have control of the national forces in peacetime on the one hand, but to cover

her interests completely in time of war—meaning general war—
on the other'. That would entail some participation in NATO
planning. It was a difficult concept to realize, with the Turks
opposing any concessions by NATO and the Americans tend-
ing to favour the Turks.

President Carter, who was elected in November 1976, had
given the impression during his campaign that he sympathized
with the Greeks rather than the Turks—not surprisingly, since
Greek-American voters were far more numerous than Turkish-
Americans. But within a few months of his inauguration *real-
politik* reasserted itself. The American Commander-in-Chief
at Izmir said in March 1977 that Greece was creating a security
problem for Turkey. In July a new US Ambassador designate
to Greece made remarks on the Aegean situation which led
the Greek government to ask for his appointment to be suspended; and in the end he never went to Athens. At the end
of the year General Alexander Haig, the Supreme Commander
of NATO forces (and future Secretary of State), said openly
in Ankara that the US embargo on arms to Turkey had served
no useful purpose. Plainly it was only a matter of time before
the embargo was completely lifted. This was the crux of the
second crisis which caused Karamanlis to go to the country in
the autumn of 1977.

Neither the United States nor Turkey was a party to the third
critical issue, which was the negotiation with the EEC; and the
Europeans were less favourably disposed towards Turkey than
the Americans were. But the Turks were still able to exercise
an adverse influence even on the preliminaries to Greek entry
into the Community, both because they were potential, if
distant, candidates for future membership themselves, and
because they could play on European fears that Greek membership would import Greco-Turkish quarrels into the Community's debates. On more than one occasion Turkish Prime
Ministers spoke openly against Greece's admission.

Karamanlis was nevertheless successful in convincing the
European negotiatiors in Brussels that the Greek application
must be treated strictly on its own merits. It must not be
judged in the light of hypothetical negotiations with future
candidates. A striking feature of the whole process was that

Karamanlis not only had complete command of the negotiations on the Greek side but also established a strong personal influence over his future European colleagues.

Early in 1975 he began visiting the European capitals to prepare the ground for a formal application. He went first to Paris in April, then to Bonn and Brussels a month later. The series of visits to members of the EEC was interrupted by a visit to Yugoslavia in June. There too he stressed that his object was not simply to join the EEC but to work for 'the political union of Europe'. Immediately after his return from Belgrade, Greece's application was presented in Brussels. In the second half of the year he continued his personal contacts with his future partners. In September President Giscard d'Estaing came to Athens; in October Karamanlis visited London, where the Labour government had lately held a referendum on membership of the EEC; in December he received the President of the EEC Commission in Athens, followed by the West German Chancellor, Helmut Schmidt, at the end of the month.

In his New Year message for 1976, Karamanlis indicated that all was going satisfactorily. But on 31 January it became known that the EEC Commission wished to impose a preparatory period of ten years before Greece became a full member, on the ground that the national economy was insufficiently developed. Karamanlis at once reacted vigorously. He summoned the Ambassadors of the nine member countries, and told them that the views of the Commission were 'morally and politically unacceptable to Greece'. He added that Greece had neither the right nor the power to force her way into the EEC, but the country would not accept membership on terms which would 'offend the dignity of the nation'. The Council of Foreign Ministers hurriedly had second thoughts. On 9 February they overruled the Commission. The next day Karamanlis expressed his satisfaction, and at the end of the month the Turkish government expressed its disapproval.

These were only the preliminaries. The formal negotiations had not yet begun; and despite many high-level flights to and fro, they did not do so until 27 July. Karamanlis marked the occasion by a statement warning his fellow-countrymen that the negotiations would be 'neither brief nor easy'. He also made it very clear that his primary motives were political: 'to change radically the destiny of this country . . . to develop the virtues of the nation and to limit its defects; to hammer together our national unity and cohesion; to safeguard the regular operation of our democratic institutions'. But although the goal was political, the subjects of negotiation were economic, and Greece would have to be ready 'for certain sacrifices which will be imposed by the reconstruction of our economy and its adjustment to the conditions prevailing in the European Community'.

During the next six months there was a steady flow of visits to Athens by future colleagues; from the Netherlands, Italy, Ireland, West Germany, the Council of Europe, and the EEC Commission. In February 1977 the new President of the Commission, Roy Jenkins, declared that 'the Greek issue is regarded as settled'. Nevertheless Karamanlis thought it wise to continue his own visits to the West, to make sure there was no backsliding. He had visited Brussels in November 1976 and planned to visit a further five European capitals in the spring of 1977. But an attack of lumbago compelled him to postpone his plans, and later even to miss the opening of the Salonika Trade Fair for the first time.

It was at this date that a series of worrying factors emerged which caused him to include the negotiations with the EEC among the impending crises in the autumn of 1977. Papandreou was threatening that a PASOK government would withdraw from the EEC, so that Greece appeared to be a divided country. At the same time the shadow of Spain was darkening the scene at Brussels. Whatever terms were negotiated with Greece would be claimed by Spain too; and whereas the competition of Greek wine, fruit, and agriculture could fairly easily be assimilated, that of Spanish products could not. The Commission had accepted Karamanlis' insistence that there should be no connection between the negotiations with Greece and any future negotiations with Spain and Portugal. But the French and the Italians would find it hard to separate the cases in practice. Karamanlis felt the need of a fresh, clear mandate to bring the matter to a conclusion. But when he sought it on 20 November, the outcome was not altogether successful. Such was the unavoidable hazard of democracy.

Chapter 11

Widening Horizons

FROM the day of his return, Karamanlis had consistently emphasized that Greece's political and psychological links were with Europe and the West. But they were not to be exclusive, nor did he mean to restrict them to the EEC and NATO. Other links, disrupted under the dictatorship, needed also to be restored. There were countries in Europe itself which belonged neither to the Community nor to the Western alliance. These too had been scarcely on speaking terms with Greece under the Junta, but the steps towards a renewal of friendship were simple and straightforward.

Karamanlis made a notable appearance at the Helsinki Security Conference in July 1975—an occasion at which it was naturally appropriate for him to make Cyprus a central theme of his speech. In November 1976 he made an official visit to Vienna; in the same years he welcomed the Swiss and Swedish Foreign Ministers in Athens; and he exchanged messages of congratulation with the Spanish and Portuguese leaders on the restoration of democracy. So the comity of nations was restored with neutrals as well as allies.

There were also other regions of the world, separated from Greece either by ideology or by distance, which were ripe for a policy of widening Greece's international horizons. First and foremost, there was the Communist world. A new attitude on Karamanlis' part was foreshadowed as early as October 1974 by lifting the ban on the KKE and restoring Greek nationality to leading Communists who returned from exile. They responded at first with warmer appreciation of Karamanlis than Papandreou did. But their internal divisions had already been formalized during the dictatorship by the expulsion from the KKE of a group which formed itself into the KKE (Interior). Euro-communism, as it was called in Western Europe, took root in this group, which approved Karamanlis' plans to join the EEC and even tolerated Greek membership of NATO.

The KKE (Exterior) remained hostile to both, but its hostility towards Karamanlis was restrained as his relations with the Soviet bloc improved.

Both natural circumstances and his own policy brought about a closer relationship with the Communist states to the north. Karamanlis had a long-standing friendship with Tito, the first and greatest of the Euro-Communists; and he in turn could be helpful in dealing with the Turks. The Soviet government also showed its intention of being active in the problem of Cyprus. Its first intervention was unhelpful to Karamanlis, when a Soviet veto quashed an anti-Turkish resolution at the Security Council in early August 1974. But once it was persuaded of Karamanlis' sincerity and goodwill, the Soviet government's interventions became more helpful.

Later in August 1974, the Soviet government proposed an international conference on Cyprus with a restricted membership. Mavros accepted the proposal on Karamanlis' behalf, and stipulated that Yugoslavia should be one of the parties. The proposal was abortive because it was impossible to agree on the composition of the conference, but the Soviet government persisted in genuine efforts to remedy the state of the island. In mid-September a Soviet Deputy Foreign Minister visited Ankara, Athens, and Nicosia, and spoke firmly against permanent partition. Still more significant was the outcome of a summit meeting at Vladivostok between Ford and Brezhnev on 25 November. The communiqué, which Karamanlis naturally welcomed, declared 'firm support for the independence, sovereignty and territorial integrity of Cyprus', and urged that a just settlement' should be based on the 'strict implementation' of the resolutions adopted by the Security Council and General Assembly of the UN. Although the results were negligible so far as Cyprus was concerned, this initiative opened the way to improved relations between Greece and the Soviet Union, which was one of Karamanlis' diplomatic objectives.

The next steps were taken with the satellites. In January 1975 talks began between the Foreign Ministries in Athens and Sofia, and in February the Bulgarian President invited Karamanlis to make an official visit. The clandestine radio station of the KKE, which had been operating north of the Greek frontier, was closed down. Next, the Romanian Foreign

Minister visited Athens and invited Karamanlis to Bucharest. When he went there in May, his speeches emphasized that the Balkans must no longer be regarded as the 'powder keg of Europe' but as an 'area of peace and co-operation'. In the same month he maintained the new mood by congratulating the organizers of the workers' May Day, which in the past had often been the occasion of violent demonstrations by the KKE.

A visit to Yugoslavia in June 1975 was for Karamanlis a matter of friendly routine rather than the opening of a new door in the Iron Curtain, but he took the opportunity of broaching with Tito his scheme for a conference on technical co-operation in the Balkans. A month later, visiting Sofia, he put the same proposal to the Bulgarian Prime Minister. Formal invitations to the proposed conference were issued in August, and accepted by the Yugoslavs, Romanians, and Bulgarians. Albania, the most difficult of Greece's neighbours, politely declined but approved the idea of bilateral co-operation. Even Turkey sent representatives when the conference took place in Athens at the end of January 1976. It was proof of Karamanlis' contention that technical co-operation was possible even when political relations were strained.

Slowly the fruits began to mature. The first commercial indication was an order placed by the Greeks in 1975 for jeeps manufactured in Romania. As they were intended for the Army, Averoff followed Karamanlis to Bucharest to confirm the order. In the New Year the Soviet Union itself joined the friendly exchanges. Twice in the first week of January 1976 the Soviet radio was heard to express interest in closer relations with Greece. An invitation was sent and accepted for Greek officers to attend manoeuvres in the Caucasus; and two anchorages off the coast of Crete were authorized for Soviet ships. Good relations had progressed so far that in February Karamanlis had to issue a denial that he intended to visit the Soviet Union. He might have added 'not yet'.

During 1976 the range of contacts spread. The Greek Foreign Minister visited Czechoslovakia and Hungary. President Ceauşescu of Romania visited Athens, and it was announced that Romanian engineers would undertake geological work on the River Nestos. The Chief of the Yugoslav General Staff visited Athens; but Yugoslav visits were now a matter of routine which hardly attracted notice. Between April and August 1976 the flow of high-level exchanges grew to a flood in all directions.

A cultural agreement was signed with the Poles; a Greek trade mission was sent to Moscow, followed soon afterwards by the head of the National Tourist Organization; a new trade agreement was negotiated with the Albanians; an agreement on industrial co-operation and another on cultural co-operation were signed with the Bulgarians. Karamanlis wrote to his colleagues in Belgrade, Sofia, Bucharest, and Ankara asking for their comments on his first Balkan conference, and proposing a repetition.

Political improvements also grew out of technical and economic contacts. The Bulgarian President visited Athens in April 1976, and Tito in May. On 11 May occurred a small but significant event which had been unthinkable for thirty years: the Soviet Ambassador in Athens openly visited the offices of the KKE (choosing naturally the Exterior rather than the Interior sect). At the same time the Soviet and other Communist governments were maintaining close contacts in Ankara, trying to alleviate the Cyprus dispute; but every suggestion was rebuffed by the Turks.

By the end of 1976 visits between the Balkan capitals had become a matter of routine at every level. Karamanlis himself received a Bulgarian Under-Secretary for Foreign Affairs in September; Averoff visited Belgrade in October; a Bulgarian parliamentary delegation came to Athens; Papaligouras, as Minister of Co-ordination, visited Sofia in December; and the leaders of the Greek Opposition, Mavros and Papandreou, both joined the circuit of visits and reported to Karamanlis on their reception. The new atmosphere in the Balkans was welcome to all parties in Greece, except the extreme right, which accused Karamanlis of fellow-travelling. He could shrug off such pinpricks in a way that no other Greek could have done.

In 1977 the network spread wider. The Hungarian Foreign Minister came to Athens in March, when an agreement was negotiated on tourism. A Polish parliamentary delegation came in the same month. At the end of March the Albanian Minister of Trade visited Athens, and co-operation in road and sea transport was discussed. In June a revised trade agreement was concluded with Czechoslovakia, after a visit to Athens by the Czech Foreign Minister. In July a Greek delegation flew to Tiranë to discuss communications by air. The growing scale of mutual activities led to arrangements for clearing agreements between the central banks of Greece and those of her new partners.

The most novel extension of Karamanlis' pioneering diplomacy was with the People's Republic of China. In June 1976 a Chinese trade delegation arrived in Athens. When Mao Tse-tung died in September, Karamanlis issued a cautious statement which opened up the possibility of friendly relations with his successors. The subject lay dormant for nearly a year, but Karamanlis noted that Tito was warmly received in Peking at the end of August 1977. Meanwhile, advancing on the technical level as was his custom, Karamanlis had allowed Chinese military observers to attend an army exercise in northern Greece. When he established diplomatic relations with Communist Vietnam, he proposed that the Greek Ambassador in Peking should be accredited to Hanoi also; and rather surprisingly, the Chinese agreed.

The diplomatic progress continued in 1978. In January the Chinese Ambassador in Athens invited a party of Greek Deputies and journalists to China. In April the Greek Minister of Trade visited Peking. In August the Minister of Co-ordination discussed an expansion of trade with the Chinese Ambassador. The most important development was a visit to Athens by the Chinese Foreign Minister in September. He was followed in April 1979 by the Minister of Trade. In September of that year Karamanlis personally received a party of Chinese journalists. It was already obvious that exchanges at the highest level were imminent.

There were consequences within the Communist world itself from the dissolution of barriers which Karamanlis was trying to promote. In July 1977 Ceauşescu openly called for a Communist Party line independent of Moscow. This coincided with the line which Tito had been preaching and practising for nearly thirty years. At the same time Western Communists, especially in Italy and Spain, were promoting the doctrine of Euro-Communism, which included acceptance of NATO. The KKE (Interior) and EDA agreed, though

Papandreou did not. Although such trends were welcome to Karamanlis, he welcomed them with caution because of the internecine feuds of the Communist world. The rupture between China and Albania occurred while he was negotiating with both. The hostility of the Yugoslav and Bulgarian Communists to each other was another embarrassment. So, of course, was the quarrel between Moscow and Peking.

Of all the newly emerging opportunities, a reconciliation with the Soviet Union was the most important prize. Discussions between Greek and Soviet officials began in April 1977 in Athens on a wide range of bilateral and international issues, which naturally included Cyprus. Next came a decision on consular representation between the two countries, which was reached in principle during August. The process was adjourned until the end of the year on account of the Greek general election, but during December a Soviet Minister visited Cyprus and gave his government's pledge to promote a 'just solution'. In January 1979, soon after the consular agreement was signed, a delegation of Soviet experts arrived in Athens for a joint committee on shipping and maritime law. This subject also had a clear relevance to Greco-Turkish disagreements in the Aegean.

The tempo of *rapprochement* accelerated in 1978. In February a Soviet trade delegation came to Athens, and Papaligouras (then Foreign Minister) was invited to Moscow. In May Karamanlis personally received the Secretary of the Soviet Politburo, which was the more remarkable because he was a party and not a government official. These friendly contacts were paralleled by simultaneous exchanges of ministerial visits between Athens and Tiranë, Warsaw, Budapest, Prague, Belgrade, Bucharest, and Sofia, culminating in an official visit to Bulgaria by Karamanlis and Rallis (who succeeded Papaligouras as Foreign Minister in May). Karamanlis' experiments in technical co-operation had already borne extraordinary fruit. The many contexts of intra-Balkan exchanges in 1977-8 now included tourism, radio and television programmes, communications by land, sea, and air, telecommunications, agriculture, oil exploration, linking of electricity grids (with Bulgaria), and even conversations between Defence Ministers (with Yugoslavia and Romania).

It was already time for preparations to go to Moscow. Rallis was the first to go, in September 1978. During a visit of six days, he signed a cultural agreement, while talks on technical co-operation continued. A striking event in October was the goodwill visit of two Soviet warships to the Peiraeus. At the end of the year it was officially announced that Karamanlis would visit Moscow during 1979. But he was anxious to maintain a balance between the different factions of the Communist world, so the announcement added: 'and possibly Peking'.

It was also declared that 1979 would be a 'Year of Balkan Tourism', and ministers were among the most active tourists. Athens welcomed the Polish Foreign Minister, a Czech Under-Secretary for Foreign Affairs, and the Deputy Prime Ministers of Romania and Hungary. Karamanlis visited Yugoslavia and Romania in March, and flew to Corfu in April to meet the Bulgarian President. In September the Soviet airline Aeroflot began a weekly service between Moscow and Athens. In the same month another Soviet trade delegation came to Athens, and an agreement was signed for the servicing of Soviet merchant ships at Syros. Finally, in October, Karamanlis set out for Moscow himself.

His visit included Hungary and Czechoslovakia as well as the Soviet Union, and he was the first Greek Prime Minister to visit any of them. As he was anxious to dispel speculation about any special significance in the tour, he pointed out that most of the Western leaders had visited Moscow before him: he was simply 'filling a gap' and setting the seal on a steady improvement of relations. In conversation with Brezhnev and Kosygin, he emphasized that Greece was and would remain a member of the Western alliance.

He had a long talk with Brezhnev alone, in which the question of new missiles in Western Europe was naturally raised. Karamanlis gave his opinion that a controlled balance of forces at the lowest possible level between the two alliances was the best guarantee of peace. Brezhnev, who appeared to be in very bad health, made no comment. He simply stated that he would be going to Berlin in a few days' time, and would there announce a reduction of the Soviet forces and armour.

The communiqué published on 4 October showed that many other topics were discussed. Apart from amicable generalities about trade, shipping, scientific and technological co-operation, and the expansion of contacts at every level, there were also specific decisions: to set up a Soviet–Greek commission on economic and technical co-operation; to examine a joint project for an aluminium plant in Greece; to consider the supply of oil, natural gas, and electricity from the Soviet Union; and to negotiate agreements on road transport and judicial assistance.

There were also political items, which were perhaps more important to the Soviet side. Both sides declared their satisfaction with the Final Act of the 1975 Helsinki Conference and the Soviet–American treaty on strategic weapons (SALT I). Both declared their support for *détente*, for a 'universal treaty on the renunciation of force in international relations', for peace, security, and co-operation in the Mediterranean area, for an early solution of the Cyprus question, for the withdrawal of Israeli troops from all Arab territories occupied in 1967, for a convention on the Law of the Sea, and in general for enhancing the effectiveness of the United Nations. The communiqué ended with a note of Karamanlis' invitation to the Soviet Prime Minister, Kosygin, to return the visit. But this never took place, for within three months the Red Army had invaded Afghanistan, and a year later Kosygin was dead.

On the day Karamanlis left Moscow for Budapest, Averoff told Parliament that Greece was in no way threatened by her northern neighbours. It was true, and it was largely the result of Karamanlis' policies during the last five years. The momentum of co-operation was becoming irreversible. In June 1979 the Yugoslav, Bulgarian, Romanian, and Turkish governments all accepted a Greek invitation to a new conference of experts on transport and telecommunications. Between July and September, Hungarian, Soviet, and Albanian trade missions visited Athens, and Mitsotakis, as Minister of Co-ordination, visited Belgrade. In October—the month of Karamanlis' visit to Moscow, Budapest, and Prague—the favourable signs multiplied: the first Soviet ship put in for repairs at Syros; a protocol on co-operation in trade, industry, transport, agriculture, and tourism was signed with the Yugoslavs; a Bulgarian economic mission led by a Deputy Prime Minister came to Athens; a party of lignite experts from the Soviet Union was also there; a Greek trade mission visited Tiranë. A few weeks later, on 8 December, a Greek official stated, in reply to a journalist's question, that 'in present circumstances' Cruise and Pershing II missiles would not be located in Greece.

Not unexpectedly, the Turkish Foreign Minister expressed disapproval of the Greco-Soviet *rapprochement*. Karamanlis needed no reminding that the *rapprochement* must not be allowed to compromise his relations with the West, nor even with China. Less than two weeks after his return from the Eastern bloc, he set out on a round of visits to Bonn, Paris, London, and Rome, in order to brief his allies on his discussions and impressions. While he was in Rome, a visit to Pope John Paul II set the seal on the reconciliation between Greece and the Vatican. It also brought Karamanlis into contact with a great patriot from the most important Eastern country— Poland—that he had not visited. Tactfully, on the previous day he had sent a telegram of congratulations to the Patriarch of Constantinople on his name-day.

There remained China. Karamanlis crowned this year of extraordinary international activity by setting out for Peking less than three weeks after his return from Western Europe. On the way he visited Thailand, and on the way back India and Iraq. In each case he was the first Greek Prime Minister ever to do so.

In Peking Karamanlis met both the Chairman of the Communist Party, Hua Guo-feng, whose days of power were over, and the Deputy Prime Minister, Deng Xiao-ping, whose star was rising. They praised his foreign policy, especially for joining the EEC and promoting Balkan co-operation. Karamanlis stressed his view that the Balkans should be kept 'outside the superpower competition'. An agreement was signed on scientific and technological co-operation, but it was recognized that trade was limited by distance. In any case Karamanlis' purpose was political rather than economic, and it was achieved. Greece was firmly placed on the map of Europe as seen from the Far East.

It was not only towards the Communist world that Karamanlis was seeking to widen Greece's horizons. Within six months of his return he was also talking of an economic opening to the Middle East, especially the Arab countries. Early in June 1975 President Sadat of Egypt made a brief stop-over in Athens. While he was there Karamanlis gave an interview to a Yugoslav journalist in which he spoke of new openings to the Middle East, North Africa, and even South-East Asia. His intention was clearly to counterbalance the imminent application to join the EEC. An interesting feature of Greece's early overtures to the Middle East was that Papandreou was making similar contacts at the same time with the more radical Arabs, such as the Ba'ath Party in Syria and the Palestine Liberation Organization.

Karamanlis' official contacts were at first with the more conservative governments. In June 1975 his Foreign Minister, Bitsios, visited Tehran and was received by the Shah. The fruit of his visit was the first trade agreement ever signed by Greece with Iran. The Iranian Foreign Minister returned the visit in October, and later came the Minister of Tourism to discuss visits to each other's monuments and cultural sites, which had so much dramatic history in common.

Meanwhile Karamanlis himself visited Cairo in January 1976 as the guest of Sadat, with whom he was developing a friendship as close as with Tito. Sadat openly supported the demand that Turkish troops should be withdrawn from Cyprus, and Karamanlis drew a comparison between the harsh fate of the Palestinians and that of the Greek Cypriots. But he was careful not to allow friendship with one Arab state to prejudice relations with another. In February an agreement was signed with Libya, a vital source of oil; and in the same month an all-embracing Greek–Arab Association opened its offices in Salonika.

At the end of 1976 Karamanlis travelled still further afield, to Pakistan. He was again the first Greek Prime Minister ever to do so, as well as the first Macedonian leader since Alexander the Great. In his speech at a state banquet he naturally reminded his host, President Bhutto, of his celebrated predecessor. 'We Greeks are prouder of Alexander as a promoter of civilization than as a military commander,' he said, and added a tribute to the teaching of Aristotle. Two years later Karamanlis was prominent among the European leaders who vainly begged the usurping President of Pakistan, General Zia ul-Haq, to spare Bhutto's life.

His contacts with the Arab world took precedence over the rest of the Middle East in 1977. He was invited to visit Libya, Tunisia, Saudi Arabia, Algeria, and Syria. The Arab Ambassadors in Athens entertained him to a formal luncheon on 4 February, at which he assured them of Greece's support for a just and speedy solution of the problems of the Middle East by the evacuation of the Arab territories occupied since 1967, by the restoration of the rights of the Palestinians, by the guarantee of the frontiers of the area and reinforcement of the right of its peoples to live in peace and security. Although he did not mention Israel, Turkey, or Cyprus by name, the implications of his speech were unmistakable.

Some time passed before Karamanlis was able to accept any of his invitations to the Arab world, but ministerial exchanges in both directions continued. In February 1977 Bitsios visited Syria and Jordan; in September the Iraqi Minister of Trade was in Athens; in October Karamanlis welcomed the Tunisian Prime Minister; in January 1978 an Iraqi trade mission followed upon its Minister's visit. Rallis visited Iraq in May 1978 and Kuwait a month later. In January 1979 Mitsotakis, as Minister of Co-ordination, visited Libya, and in October his Minister of Trade visited Iraq and Kuwait. In the opposite direction, the Syrian Minister of Planning came to Athens in July 1979; the Deputy Prime Minister of Kuwait in August; the Egyptian Foreign Minister in October.

In addition to all these bilateral contacts, Karamanlis had appointed a distinguished academic, Professor Yanni Giorgakis (once private secretary to Archbishop Damaskinos during and after the German occupation) as a roving super-Ambassador to the Arab states. He also enjoyed the somewhat unpredictable help of Papandreou, who kept him in touch with his own more radical contacts in Tripoli, Baghdad, and the PLO. The outcome of all these multifarious exchanges was a series of agreements on trade, technology, and culture. Even more important was the interest which the wealthier Arab states began to show in investment in Greece. Their interest grew when the Lebanon, once the financial centre of the Middle East, disintegrated into civil war, and many Arab entrepreneurs shifted their offices to Athens.

Sometimes Karamanlis' new friendships led to unforeseen advantages. In March 1978, for example, after an Egyptian journalist was murdered in Nicosia by Palestinian terrorists, Karamanlis was able to help in the delicate task of restoring relations between Egypt and Cyprus. Occasionally, on the other hand, there were potentially more embarrassing episodes involving Greece in the revolutionary situations of the Middle East. After Arab terrorists extended their activities to Athens, an anti-terrorism law had to be passed in Parliament. After the fall of the Shah of Iran, the new Foreign Minister paid an unwelcome visit to Greece, on the invitation of a body calling itself the Group for Solidarity with the Iranian Revolution.

Iran had fortunately not been on Karamanlis' schedule of visits. He had been there as a private citizen in 1964, and had not liked what he saw. But the Arab countries had a stronger attraction for him. Although there was too little time to accept all his invitations, he visited Saudi Arabia, Syria, and Iraq during 1979. Early in 1980 he allowed the Palestine Liberation Organization to open an office in Athens; and the Ministry of Trade set up a department for trade relations with the Arab world.

Karamanlis' primary object was to promote goodwill and trade, to secure support for Greece at the United Nations, and to establish Greece in the eyes of his hosts as a significant member of the EEC. In the case of the major oil-producers, there was also the prospect of attracting investment. In all this he was helped by the fact that Greece had never had full diplomatic relations with Israel. But he had no thought of compromising the principle that Greece belonged to the democratic West. As with his overtures to the Communist world, nothing in Karamanlis' dealings with the Middle East derogated from that position.

After the general election of November 1977, Karamanlis' first statements to his Deputies, to the Council of Ministers, and to Parliament reminded them bluntly of the unfinished business which had to be resumed. There were still the crises which had accelerated the election—Cyprus, the Aegean, the EEC; there were the defence problems—NATO, the US facilities, the cost of armaments; and there were the domestic problems—the impact of a world-wide recession, the need to modernize Greek institutions, administration, and education. It was too much to hope that these would all be solved during Karamanlis' final term of office.

For some of them there could never be a solution in the ordinary sense, because they were perennial. Such were the disputes with Turkey over Cyprus and the Aegean, which again occupied interminable stretches of Karamanlis' time in the next two and a half years, without yielding the slightest progress. But elsewhere there could be a steady improvement across a broad front, which was reinforced by the two unquestionable successes of Karamanlis' last administration: entry into the EEC and reintegration into NATO. The latter, however, was completed not under his premiership but under his Presidency.

Negotiations at ministerial level with the EEC were resumed in Brussels during December 1977. Difficulties were still being found over the enlargement of the Community. Karamanlis told Parliament on 15 December that there were two obstacles; the prospect of applications from Spain and Portugal, and the question of Mediterranean agricultural produce. But in answering criticisms from Papandreou, who was now the leader of the Opposition, he reiterated that he had 'succeeded in detaching the case of Greece from these two issues'. Papaligouras, who was now Foreign Minister, and Kondogiorgis, the Minister without portfolio in charge of the negotiations (and future EEC Commissioner), went to Brussels on 18 December and returned two days later with a report which confirmed Karamanlis' optimism. In particular, quotas had been settled for Greek wine—a crucial point for the French and Italians. As a further sign of confidence, the EEC had made a grant of 300 million dollars to Greece, restoring and increasing a grant which had been made under the Treaty of Association but suspended under the dictatorship. The protocol ratifying this agreement was approved by Parliament on 16 January 1978, with the qualified support even of PASOK.

Although the negotiations were going well, Karamanlis

thought it best to tour the European capitals himself, to ease any outstanding obstacles out of the way. At the end of January 1978 he visited London, Brussels, Paris, and Bonn. After meeting Roy Jenkins, the President of the Commission, he predicted that Greece would be in the EEC by the end of 1979, but this forecast proved over-optimistic. On his return to Athens he took the chair at two ministerial meetings in the Ministry of Coordination, on 7 and 10 February, to make sure there was no slippage that could be blamed on the Greek side. A detailed statement was issued after the second meeting, urging both public servants and private industrialists to hasten their preparations for entry into the Community.

At the end of March Karamanlis resumed his travels, visiting Copenhagen, Luxemburg, the Hague, and Rome. His visits were naturally concerned with the EEC, but the negotiations no longer had the same urgency on his personal agenda, and there were less taxing occupations for him. In early May he revisited West Germany, to receive the Charlemagne Prize at Aachen in recognition of his services to the unification of Europe. Before returning, he also spent two days in Switzerland, where he again spoke, at a banquet in his honour, of the ideal of a united Europe. Later in the month he flew to Washington for a summit meeting of the NATO powers, followed by the General Assembly of the UN in New York. Once more he took the opportunity of proposing a non-aggression pact with Turkey.

For several months the negotiations in Brussels seemed to be going smoothly. Papandreou was calling for a referendum before Greece was committed, but Karamanlis brushed aside the proposal. More serious difficulties than that were to arise, however. In August 1978 Jenkins visited Athens and emphasized the problem over agriculture. In October Karamanlis again felt obliged to make a personal intervention. He visited Italy, France, and Ireland—all of them agricultural countries—and he sent Rallis to Brussels to lend weight to the negotiations. Then, on seeing the final proposals of the EEC negotiators for Greek agriculture, he addressed a strong letter of dissatisfaction to the Prime ministers of all EEC members on 12 December.

As so often in the affairs of the EEC, a vigorous intervention by a determined national leader quickly resulted in success.

The argument was resolved within ten days. On 21 December it was announced that agreement had been reached on the terms of entry, including the transitional period for Greek agricultural products. Karamanlis was able to tell Parliament, in a debate on foreign policy on 16 January 1979, that his objective was achieved. With characteristic frankness, he emphasized that the underlying purpose was political: 'On joining the mighty European family as an equal member, Greece will no longer be obliged to seek protection from one or another superpower.' There followed, however, a long and acrimonious argument in the Chamber with Papandreou. Karamanlis offered to show him confidential documents on the negotiations, but Papandreou declined.

Apart from Papandreou's intransigence, the rest was straightforward. Early in April 1979 Rallis and Kondogiorgis went to Brussels for the last ministerial meeting before the signature of the Treaty of Accession. A series of visits to Athens by leading figures from the West set the seal on the agreements. On 28 May the treaty was signed in Athens in the presence of Heads of State, Prime Ministers, and lesser dignitaries. In a moving and quietly jubilant speech, Karamanlis gave his new colleagues a lesson in Europeanism.

It was, he said, the end of a journey; it was 'the identification of our destinies'. He spoke of the innumerable difficulties that had been overcome, and paid tribute not only to the current negotiators but to 'the pioneers, near and far, of the European idea'. He spoke of his personal emotion, of his 'steady vision and unwavering faith in the need for a united Europe', of the fulfilment after eighteen years of his belief in 'the European destiny of my country'. It would involve no change of environment, for 'Europe is our own place', where Greek and Roman and Christian spirit was synthesized, and to which Greece brought 'the ideas of freedom, truth, and beauty'.

The Community, he emphasized, was not a rich men's club. It was there to safeguard Europe's independence, to guarantee a balance of power, to contribute to peace and order. Greece too would contribute through her economic and cultural relations with the Balkans and the Mediterranean area. Much as Peter the Great once called his new capital 'a window to the West', Karamanlis called Greece 'the Mediterranean balcony of Europe'.

He assured his colleagues that there would be no turning back, for he was following the 'logic of history'. Europe had once been a scene of war, and the Balkans had been 'the powder keg of Europe'; but today 'nationalist prejudices were abandoned'. Yet there were still difficulties ahead, for technical and scientific advances had not been matched in the political sphere. Europe's problems were still those once analysed by Thucydides and Plato: they still had to realize Aristotle's model of 'the citizen who knows both how to rule and how to be ruled'. European union had still to create the new man, whom he symbolized in the merger of 'the reason of Apollo and the feeling of Dionysus'. Recalling his own reading of Goethe and not forgetting that Mistra in the Peloponnese was the scene of Faust's union with Helena, he declared that it was 'time for Europe's Faust to make a new journey to the land of harmony and proportion, there to beget a new Euphorion'.

After this flight of imagination, he returned to mundane affairs. Economic union must gradually follow. Europe must promote economic justice and help developing countries. There must be no isolationism; progress must be collective; without unity of action, the problems which had lately caused disillusionment would be worse still. He pointed to a few encouraging signs: direct elections to the European Parliament, the establishment of a European Monetary System; though neither was yet extended to Greece.

In his peroration he reverted to the sense of commitment in his own country:

From today Greece accepts once and for all the historic challenge, her European destiny, without losing her national identity. We have confidence both in Europe and in Greece. We have resolved that we will be all Europeans, as Churchill would say, and as Shelley would say, all Greeks. For in the words of Isocrates, Greeks are not those who were born in Greece but all those who have adopted the classical spirit.

His words were addressed as much to his own people as to his foreign guests, for there were still hesitations about membership of the EEC, especially on the left. The final stage of Greece's entry was an anti-climax. Legislation to ratify the treaty was tabled on 4 June and debated in Parliament from the twenty-fifth to the twenty-eighth. After a speech by Papandreou denouncing the treaty 'unreservedly', the PASOK Deputies absented themselves from the further debate. The KKE (Exterior) acted similarly soon afterwards. After they had left, Karamanlis began his speech by regretting that he was 'obliged to debate with absentees'. The ostensible reason for their absence was given as the government's refusal to table the minutes of the negotiations; but Karamanlis replied that there were no minutes, only conclusions, which were embodied in the treaty. In this respect the government had simply conformed with the normal practice of the EEC. Papandreou had in fact, he said, known that this was the case for more than a month.

The rest of Karamanlis' speech was divided between castigation of PASOK's attitude and exposition of the benefits of belonging to the EEC. He argued that Papandreou was wrong in claiming that Greece's independence was at stake. The promises which Papandreou had made of a future referendum on membership was fraudulent, since only the President could, under the constitution, order a referendum. Papandreou was also wrong in arguing that Greece would be harmed economically, since the reverse had happened under the Treaty of Association. He was wrong again in talking of damage to Greek agriculture and of danger from monopolies and foreign capital, since any such risks were averted by the terms of the treaty. It was a delusion to imagine, as an alternative, that a 'special relationship' could be established with the EEC, since that could neither guarantee Greek exports nor maintain agricultural prices. The significant facts were that all the 'productive elements' in the national economy favoured entry; that Spain and Portugal were impatient to join too; and that no existing member really wanted to leave the EEC.

The benefits were those already outlined by Karamanlis at the ceremony of signature, though now phrased in less exalted language. Entry into the EEC was a 'revolutionary change' which would end Greece's 'age-long isolation'. In a time of uncertainty, when small nations were vulnerable, it would be dangerous to be left outside. Greece should join for these reasons even without the economic advantages, which were also considerable: the opportunities for social and industrial progress, especially in the agricultural sector; the attraction of foreign capital and expertise; the stimulus of competition. But the advantages would not come automatically. There followed the familiar warnings about the need for efforts and readiness for change.

There were real difficulties, he admitted, as the British and the Irish had found. But they caused him no anxiety provided that the Greeks could avoid 'political adventures and social disturbance'. His final words looked to the far future: 'We shall open new horizons for our race, and a better and safer life for coming generations.'

The treaty was ratified on the twenty-eighth by 191 votes to two, with three blank votes and 104 abstentions. Ratification by the existing members followed during the last months of 1979, with the British government for once leading the way. The treaty was to come into effect on 1 January 1981, a year later than Karamanlis had predicted in a moment of optimism at the beginning of 1978.

It was too early, even when he retired from office, to estimate the economic consequences of membership. In any case the political factors weighed more heavily in Karamanlis' mind and of these he was certain. But he had a last opportunity to present the balance sheet of his government's achievements in the economic field at the Salonika Trade Fair, which he opened on 8 September 1979. Two facts dominated his report: Greece's entry into the EEC and the world-wide crisis caused by energy costs and inflation. On the first point he repeated his familiar lesson, that the benefits would depend on hard work, sacrifices, and changes in both public and private attitudes. But the initial prospect was encouraging, thanks to the advances made in the past four years. Greece, which was once the poorest country in the Balkans, was now the richest, as well as being the only democracy.

Evidence of these advances was to be seen in most of the key indicators. National income had increased at a rate above five per cent per annum (compared with two per cent in the EEC); and the level per caput had risen from 2,165 dollars in 1974 to 3,430 dollars in 1978. Investment had also risen at five per cent per annum; savings had risen by 170 per cent over four years, and consumer expenditure by over 100 per cent. The budget was nearly in balance, and tax evasion was being overcome. The general improvement in the standard of living was plain for all to see.

As examples, there were considerably more than twice as many private cars in circulation as in 1974—though this was not an unqualified benefit—and more than a million television sets. Workers' wages were maintaining their value in real terms, and rather better than maintaining it in the case of agricultural workers. At the same time incomes policy was protecting the weaker classes. Not everyone was equally prosperous, but all were more prosperous than five years earlier. 'Who has benefited from this spectacular progress?', asked Karamanlis rhetorically: '900 capitalists or nine million Greeks?'

But some dark clouds could not be overlooked. Owing to inflation and fuel costs, some of the indicators were likely to slow down. The balance of payments was at risk, though Greek credit abroad stood high. Oil was costing Greece over a billion dollars a year. Prices were rising at nearly twenty per cent per annum. Comparatively mild restrictions on consumption were leading to disproportionate reactions—strikes, demonstrations, and extravagant wage demands, encouraged by the 'demagogy of the left'. Karamanlis appealed to the maturity of the Greek people: 'We must accept small and, I hope, temporary sacrifices to avoid painful deprivations in future.'

The future also depended on Karamanlis' own stewardship, which was nearing its end, and his foresight, of which there were happily good auguries in his last months as Prime Minister. Towards the end of 1979 he completed the task of assuring Athens' water-supply, which he had begun more than a quarter of a century earlier, by opening a major dam on the River Mornos. In the last weeks of the year came confirmation that uranium had been found near Serres, and that oil was being extracted in commercial quantities from the sea-bed near Thasos, with the prospect that by the 1990s Greece would be self-sufficient for twenty per cent of her consumption. It was a stroke of fortune that both these new discoveries —like the great archaeological discoveries of the 1970s—were made in northern Greece, Karamanlis' own homeland. Fortune favours not only the brave but the man of vision.

Once it was clear that the issue of the EEC was approaching its conclusion, Karamanlis was able to devote more of his time to the concurrent issues of Greek relations with NATO and the United States. The peculiarity of the position in NATO was illustrated at two ministerial meetings in Brussels soon after the election of 1977. When the NATO Ministers of Defence met on 7 December, Greece was unrepresented; when the NATO Foreign Ministers met two days later, Greece was represented by Papaligouras. Karamanlis took the opportunity to convey through Papaligouras a strong message of protest at the pro-Turkish bias shown by his NATO colleagues, especially the Americans and Dr Luns, the Secretary-General. To reinforce his protest soon afterwards, he sent General Davos, the Chief of the Defence Staff, to the allied GHQ with instructions to discuss Greece's 'special relationship' with NATO.

He knew, however, that in the long run a 'special relationship' would not be enough. Eventually a full reconciliation and re-entry would be necessary, but there were two obstacles: the opposition of the Turks and the hostility of Greek public opinion to the United States. Soon after his return in 1974, Karamanlis had remarked ironically that he was the only friend the Americans had in Greece, and he dared not admit it. The hostility had shown itself in the murder of two American diplomats—the Ambassador in Nicosia and an attaché in Athens. Feeling was particularly strong against Dr Kissinger personally. After the general election of 1977, it was further aggravated by the transfer of the leadership of the Opposition from the mild and conciliatory Mavros to Papandreou, whose anti-Americanism was uninhibited by the fact that he had enjoyed an American education and had married an American wife.

The belief that the American authorities were fundamentally pro-Turkish did not lack evidence. Early in 1978 President Carter made statements which seemed to minimize the harshness of the Turkish occupation of northern Cyprus, and to endorse Turkish complaints about Greek oppression of the Muslim minority in western Thrace. More serious, however, was the increasingly plain intention of the President to lift the embargo on arms for Turkey. When the State Department announced the President's intention on 3 April, the one concession to Greek opinion was the inclusion of conditions linking the end of the embargo with negotiations over Cyprus. But all that was required was the President's certificate that the Turks were pursuing the negotiations 'in good faith', which he could not easily refuse. Karamanlis issued a reproachful statement on US policy on 7 April, but he could not hope to change it. By the middle of August both Houses of Congress had approved legislation lifting the embargo, though only after fairly close votes.

It was easy to see the logic of the US government's decision. The embargo had deprived it of the use of the bases in Turkey and had done nothing to win concessions in Cyprus. It was even argued that the Turks would prove more flexible over Cyprus if the embargo were lifted. The Americans actually initiated private proposals to this effect, which unfortunately, against Karamanlis' advice, the government of Cyprus rejected. Thus the US government was released from the obligation to press for a solution, and the Turkish government from the obligation to make concessions.

Greece's relationship with NATO therefore remained to be settled in circumstances which were more than ever favourable to Turkish objections. In July 1978 Averoff reaffirmed the government's policy of seeking a 'special relationship' similar to that of France. The negotiations moved slowly over the next two years, marked by many visits to Athens of ministers and senior officers from the NATO powers. In the summer of 1979 an agreement on terms for Greece's re-entry into the military organization had been worked out by General Davos and General Haig, which was accepted by all members of the alliance except the Turks. That exception was decisive, and the deadlock was complete.

Turkey's position was fortuitously strengthened in that year by the revolution in Tehran, since the eviction of US bases from Iran made those in Turkey even more important. Karamanlis, on the other hand, had only one asset, which was to refuse to conclude discussions on the US facilities in Greece until relations with NATO were finally settled. In September 1979 a military delegation from NATO visited Athens, followed within a few days by the US Deputy Secretary for Defence. The Opposition assumed that pressure was being put on Karamanlis, and Papandreou ironically congratulated him on resisting it. But Karamanlis needed no encouragement to stand firm. The deadlock continued until almost his last days as Prime Minister.

It was broken only after changes in the high command both in Greece and in NATO. General Gratsios, who succeeded Davos as Chief of the Defence Staff, met General Rodgers, the new Supreme Commander, at Brussels on 11 February 1980. The American General put forward a new proposal, which was considered at a meeting of Ministers and Chiefs of Staff under Karamanlis' chairmanship on the twenty-second. It was found unsatisfactory, and the Greek government's reply insisted that only the proposal agreed between Davos and Haig would be acceptable. At last the Americans found it necessary to put pressure on the Turks. Turkey was in a state of anarchy, as the alternating governments of Ecevit and Demirel had completely broken down. Fortunately for the negotiations, the Turkish Chiefs of Staff, who wanted to reach an agreement, overthrew the nominally democratic government on 12 September 1980 and took power themselves. Military rule, which was abhorrent in Greece, was welcomed in Turkey as a lesser evil.

In great secrecy the negotiations were then brought quickly to a conclusion. General Rodgers was at last able to persuade the Turkish Generals to agree to the re-entry of Greece into the military structure of NATO on terms acceptable to the Greek government. No problem of ratification presented itself in Ankara, where Parliament had ceased to exist. In Athens there was a problem in putting a secret agreement to Parliament for ratification, but it was overcome by a simple vote of confidence in the government on 24 October.

The agreement also made it possible to pursue more actively the concurrent discussions on the US facilities in Greece. They consisted of four major sites: an anchorage at Souda Bay in Crete, an electronic-surveillance station also in Crete, an air-support base at Athens airport, and a fleet communications centre near Marathon. There were also a number of relay posts and early-warning stations visibly situated on Greek hilltops; and there was an undisclosed stockpile of nuclear warheads. Karamanlis insisted that these facilities should be, and should be known to be, under Greek control.

A new factor in the discussions had been introduced by the terms negotiated for the reactivation of the US bases in Turkey. Originally the availability of US facilities in Greece had not been linked to economic aid. But the grant of a billion dollars to the Turkish government as the price of the settlement, followed by the corresponding grant of 700 million dollars to the Greek government, had established a new principle. As a matter of national security, Karamanlis was in effect asking the Americans to maintain a proportion of ten to seven between Turkey and Greece in the allocation of military support; and that proportion took on an accepted permanence from then on.

The negotiations were protracted and difficult. The Opposition again compounded the difficulties, for Papandreou argued that the 'imperialist bases', as he called them, would give Greece no security but carried the threat of nuclear annihilation. Like the agreement with NATO, a settlement of the US facilities had not been reached when Karamanlis retired from the premiership, and was even longer delayed. His last two and a half years in office therefore did not achieve all of his objectives, but he had set Greece on a course from which it would not be easy to depart. The option of a withdrawal from either the EEC or the Western alliance remained open for a future government, but Karamanlis remained confident that in the long run such isolation would not prove attractive.

In other respects as well, Karamanlis' last administration was one of consolidation. Greece's international reputation stood high. Even if Karamanlis insisted that he was not irreplaceable, he was its undisputed architect. One simple illustration of his prestige was the fact that at the beginning of 1978 he had seventeen invitations abroad to consider, only a few of which could be fulfilled. They included not only politically important visits to Europe, the USA, the Soviet bloc, the Middle and Far East, but also honorific occasions: to Strasbourg to receive the Schuman prize for services to European unity (which Averoff went to accept on his behalf), and to Geneva to address the annual conference of the International Labour Office (which was to be his first foreign engagement as President). His fame also attracted many visitors to Athens, no longer on matters of urgent policy: ex-Chancellor Willy Brandt, the French Socialist leader (and future President) François Mitterrand, Senator Edward Kennedy, the Speaker of the House of Commons, the Chancellor of Austria, the President of Senegal, the Foreign Ministers of Zaire, New Zealand, and Australia, the President of the European Parliament, and many others.

There was one notable exception in his travels. He never set foot in Cyprus as Prime Minister. In Makarios' lifetime, this was because he was never invited. But later it was because he was anxious not to appear to be acting as Big Brother to the Greek Cypriots, either to dominate them or to relieve them of the responsibilities which accompanied independence. After President Kyprianou succeeded on the death of Makarios, he invited Karamanlis to Cyprus in February 1978. But Karamanlis replied only that he would be willing to accept 'when the time is opportune'. It never proved opportune during the remainder of his premiership.

He was still, however, just as active in travelling at home as abroad. Soon after the election of 1977, he revisited Macedonia to inspect the archaeological excavations at Vergina, as well as the public works in progress at Salonika. He was in Macedonia again at the end of June 1978, attending a military parade at Serres, only a few days before a disastrous earthquake struck Salonika. In September he made an extensive tour of the Aegean islands, from Mitylini through the Dodecanese to Crete. The anniversary of the liberation of Ioannina drew him there for a military parade in February 1979. In September he made a tour of Macedonia and western Thrace. His last provincial visit before relinquishing office was to the Peloponnese, where he accompanied Olympic officials to inspect the site which he had proposed as the permanent home of the Olympic Games.

Such occasions at home and abroad might have been given a valedictory character if Karamanlis had not at the same time kept a tight grip on policy, domestic as well as foreign. Besides taking the chair at the full Council of Ministers, he presided regularly at ministerial committees in the different departments. His assessment of the urgency of national problems can be seen, as usual, from the frequency of such occasions and the departments in which they took place. Some of the priorities were predictable: economic policy, inflation, fuel prices, defence, agriculture, public health, and education. Others were more unexpected, either due to sudden emergencies—such as the earthquake at Salonika, the floods in Macedonia, or the wave of international terrorism—or because they reflected new and growing personal interests: the environment, national culture, research and technology.

For Karamanlis was widening not only Greece's horizons but his own. His concern for Greece's cultural heritage and national monuments stood out in his last term of office just as prominently as his commitment to Greece's survival and modernization did in earlier terms. The discoveries at Vergina, the preservation of the Acropolis, and the prospect of bringing the Olympic Games back to Greece particularly caught his imagination. He first took the chair at a ministerial meeting in the Ministry of Culture on 23 November 1978, and announced his intention to preside at two further meetings. He took a close interest in projects such as the Bodosaki Institute and the European Cultural Centre at Delphi; and he made the foundation of the National Cultural Centre in Athens the occasion of a major speech in October 1979. In the same month he had the pleasure of congratulating his friend Odysseus Elytis on the award of the Nobel Prize for Literature, with a telegram which declared that 'the Committee has rightly honoured you as your work honours Greece.' In one of his last public statements as Prime Minster, on 1 February 1980, he recalled his lifelong belief that 'the place of nations in history is primarily determined by their cultural traditions,' and that 'no people ever imposed itself on the history of the world by material achievements.' It was the justified claim of a Greek patriot, echoing the voice of a Macedonian schoolmaster from seventy years before.

This was an appropriate note on which to end his career in active politics. But even his last months in office were not uncontroversial. In the first quarter of 1980, Karamanlis had to make a crucial decision about his future. The five-year term of Costa Tsatsos as President was due to end in June. If Karamanlis wanted to succeed him, the decision had to be taken soon; but he no longer commanded the 200 votes needed to ensure election on the first ballot. No one except Tsatsos had a definite idea of Karamanlis' intentions. Nor was it clear how the important votes of PASOK would be cast when the time came.

In the meantime the normal business of government had to be carried on. Negotiations with NATO, the Turks, and the Americans were still in progress with variable hopes of a conclusion. The usual stream of eminent visitors came to Athens, and the customary routine of ministerial meetings continued. During the first three months of the year, Karamanlis gave his guidance to the Ministry of Defence on relations with NATO, to the Ministry of Communications on the proposed international airport at Spata, to the Rectors of the Universities on student grievances, to the State Property Organization on the building programme, to the Ministry of Agriculture on the reafforestation of Attica. But on his own intentions he kept his own counsel.

There were two meetings of the full Council of Ministers during April. At the first, after dealing with routine business, Karamanlis gave his colleagues a *tour d'horizon* of domestic and foreign affairs. It might, or might not, have been the prologue to a decision. On the fourteenth he paid a visit to the Acropolis, to examine the deterioration of the monuments and the plans for saving them. It might, or might not, have had a valedictory signficance. Only on the seventeenth did he reveal to a second full meeting of the Council of Ministers his intention to accept nomination as a candidate for the Presidency.

Two days later he published a short, revealing statement:

As I have said in the past, I have no personal ambitions. If I had, I should have satisfied them in 1975, when I was reshaping the constitution of our country. It was possible for me then to strengthen the powers of the President of the Republic, to ensure his direct election by the people, and to secure my own election by a large majority. It was also possible for me to be elected easily by the last Parliament, in which New Democracy held 220 seats.

Instead, I thought it my duty to remain in active politics in order to consolidate our still precarious democracy and to confront the critical problems at home and abroad which we inherited from the dictatorship.

So I have neither personal nor party objectives in view. And it would be in conformity with my wishes to withdraw from politics at some point after forty-five years' service. For in our country no one knows how he will end his political life.

Nevertheless it is also possible for me to accept candidature and to put myself at the disposal of the representatives of the nation and thus of the country. But I would pray in that case that a politicization of the election should be avoided, and that Deputies should be free to vote according to their conscience. For only thus would it be possible for me, if I am elected, to stand beyond and above the parties and to exercise my political duties without constraint and with increased prestige.

I believe that this position, if it is accepted, will liberate us all from unnecessary dilemmas and will contribute to the stabilization of our political system.

But that prayer was not to be answered as he hoped, and as he had intended when he drafted the constitution.

The first ballot took place in Parliament on 23 April. It was inconclusive: Karamanlis received only 179 votes out of the 200 he needed. A week later, in the second ballot, the result was nearly the same: 181 votes out of the 200 needed. On both occasions PASOK abstained *en bloc*. So they did again in the third ballot on 5 May; but this time Karamanlis needed only 180 votes to be elected, and he gained 183. The threat of the alternative—a dissolution and a general election— rallied enough of the Opposition to his side.

Next day he addressed the Council of Ministers for the last time. Then he went to Parliament to be received for the last time by the President of the Chamber. In his final speech he defined his new duties as 'arbiter of the constitutional system'. He would have two fundamental aims: 'first, the consolidation of our democratic constitutional system and the smooth operation of its institutions; second, the preservation and strengthening of our national unity, above political antago- nisms'. It was thus only in a nominal sense that he could be said to be retiring from active politics.

On 8 May New Democracy held a ballot to choose its new leader. George Rallis won by the narrow margin of eighty-eight votes to eighty-four for Evangelos Averoff, who thereupon declined the post of Deputy Prime Minister but retained the Ministry of Defence. Karamanlis made no attempt to influence the election, and rebuffed suggestions from his followers that he should name his own successor: the rules of the party's charter were strictly followed. Tsatsos, in his last major act as President, appointed Rallis Prime Minister the next day. A week later he resigned from the Presidency without waiting for the expiry of his full term in June. On 15 May Karamanlis took the oath as President.

His conception of the Presidency under the constitution which he had devised himself remained to be tested; and the crucial test was still to come, with the change of government from New Democracy to PASOK at the general election in October 1981. But nothing could alter the fact that Karamanlis relinquished the premiership with a higher reputation than any man since Venizelos. His achievement was indeed greater than that of Venizelos: not only because Venizelos' career ended with a fatal error of judgement in sanctioning the revolution of 1935; but also for a further reason.

The prestige of Venizelos had been purely personal; that of Karamanlis was also the prestige of Greece. In the 1920s Greece was simply a minor object of European policy. The country had not the capacity to be anything more. Venizelos, with his intellectual charm, could persuade European statesmen to take him but not his country seriously. His charm itself led him and his country into adventures which it could not sustain. There were no such errors in Karamanlis' record.

He avoided Venizelos' error of imposing the commitments of a major power on the infrastructure of an underdeveloped country. He first advanced its infrastructure to the level of a secondary power, and then sought commensurate responsibilities. He recognized that in association with major powers, through NATO and the EEC in particular, he could exercise greater leverage on international affairs than a secondary power could exercise on its own. At the same time he could enhance Greece's standing with her associates by providing them, through Athens, with a window to the East, looking out in particular on the Arab world and the Communist bloc. This was his achievement abroad.

At home his success lay, first and foremost, in being a Greek through and through but also transcending his nationality, so that he could be, like no other contemporary, a perceptive and unsparing critic of his people. He knew all the Greeks' weaknesses, and frequently told them so. In forty-five years as a politician he had learned, as the sardonic philhellene George Finlay put it a century earlier, that it was impossible to govern the Greeks except constitutionally. But he had also learned that democracy, for all its Greek origins—origins which it shared with anarchy, demagogy, oligarchy, and tyranny— was still a precarious system in Greece; and that the only constant factor in Greek politics was the desire for change— preferably through the ballot-box, but if necessary by revolution. He had tried strenuously to correct these weaknesses, but when he moved up to the Presidency he could not yet be sure that he had succeeded. His last task was, as 'arbiter of the constitutional system', to mitigate the consequences—a task in which many heads of state before him, whether hereditary or elected, had failed.

He might justly have recalled a famous saying attributed to Archimedes, the greatest of Greek engineers: 'Give me a place to stand, and I will move the earth.' Politics, for Karamanlis, was a kind of engineering; and he had given the Greeks a place to stand. Whether he had also cured them of the belief that Greece is the 'navel of the earth' remains an unanswered question.

Index